T0329959

Work and Citizenship in the New Europe

Work and Citizenship in the New Europe

Edited by

Harry Coenen

Professor of Labour Studies

and

Peter Leisink

Lecturer in Labour Studies, Utrecht University, The Netherlands

Edward Elgar

Published by
Edward Elgar Publishing Limited
Gower House
Croft Road
Aldershot
Hants GU11 3HR
England

Edward Elgar Publishing Company
Old Post Road
Brookfield
Vermont 05036
USA

Library of Congress Cataloging-in-Publication Data

Work and citizenship in the New Europe / edited by Harry Coenen and
    Peter Leisink.
    272 p.   21 cm.
        Papers presented at the international conference on the quality of
    citizenship.
        Includes bibliographical references and index.
        1. Labor market–Europe–Congresses.   2. Citizenship–Europe–
    Congresses.   3. Alien labor–Europe–Congresses.   4. Employment in
    foreign countries–Congresses.   I. Coenen, Harry.   II. Leisink,
    Peter, 1952–
    HD5764.A6W67   1993
    331.12'094–dc20   93–9712
                                                                   CIP

ISBN 978 1 85278 739 4

Printed and bound by CPI Group (UK) Ltd, Croydon, CR0 4YY

Contents

v

List of Tables and Figures

Tables

Figures

List of Contributors

Hans Adriaansens is Professor of General Social Sciences and Dean of the Faculty of Social Sciences at the Utrecht University, the Netherlands. He is also a member of the Netherlands Scientific Council for Government Policy.

Gregory Andrusz teaches at the Faculty of Social Science at Middlesex University, United Kingdom.

Jens Bastian is a Researcher at the European University Institute, Department of Political and Social Sciences, in Firenze, Italy.

Leni Beukema is a Lecturer in Labour Studies at the Department of General Social Sciences at the Utrecht University, the Netherlands.

Harry Coenen is Professor of Labour Studies at the Utrecht University, the Netherlands.

Willem Dercksen is Professor of Socio-Economic Policy at the Utrecht University, the Netherlands. He is also a member of staff of the Netherlands Scientific Council for Government Policy.

Stefan Dimitrov is Assistant Professor of Philosophy and Sociology at the Technical University of Sofia, Bulgaria.

Dimitrina Dimitrova is a Researcher at the Bulgarian Academy of Sciences in the Institute of Sociology, Sofia, Bulgaria.

Godfried Engbersen is Associate Professor of General Social Sciences at the Utrecht University, the Netherlands.

Stephen Heycock teaches in the Department of Industrial Technology at the University of Bradford, United Kingdom.

John Jacobs is a Lecturer in Social Policy at the School of Cultural and Community Studies, University of Sussex, United Kingdom.

Peter Leisink is a Lecturer in Labour Studies at the Department of General Social Sciences, Utrecht University, the Netherlands.

Robert Moore is Eleanor Rathbone Professor of Sociology at the University of Liverpool, United Kingdom.

Claus Offe is Professor at the Centre of Social Policy at the University of Bremen, Germany.

Romke van der Veen is Associate Professor at the Department of Public Administration and Public Policy, Faculty of Social Sciences, Leyden University, the Netherlands.

Jacques Vilrokx is Professor of Sociology and Labour Economics and Director of the Study Group in Technological, Economic and Social Change and Labour Market Research (TESA) at the Free University of Brussels, Belgium.

Foreword

After some five years in which we focussed on backstage activities to develop a new Department of General Social Sciences at the Utrecht University, the time was ripe in 1991 for a public display of the research that was being carried out. The department accommodates social scientists, many of them psychologists and sociologists, who co-operate in an interdisciplinary research programme concerning current social problems with the aim of providing theoretical analyses and empirically-founded scenarios for policy interventions. Hans Adriaansens should be given credit for promoting the issue of citizenship as the general theme integrating the various research projects and for waking us up to the heritage of social and political theory with respect to issues of community membership and social participation. Under his chairmanship the international conference on 'the quality of citizenship' attracted some two hundred scholars from all over the world. It offered an exciting opportunity to present the research of our department, but above all it was proof of the rapidly growing importance of citizenship.

The workshop on 'work and citizenship' which we chaired hosted a number of papers and debates on topics which have attracted even more interest since then. The economic crisis has affected the basis of the modern welfare state and attempts at reform have caused considerable concern about the state of citizenship. Any serious reform of the welfare state inevitably raises the issue of the social contract itself, the rights and duties of citizens and the state. In addition, the Western sensitivity about the concept of citizenship has increased due to the recent changes in Central and Eastern Europe, which have contributed significantly to a revaluation of civil and political citizenship rights. In the New Europe the concept of citizenship will, therefore, be pivotal. It will accompany any public debate on redressing the balance of rights and duties in the context of changing cultural, economic, political and technological circumstances. Exploring the contours of such a balance in relation to work is the task we have set ourselves with this collection of essays by authors from different states from the East and the West of the New Europe.

Notwithstanding our intellectual belief in the significance of the issue of work and citizenship, there were more practical demands to be met in order to achieve our aim. The first of these was solved by Edward Elgar, to whom we are very grateful for the trust he put in the quality of our project. We would like to thank David Clark and Julie Leppard of Edward Elgar Publishing Ltd for their quick replies to our questions and for their helpful editorial assistance. We would also like to thank Rikkert Stuve of the University Language Centre Nijmegen, who thoroughly corrected many of the chapters. He proved to be a conscientious proofreader who did not restrict himself to translation matters but also raised substantial questions when he thought fit.

Cees de Wit participated on our behalf in the organizing committee of the conference and Karin van Vliet did a lot of organizational work preparing our workshop. Sabine Jansen acted as an efficient secretary to the project of this book, performing a lot of useful editorial work and providing administrative assistance throughout this project, for which we are grateful. We would like to thank the Department of General Social Sciences for its generous financial and organizational support of our project. Our colleagues of the research group Work and Participation inspired our project intellectually with their questions and comments on ideas and draft parts of the book. We are grateful to them for their contribution. In spite of all the support we have had, this book may nevertheless have its defects for which, as usual, we are entirely responsible.

Harry Coenen
Peter Leisink

1. Work and Citizenship in the New Europe

Peter Leisink and Harry Coenen

The Topicality of Work and Citizenship

If one compares the number of publications on 'citizenship' by the middle of the 1980s with the present number, the topicality of the subject presents itself irresistibly. The second half of the 1980s did indeed witness a strong revival of interest in citizenship. (Held 1991 p. 19; Lister 1990 p. 22)

The current interest in citizenship, both in the political community at large and in the social and political sciences, is related directly to the major social developments which have taken place in Europe during the past few years. The first to be mentioned is the crisis of the Western welfare states and the concomitant erosion of social citizenship rights. (Dahrendorf 1988a) Almost all Western economies suffered from major economic recessions in the early 1980s and the early 1990s. The economic crisis has been reflected in declining or stagnating Gross National Products and in overall high unemployment. It has induced governments on the left and the right to embark on policies of retrenchment and control of public expenditure. Where such policies were firmly implemented, social security, which the welfare state was meant to provide for, was gradually eroded resulting in a growing number of people facing poverty. We even witnessed the gradual emergence of an underclass in some Western countries like the United Kingdom and the Netherlands. As social citizenship rights had once been intended to enable all citizens to be full members of the community, the emergence of an underclass was consequently seen as giving rise to an 'exclusive society'. (Lister 1990; Turner 1991 p. 216)

In addition, the economic crisis of the Western societies and the pressures which are put on the welfare states were and still are to a large extent responsible for a rather hesitant attitude towards Central and Eastern Europe when it comes to providing financial support during their transition process towards a market economy.

The demise of 'really existing socialism' is indeed the other major development which boosted the renewed interest in citizenship. (Andrews 1991 p. 11; Dahrendorf 1991 pp. 8–11) The overthrow of Communist rule and the introduction of a multi-party parliamentary system as well as the intended transition to a market economy (entailing among other things the right to private property and freedom of contract) were claimed by the West as a victory of the Western type of citizenship. One might have hoped that this euphoria would have led to the recognition of common history and culture and to the establishment of citizenship rights on a European level. This is what Michail Gorbachev, the former president of the former Soviet Union, may have meant by the idea of a 'common European home'. Rather, the common home appears to be a block of flats without a freely accessible lift. Eastern European citizens who wished to make use of their newly gained freedom and made plans to migrate to the West were stopped. At the same time when Western European states were moving towards a European Community (EC) which should grant its citizens freedom of travel within the Community, they decided to virtually close their outside borders. The citizenship rights of the Community's insiders contrast sharply with those granted to outsiders. As is so often the case, the establishment of insiders' rights entails the exclusion of outsiders.

The developments which have taken place during the 1980s and the early 1990s have brought up various dimensions of citizenship, which Marshall classified as civil, political and social rights. Civil and political rights were clearly the primary issue of civil rights movements in Central and Eastern European states, like Charta 77 in Czechoslovakia. (*cf.* Bloomfield 1991) Social rights were the issue of trade unions and anti-poverty groups in Western European states. These respective issues have attracted a specific interest of their own. For instance, a number of publications raise the conditions which underpin the civil and political rights of citizens such as the free press (Dahlgren and Sparks 1991) and education. (Heater 1990) The crisis of the welfare state has generated a growing number of publications on social citizenship rights. (Esping-Andersen 1990; Lister 1990; Taylor-Gooby 1991) Whereas the topic of work is touched on by most publications in one way or another, the relationship between work and citizenship as such, has not become the focus of substantive analysis however.

The neglect of work may have to do with the fact that citizenship is commonly associated with the public relationship between state and citizens and is situated in the field of politics, whereas work is regarded as a private relationship between employers and employees and is situated in the field of the economy. Nevertheless, the disregard of work is curious since the two major developments which have made citizenship topical are clearly related to work. The crisis of the welfare state is directly related to work, notably to the transformation of work by technological innovation and economic restructuring. In the debate about the state provision of welfare which accompanies this crisis, work is a key issue. The suspicion that the provision of state welfare might have the perverse effect of acting as a disincentive to work has even been brought up as an argument to distinguish principally between civil and political rights on the one hand and social rights on the other. (Taylor-Gooby 1991 pp. 198–199)

Likewise, the market economy, including private property, is one aspect of the attraction of West European welfare states to many East European citizens, the other one being civil and political liberty. In fact, not willing to wait until privatization of the state enterprises has generated wealth in Eastern Europe, many of its citizens try to find work in the West, even if it is only a temporary job. For instance, for many years Polish workers have come to assist in the harvest of tulip bulbs, strawberries and asparagus in the Netherlands. Many still do this kind of seasonal work, be it now illegally because the Dutch government wants to reserve work permits to citizens of European Community member states.

The sheer fact that work seems to be a blind spot in many analyses may be regarded as an invitation to examine the relationship between work and citizenship more closely. The position of work in relation to citizenship does not appear to be quite clear. Is work to be subsumed under citizenship rights in the economic field, or under citizenship obligations? It may be noted that Central and East European states, such as Bulgaria and the former Soviet Union, used to grant their citizens a right to work. However, in the Western concept of citizenship social rights concern an entitlement to benefit payments in case one is not able to support oneself through work because of unemployment, illness, disability or age. In all West European states the economic crisis has again given rise to an emphasis on the obligation to work.

It will be clear from this summary exploration of work and citizenship that, in social policy, 'work' is defined as paid work or employment. No Western welfare state has regarded housework or community service as a ground for granting benefit payments. On the contrary, welfare states ignore the contribution to the common good made by the unpaid carework carried out for the most part by women. (Taylor-Gooby 1991 pp. 202–206) Our focus on the relationship between work and citizenship will, therefore, also imply a critical reassessment of the concept of work, differentiating between paid and unpaid work.

The fact that major social developments are related to citizenship and work in one way or another whereas this relation is not dealt with explicitly, as well as the indication that there is something unclear in the relationship of citizenship and work, are strong arguments to warrant the analysis of work and citizenship as a central issue. This is what we will do in this collection of essays.

In this introductory chapter we will first set out how we approach the concept of citizenship. Second, we will focus on the multiple relationships between work and citizenship. The various relations we will deal with are: work as a form of participation in society, work as a citizenship right and work as a citizenship obligation. Then we will concentrate on the meaning of work and citizenship in the context of the 'New Europe'. Finally we will introduce the outline of this volume.

Citizenship: Membership and Participation

The historical origins of citizenship have been traced to Aristotle's *Politics* (Barbalet 1988 p. 2; Heater 1990 p. 3), but most sociologists begin their analysis with T.H. Marshall's 1949 lectures on *Citizenship and Social Class*, which were reissued recently. (Marshall and Bottomore 1992)

Marshall regarded citizenship as 'a status bestowed on those who are full members of a community. All who possess the status are equal with respect to the rights and duties with which the status is endowed.' (Marshall 1973 p. 84) He divided citizenship into three sets of rights – civil, political and social rights – and connected these to the institutions of the courts of justice, the parliament and councils of local government, the educational system and the social services. (Marshall 1973 pp. 71–72)

Whereas the rights are 'precise' according to Marshall, the duties are less unequivocal.

> The duty whose discharge is most obviously and immediately necessary for the fulfilment of the right is the duty to pay taxes and insurance contributions. ... Education and military service are also compulsory. The other duties are vague, and are included in the general obligation to live the life of a good citizen, giving such service as one can to promote the welfare of the community. (Marshall 1973 p. 117)

As regards this general obligation Marshall considered the duty to work 'of paramount importance' but he was well aware that it is 'no easy matter' for the citizen to identify himself with this personal obligation. (Marshall 1973 pp. 117–118)

Although Marshall defined citizenship as a status, his analysis supports a reading of citizenship as 'participation in or membership of a community' (Barbalet 1988 p. 2) or as 'social membership and participation in society as a whole'. (Turner 1986 p. 85) Regarding citizenship as essentially concerned with participation in a community or society draws attention to the fact that citizenship is not merely a matter of having formal rights. These rights are important, of course, because they define the domains in which citizens may pursue their activities. However, one should also pay attention to the conditions under which citizens' rights are actually enacted. The examination of both formal rights and social conditions constitutes what Held has called a 'double focus' which 'makes it possible to grasp the degrees of autonomy, interdependence and constraint that citizens face in the societies in which they live'. (Held 1989 p. 175) In connection with work this approach means that we will have to study the participation of citizens, or the non-participation for that matter, in relation to the division of labour and the structure of labour markets among other things. (*cf.* Harrison 1991 p. 211)

Marshall analysed the structure of modern society as the outcome of the rise of capitalism on the one hand and the development of citizenship on the other. While capitalism created class inequalities, citizenship progressively provided for an equality of status. Social citizenship rights in particular had a strong impact on class inequalities. Although social rights did not remove class inequality as such, they tended to reduce social inequalities. The provision of social services, such as health care and education, and a guaranteed minimum income as in the case of old-age pensions, introduced a measure of social justice and protection against the freedom of the market. Thus, according to Marshall, citizenship has imposed profound modifications on the capitalist class system. (Marshall 1973 p. 110)

Marshall's framework of study, in which citizenship is analysed in relation to class divisions, has been accepted by sociologists such as Dahrendorf (1988a pp. 29, 36) and Giddens (1985 p. 204), although Giddens (1989 p. 268) now agrees that this framework is insufficient. Recent reassessments of citizenship, however, have criticized Marshall's framework as too restrictive. (Barbalet 1988 p. 97; Held 1989 pp.

172–176; Turner 1986 pp. 85–92) The importance of class in relation to citizenship is not denied and the historical contribution of the labour movement to the expansion of citizenship rights is recognized. However, the development of citizenship may not be reduced to class conflict only. As Held aptly puts it:

> If citizenship entails membership in the community and membership implies forms of participation, then it is misleading to think of citizenship primarily in relation to class or the capitalist relations of production. Citizenship is about involvement of people in the community in which they live; and people have been barred from citizenship on the grounds of gender, race and age, among many other factors. ... If citizenship involves the struggle for membership and participation in the community, then its analysis involves examining the way in which different groups, classes and movements struggle to gain degrees of autonomy and control over their lives in the face of various forms of stratification, hierarchy and political oppression. (Held 1989 p. 173)

We agree with this broader conception of citizenship. Our intention to focus on the relationship of work and citizenship should not be read as an approach to citizenship in terms of class analysis only. In fact, we will argue that the relationship between citizenship and work has been changing and must change further not only because of economic and technological factors, but also because of the demands put forward by different social movements, the labour movement being only one of them. For instance, the claim of the feminist movement to labour participation as a major form of participation in society has led to the demand for a redistribution of paid and unpaid work, among other things by a reduction of working hours. The demands made by the ecological movement can only be complied with when sustainable growth and ecologically-sound production processes will be achieved, although this will have consequences for employment and the organization of work.

Having introduced our approach to citizenship as concerning membership of and participation in society, we will now go on to analyse the multiple relationships of work and citizenship in more detail. We will begin with the analysis of work as a form of participation in society.

Work as a Form of Participation in Society

Work itself is a major form of social participation. Through their work people enter into social networks. Indeed, the loss of these networks is one of the most painful consequences of losing one's job. Under conditions as they exist in the American inner cities where only unemployed

live because those who have a job have moved to another neighbourhood, the loss of networks with people having a job and knowing
vacancies may virtually eliminate access to work and to society. (Wilson
1987 p. 60) Unemployment is one of the key factors in causing social
isolation.

The importance of work as a form of participation in society in itself
and as a condition of participation in society as a whole is borne out by
the characterization of modern societies as 'work societies'. (Dahrendorf
1988a p. 143) Modern societies, according to Dahrendorf, are built
around the work ethic and occupational roles. Work is a 'central social
institution and an essential part of most people's lives'. (Grint 1991 p.
46) The implications of the importance of work as a form of participation
may be spelled out in more detail.

Work has many functions for the individual which have been summarized by Jahoda in five categories. These categories have been singled
out on the basis of the experience of unemployment. In other words, the
positive aspects of work have been established by examining the social-
psychological consequences of unemployment. In the following aspects
the unemployed felt psychologically deprived: the experience of time,
the reduction of social contacts, the lack of participation in collective
purposes, the absence of an acceptable status and its consequences for
personal identity, and the absence of regular activity. (Jahoda 1982 p.
39)

Most of these aspects overlap with social participation or membership
of a community, which we have taken as the essential concern of
citizenship. These aspects of work as social participation are not what
employment is for, rather they are its unintended consequences: '...it
enforces these categories of experience on all participants. While the
unemployed are left to their own devices to find experiences within these
categories if they can and suffer if they cannot, the employed take them
for granted.' (Jahoda 1982 p. 39)

Jahoda explicitly restricts her analysis to employment, that is to say
to jobs or 'work under contractual arrangements involving material
rewards'. (Jahoda 1982 p. 8) When one examines the different functions
of employment which Jahoda lists it is evident that these do not equally
pertain to housework. Generally speaking housework does not offer
social contacts, participation in collective purposes, a positive status and
identity in the way a professional job does. (Oakley 1974) Or, as Gorz
has put it:

It is by having *paid* work (more particularly, work for a wage) that we belong to the public sphere, acquire a social existence and a social identity (that is, a 'profession'), and are part of a network of relations and exchanges in which we are measured against other people and are granted certain rights over them in exchange for the duties we have towards them. (Gorz 1989 p. 13)

Having a job is obviously a major form of social participation. Yet there is no clear-cut distinction between employment and work. On the one hand work which is not organized as employment, such as domestic labour, qualifies as social participation at least in some respects and to a certain extent, but it has less status according to the capitalist and patriarchal model of work. (Grint 1991 pp. 32–40, 46) On the other hand paid work does not yield the positive aspects of work indiscriminately either. Jobs differ considerably for instance with respect to the opportunities they offer for communication and participation at work.

To sum up our argument so far, through their very work individuals constitute themselves as members of society. However, significant differences which go into the make-up of work, notably the difference between paid work and unpaid work as well as the internal differentiation of paid work, determine the differential nature of social membership through work.

To underline the significance of work, particularly employment, as a major form of social participation, it must be added that it also appears to be a condition of full participation in society as a whole in a way which cannot be equalled by social security rights. We will now explore this significant function of work to participation.

Besides work there are other forms of social participation such as participation in political life, being on the board of a school, doing social work for the elderly, and so on. Given the ample amount of time on their hands one might expect the unemployed to engage far more actively in these forms of social participation than those having a job. However, the opposite rather appears to be true when long-term unemployed and employees are compared, as empirical research of participation in clubs and community activities demonstrated for the Netherlands. (Becker and Vink 1984; Kroft, Engbersen, Schuyt, Van Waarden 1989) For instance, twice as many employees are members of sports clubs as long-term unemployed, and the former also participate in voluntary community work twice as much (about 40 per cent versus 20 per cent).

Apparently employment is significantly connected with other forms of participation in society. To put it differently, those who lose their job also lose access to other forms of social participation to a considerable extent. This loss of social contacts may even amount to a level of near social isolation, as in the case of about one-third of welfare claimants who can no longer afford a telephone. (Engbersen 1990 p. 130) In this context the emergence of an underclass has been pointed out.

This paradoxical outcome raises questions with respect to the degree in which social security benefits allow those who are dependent on them to stay full members of society, the aim which they are officially intended to achieve. It is true that citizens who lose their job and are on unemployment benefit do not lose their political rights, whereas in the nineteenth century paupers placed in the workhouse forfeited the rights possessed by other citizens. (Giddens 1982 p. 169) Social security benefits are structured in such a way, however, that they limit social participation opportunities both substantially and formally.

The substantial limits to participation can be assessed most easily. From the early 1970s onwards the economic crisis has confronted the Western welfare states with declining revenues and increasing expenses. To tackle the rising public debt governments have favoured cutting down social security expenditure. In the United Kingdom this cut went together with discussions about what was to be considered as the biological subsistence level. In fact the number of people who do not have a hot meal once a day and the number of homeless has increased very sharply during Thatcher's term of office. Between 1979 and 1987 the proportion of the population living below or at the minimum subsistence supplementary benefit level rose from 12 to 19 per cent. (Taylor-Gooby 1991 pp. 86–91)

In other Western countries, like the Netherlands, with less ideologically-marked conservative governments and even in states led by socialist governments, like France and Spain, cuts on social security benefits have not been much less. The cuts have caused at least 10 per cent of Dutch households to be poor. (Berghman, Muffels, de Vries 1988) The loss of income affects the social participation of claimants substantially, as has been indicated above. All forms of community membership that entail financial costs, such as subscription to newspapers or membership of a sports club, tend to be dropped by households on benefit.

This deficiency of social security benefits of achieving full membership, which they are intended to underpin, is connected with the very nature of social citizenship rights. Whereas civil and political rights are embodied in constitutions, social rights are not similarly entrenched. (Dahrendorf 1988a p. 40) This is not to say that all civil and political rights are determinately defined and implemented. (Plant 1991 pp. 55–56; Taylor-Gooby 1991 p. 198) In addition, civil and political rights are universal rights concerned with protecting the space for citizens to pursue their activities unimpeded by state action without regard to individual conditions. With respect to social rights, however, the right to social services as such is universal but the services which are provided are particular in order to meet different needs of different categories of claimants. (Barbalet 1988 pp. 18–20, 67–72) Moreover, whereas civil and political rights demand state action and expenditure that benefit all citizens, social rights entail state intervention to secure the provision of benefits for particular categories of welfare claimants. As a consequence of this nature of social rights, the social right to 'a modicum of economic welfare and security' (Marshall 1973 p. 72) and, based on that, the full membership of society appears to fluctuate in relation to political and economic circumstances in a way in which civil and political rights generally do not.

In yet another way social rights are different from civil and political rights. Although every citizen has an obligation to comply with the law, a citizen who is suspected of not having fulfilled this obligation in a particular instance has the right to a due process of law. Civil rights are unconditional. Similarly political rights are rights that are not themselves tied to specific obligations. Political rights enable citizens to partake in the political life of their community without compelling them to do so. Or, as Dahrendorf puts it, 'compulsory voting is a dubious interpretation of citizenship rights'. (Dahrendorf 1988a p. 34)

Social policy treats welfare benefits, particularly unemployment benefits, as conditional, however. It is obligatory on citizens who are on unemployment benefit to apply for jobs actively and to be available for work at short notice. Unemployed who do not actively search for work will be sanctioned and may even forfeit their benefit right.

The conditional nature of unemployment benefits has indeed been intensified throughout the 1980s. Many Western states have introduced all kinds of employment policy programmes, offering training, work experience, community service projects and so on while at the same time forcing sanctions on unemployed claimants who are unwilling to accept such offers made to them. (*cf.* Baglioni and Crouch 1990; Watts 1983) For instance, in the Netherlands unemployed face a cut of their monthly allowance when they refuse a training offer which is considered necessary.

The point that is relevant within the context of this paragraph is that the specific obligations to which unemployment benefits are tied can become a barrier to other forms of participation in society. Unemployed who would like to engage voluntarily in community activities, which are often unpaid, are prevented from doing so by the same obligations to which they are tied because of their benefit. For instance, the argument not to allow unemployed claimants to engage in community work is that these activities might keep them from actively searching for a job and from being available at short notice. In this way the conditional nature of the social security entitlements constitute another barrier to social participation and to community membership.

The very nature of the social security rights threatens to turn them into the opposite of what they are intended to effect. Instead of providing a means of enabling citizens to partake in the community (Barbalet 1988 pp. 68–69), social rights may for some categories of citizens turn out to be a barrier to it. Work, especially employment, is not only a major form of social participation in itself but it is also a condition of full participation in society in a way which is not equalled by social security rights, given their actual structure. One way of reading this analysis is that if the state is looked upon as the guarantor of citizenship rights then it has the duty too to offer its citizens the right to work.

Work as a Citizenship Right

In Marshall's theory of citizenship the right to work is not absent. Indeed, according to Marshall 'in the economic field the basic civil right is the right to work', but he qualifies its sense in the context of his historical analysis of the development of citizenship. (Marshall 1973 p. 75) The right to work entails 'the right to follow the occupation of one's choice in the place of one's choice, subject only to legitimate demands for preliminary technical training'. The right to work, as Marshall conceives it, takes its meaning from the abolition of guilds and local regulations during the seventeenth and eighteenth century which reserved employment to their members and which used apprenticeship as an instrument of exclusion. (Marshall 1977 pp. 75–77)

The significance of this right to work should not be underestimated. For instance, only in 1994 will Russia abolish the internal passport and residential permit which the state used as an instrument to prevent citizens from moving to a particular town to look for a job. Nevertheless, Marshall's right to work does not enable the citizen to partake in economic life in the same way as political rights enable him or her to participate in the exercise of political power as an elector, as a member of a political party or as a member of a body invested with political authority. Citizens do not have a substantive right to work. Although the Universal Declaration of Human Rights, which was accepted by the United Nations in 1948, states in article 23 that 'everyone has a right to work', no Western nation-state has entrenched this right in its constitution, as far as we know. The 1983 constitution of the Netherlands only has it that 'the promotion of sufficient employment is an object of care of the state'. The right to work is largely defined negatively, that is to say there are no customs or statutes as in the seventeenth century preventing citizens from applying for jobs. (Held 1991 p. 21)

Dahrendorf has argued against a right to work on the grounds that 'no judge can force employers to hire unemployed people'. (Dahrendorf 1988a p. 148) He favours another option: 'In terms of liberty, it is more important to establish the right not to work, so that governments cannot force people into a dependence which they want to escape'.

Dahrendorf regards the employment relationship as a private contract and therefore rejects a right to work. Although this is legally correct, the purely private nature is not always as private as Dahrendorf states. In the Netherlands as well as in other welfare states, the state subsidizes an employer for a number of years if he is willing to hire a long-term unemployed for a job. Nevertheless, Dahrendorf's alternative to establish a right not to work deserves serious attention.

Surely the right not to work would do away with a basic asymmetry which currently exists. On the one hand employers are not forced to hire unemployed people, but on the other hand unemployed are forced to search for work actively and to accept a job vacancy which a manpower service consultant thinks appropriate, even though it may not match their educational qualifications. Moreover, the right not to work would also put an end to the paradoxical situation which we noted in the previous paragraph that the obligations to which the use of social security benefits are tied tend to block rather than to facilitate the participation in community life. However, there are two main arguments against the outright acceptance of a right not to work.

First, we should acknowledge that employment has become a scarce resource in itself, which in its turn offers access to other scarce resources in society. As Dahrendorf has put it himself: 'Jobs are the entry tickets to the world of provisions', provisions being the goods and services available for consumption. (Dahrendorf 1988a p. 143) Replacing the obligation to work by the right not to work does not change the inequality of conditions on the labour market, it may even be used to legitimize it. Second, Dahrendorf's suggestion to establish the right not to work uncritically accepts the dominant definition of work as employment. It foregoes the fact that a lot of work is done and must be done, such as domestic labour and community work, without being paid and without being recognized as work.

Concluding we are in favour of a qualified right not to work, that is a right to refuse work, for instance in the case of work that may pollute our habitat severely. However, if 'citizenship involves essentially the question of access to scarce resources in society and participation in the distribution and enjoyment of such resources' (Turner 1986 p. 85), then citizenship should entail the access to work in a differentiated sense. (Berkel and Hindriks 1991; Gorz 1989) This would imply a redistribution of employment, for instance by a reduction of working hours. It also implies the recognition that those unemployed who engage in community work do not have to search for a job because they do work. These implications cannot be stopped by the kind of objection that Dahrendorf raises against a right to work because that would entail the intrusion of judges on the domain of employers. Indeed the implementation of these implications remains within the competence of the state as the historical record of working hours legislation and social security legislation testifies. Obviously there are more implications of a right to work. We will deal with them in the next paragraph.

Work as a Citizenship Obligation

When we introduced the concept of citizenship we noted that there is no unequivocality with respect to citizenship duties. (*cf.* Heater 1990 p. 193) Marshall himself was explicit about the duty to pay taxes and insurance contributions. In his opinion education and military service were also compulsory. However, 'the other duties are vague, and are included in the general obligation to live the life of a good citizen, giving such service as one can to promote the welfare of the community'. (Marshall 1973 p. 117) In this latter context Marshall elaborated the duty to work.

It is important to note that Marshall regards citizenship duties as general duties. He does not distinguish duties into specific obligations each of which is a condition of a specific set of rights. To be precise, he has not made the duty to work a condition of the consumption of social rights. Indeed Marshall held the opinion that 'social rights imply an absolute right to a certain standard of civilization which is conditional only on the discharge of the *general* duties of citizenship.' (Marshall 1973 p. 94; italics ours)

It is worth emphasizing this point since contemporary debates focus strongly on the obligation to work as a condition of the right to welfare. Mead for instance regards as the fatal weakness of welfare programmes 'that they award their benefits essentially as entitlements, expecting next to nothing from the beneficiaries in return.' (Mead 1986 p. 2) He defends the thesis that 'only those who bear obligations can truly appropriate their rights'. (Mead 1986 p. 257) In his opinion the obligation to work is the most important social obligation. Unemployed who do not actively look for a job should therefore not be entitled to welfare provisions.

The social policies of many Western welfare states have shown a shift from welfare entitlements to claimants' obligations and sanctions against those who are not willing to accept a training or work-experience offer. The arguments underlying the emphasis on work as a citizenship obligation are threefold. They can be taken from the 'working perspective' programme by the Netherlands Scientific Council for Government Policy (WRR 1990), the general outline of which has been accepted by the Dutch government.

First, work itself is an important form of social participation. Work has a number of functions for the individual, such as we have elaborated above. (WRR 1990 pp. 39–41) Second, work has functions for society as well. By working, people enter into social networks and contribute to the integration of society. The less people have a job, the more other institutions are called upon to generate social integration. Since many traditional institutions, such as the family household and the church have been eroded in modern societies, work is increasingly essential in providing for social cohesion. (WRR 1990 pp. 7, 41–44)

Third, a high rate of labour participation is considered necessary as an economic condition of a sustainable welfare state. Only if more people have a job can we continue to afford the social rights which the welfare state offers. (WRR 1990 p. 8) This argument is pressed home by pointing to demographic developments leading to a diminishing number of young people and a growing number of older, retired people.

The 'working perspective' programme from which these arguments for labour participation are taken, differs from Mead's analysis in that it does not stress the obligations of the citizen only but pays attention to the state's obligations as well. The policy scenario which was elaborated includes such state obligations as providing training, child care and parental leave facilities, affirmative action and so on. Against the background of individual and collective obligations the need is stressed to activate the unemployed themselves. When unemployed get more and more opportunities for training, work experience or temporary jobs through all kinds of programmes, it is considered fair to impose sanctions against those who do not comply. Sanctions of up to a quarter of an unemployment benefit are proposed to discourage unemployed from preferring unemployment benefit to work at a minimum wage level.

Evidently this argument for labour participation is far more balanced than Mead's, but is it enough to underpin a citizen's obligation to work? The first argument that work is an important form of social participation and has a number of functions for the individual may well be accepted without converting work into an obligation. The state that compels its citizens to do something which is in their own interest may soon find itself behaving like Big Brother, stifling any liberty of choice.

The function of work to society, which is referred to by the second argument, goes back to the Durkheimian analysis of social cohesion. In modern societies, Durkheim argued, social cohesion is less dependent on mechanical solidarity, which is based on people conforming to the same set of social values, and becomes more dependent on organic solidarity, which is based on the increasing interdependence of people through the progressive division of labour. (Durkheim 1984) The labour participation scenario adopts this institutional and functional approach to social integration, with citizenship being called upon to provide some moral tissue. This kind of policy has been criticized by Dahrendorf, who also refers to the Durkheimian argument of social integration: 'Worried neo-conservatives join forces with bewildered socialists in extolling the virtues of hard work when neither have enough employment to offer to all. They are really talking about social and political control, for which no other mechanism than the discipline of employment has yet been found.' (Dahrendorf 1988a p. 144)

The modern conflict between the effort to create wealth and the effort to extend rights to those on the margins of society is reflected in the aims of the labour participation scenario. Labour participation is necessary, as the third argument states, as an economic condition of a sustainable welfare state. But is the citizen's obligation to work, which follows from it, balanced by the state's obligation to provide enough training programmes, child care and parental leave facilities, opportunities for work experience and so on? The intended reciprocity of citizen and state obligations cannot be achieved at all at this moment. The state's capacity to offer provisions is failing in all areas which the 'working perspective' programme indicates as essential. This should caution us to lay down a citizen's obligation which cannot really be fulfilled. Yet the obligation to work is not lifted for the long-term unemployed and sanctions against non-compliant claimants are stressed even more than ever before. Politically, then, the emphasis on work as a citizenship obligation tends at present to topple the balance towards reserving rights to those who meet their obligations.

Contrary to Mead who regards work as the primary obligation, Dahrendorf argues that work is not a citizenship obligation. Dahrendorf believes that Mead is 'fundamentally mistaken and destroys an important concept if not, by its application, the rights of people'. (Dahrendorf 1988a p. 33) According to Dahrendorf:

> Citizenship is a social contract, generally valid for all members; work is a private contract. ... when the general rights of citizenship are made dependent on people entering into private relations of employment, these lose their private and fundamentally voluntary character. In an indirect but compelling manner, labour becomes forced labour. It is imperative that the obligations of citizenship are themselves general and public as it were. (Dahrendorf 1988a p. 33)

In Dahrendorf's conception work is not a citizenship obligation because work is a different social category belonging to the sphere of private contract. Although he is hesitant about the extent of obligations, thinking that 'in principle the rights of citizenship are not conditional' (Dahrendorf 1988a p. 34), there are a number of public obligations which he recognizes. These include compliance with the law and paying taxes. He goes on to state:

> It may well make sense to ask citizens to give some time of their lives to the community. Conscription is the obvious example, though some form of community service could be one method of dealing with issues which the market does not resolve by itself. Such service, whether military or civilian, is of course also 'forced labour'. But it is strictly circumscribed and in all respects a part of the public domain in which citizens exist. (Dahrendorf 1988a p. 33)

The interesting point of Dahrendorf's analysis is that he takes up the original idea of Marshall about the 'general obligation to live the life of a good citizen, giving such service as one can to promote the welfare of the community'. In our opinion Marshall's realization of this general obligation in terms of the duty to work (read: to take a job) must be understood within the context of the post-Second World War economy.

The 1950s and 1960s were a time of full employment, and unemployment, if it occurred, was mostly temporary. However, since the late 1970s we face structural unemployment, in terms of the numbers of registered unemployed, even more in terms of the numbers of job-seekers who are not registered, and still more in the context of a distribution of labour on a global scale. We think, therefore, that the general obligation 'to live the life of a good citizen' is now more adequately realized by doing 'community service' (Dahrendorf) which promotes 'the welfare of the community'. (Marshall) This approach has additional advantages because it recognizes contributions to the common good which are ignored by the dominant conception of citizenship.

According to this dominant conception which at bottom is based on the obligation to take a job, a workaholic who works sixty or more hours a week and has no time to do community service like being on the board of a school is considered a good citizen, whereas the unemployed who is full-time engaged in community service activities but cannot find a job is not considered a good citizen. Yet, the unemployed citizen engaged in community service may be said to promote as much, if not more, the welfare of the community as his workaholic colleague. Similarly, the dominant conception of citizenship ignores the unpaid care-work which is mostly carried out by women, although care-work, notably the upbringing of a new generation, is vital to the continuance of society. (Taylor-Gooby 1991 pp. 200–202)

In the previous section we noted two arguments against accepting an outright right not to work. To our argument that every citizen should have equal opportunities to find a job, we can now add that in our opinion all citizens should have the obligation, or rather responsibility (*cf.* Heater 1990 pp. 197–202; Mulgan 1991) to contribute to the welfare of the community. As Mulgan has argued: 'a libertarianism that leaves the individual with no obligations looks like a cul-de-sac. It leaves community as contingent, social responsibility as nothing more than an effect of free-floating conscience.' (Mulgan 1991 p. 43) The idea that property rights provide the best means for creating a responsible society must be refuted because they 'seem to foster care within narrow limits only at the price of carelessness in relation to the rest of society', as environmental pollution, to name but one example, testifies. (Mulgan 1991 p. 44) Therefore, we should introduce a new moral sense of social responsibility.

Against this background we bring up work as a citizenship obligation, that is to say work not in the orthodox restricted sense of employment but in a broad sense which includes unpaid work such as care-work and community service.

Towards Economic Citizenship Rights

Before going on to broaden our scope of analysis to the New Europe, we will sum up our argument. We regard citizenship as essentially concerned with membership of and participation in society. Taking into account that having a job is a major form of social participation and a condition of full participation in society, every citizen should have a right to work. Since there are objections to legally enforcing this right, one might consider a right not to work. However, such a right would leave the inequality of access to the scarce resource of employment as it is, and, in addition, it ignores the issue of citizens' responsibilities towards their community.

Therefore, we argue in favour of a citizenship right to work in a broad sense, ranging from employment to care-work and community service. We are in favour of a redistribution of paid work so that every citizen can have a job as well as have a share in care-work and community service. However, as long as this is not realized we think that every citizen who cannot find a job but engages in care-work or community service should not be harassed by the obligation to look for a job actively and to be available at short notice or forfeit his or her welfare benefit.

The membership of a community demands that all members share in the responsibility towards the welfare of their community. This original sense of citizenship duties is more adequately realized by the obligation to work in a differentiated sense than in the orthodox restricted sense of employment. In this context work is a citizenship right and a citizenship obligation, and citizenship entails a certain reciprocity as it has always meant to do. (Held 1989 p. 172)

So far we have concentrated on the relationships between work and citizenship without bothering about the question how work as a citizenship right might be fitted into the conventional conception of citizenship. To put it differently, does giving work the status both of a citizenship right and of a citizenship obligation call for a revision of the conception of citizenship itself?

We agree with Held (1989 pp. 175–176) that there are good reasons for regarding the conception of citizenship as consisting of civil, political and social rights as too restricted. Held has suggested adding other sets of rights such as economic rights and reproductive rights. These rights may be understood as the result – and the goal as far as they have not yet been fully achieved – of the struggle of different social movements over the nature and extent of citizenship. (Held 1989 p. 173) Economic rights concern us in the present context of work and citizenship.

We can only indicate here what we consider as constituting economic rights of citizenship, which should in our opinion form part of the future agenda of social movements like the labour movement. Following Giddens, Held suggests including 'all those rights which have been won by the labour movement over time and which create the possibility of greater control for employees over the work-place.' (Held 1989 p. 175) These rights concern economic and industrial democracy and include such issues as collective bargaining, participation and autonomy at work. We would like to add two more rights, namely the right to work in the broad sense which we have indicated and the right to a basic income. Since we have dealt rather extensively with the right to work, we will restrict ourselves here to making some remarks about the right to a basic income.

Dahrendorf has argued in favour of a basic income guarantee for all citizens. (Dahrendorf 1988a p. 177) In his opinion this should form part of general policies to prevent the formation of an underclass. In addition, a basic income guarantee would enhance the liberty of the citizen, which fits in with his conception of a free society which offers opportunities and does not impose ways of making use of them. (Dahrendorf 1988a pp. 17–18, 176)

The argument for a basic income entitlement as such, however, entails what Taylor-Gooby calls the moral hazard problem, which may be elucidated by the liberal argument against granting welfare entitlements: 'This opens up the road to scroungers who will exercise welfare rights rather than toil in order to subsist, and will speedily bankrupt the collective purse to the detriment of all.' (Taylor-Gooby 1991 p. 198) To approach the problem from another direction we refer to the argument we pointed out before that a libertarianism that grants rights but imposes no obligations leaves the issue of social responsibility towards the community as contingent. In our opinion Dahrendorf's case for a basic income guarantee does not entirely escape these problems. In fact, he is explicit about a right not to work but he is not equally strong about the obligation of every citizen to contribute to the welfare of the community. He seems rather cautious when he states that 'it may well make sense to ask citizens to give some time of their lives to the community.' (Dahrendorf 1988a p. 33)

Our inclusion of a basic income guarantee in the economic citizenship rights does not run the moral hazard risk since we have also laid down the general obligation to contribute to the welfare of the community by work. It should be emphasized that we regard a basic income guarantee as a general right. Unlike unemployment benefits under the current social security system a basic income guarantee is not a conditional right which citizens will lose when they do not work. Citizens who do not live up to their obligation to work will not automatically lose their basic income guarantee. Just as citizens who do not fulfil their citizenship obligation to comply with the law may be fined or sentenced to imprisonment, citizens who do not work may be sentenced in one way or the other.

The practical realization of this right to a basic income might take different forms which we will not deal with here. We just want to observe that if welfare claimants who engage in community service were granted their social security benefits without having to look for a job, their benefits might be regarded as a kind of basic income. It would be more attractive, however, to have a negative income tax system which guarantees all citizens a basic income and leaves it up to themselves whether they supplement this by looking for a job. This approach to a basic income system might be elaborated further by examining which kind of work should be organized as employment, which should be organized as work-for-oneself and which should be unpaid community service. (*cf.* Gorz 1989)

The New Europe

So far we have discussed relationships between work and citizenship which may have raised some new aspects but which must be familiar in the sense that they do not transcend the traditional association of citizenship and the nation-state. The history of citizenship is closely connected with sovereignty and nationalism. (Gellner 1983; Giddens 1985) Against this background the meaning of the catchword the 'New Europe' must be explained. In fact, different developments may be covered by this term.

The transitional processes which Central and East European states currently go through are in part closely connected with the citizenship rights which we have discussed. For instance, they concern the recognition of civil rights, such as the right to property and freedom of expression, and political rights with their institutional locus in a parliamentary democracy. Our 'common European home' in this respect means that Central and East European nation-states have joined the family of West European nation-states with their realization of these rights in terms of a market economy, private property, a multi-party system and so on. However, the outcome of this transition process should be understood properly. Well before the end of really existing socialism in Eastern Europe Giddens observed:

> What has happened in modern history, as I would see it, is that many types of citizenship rights (such as rights of political participation) have in fact become more or less universalized. That is to say, they have been acknowledged almost everywhere. However, this has come about, not because of a globalization of these rights themselves, but because of a universalizing of the nation-form. Virtually all modern states, for example, are in some sense 'democratic', and as such accord a range of rights to their citizens. But by this very process, these rights are institutionalized only in sectional fashion, within the confines of discrete states. (Giddens 1989 p. 269)

In this respect the term 'New Europe' does not entail a transcendence of the nation-state. On the contrary, the summer of 1992 confronted the world painfully with the sovereignty of nation-states in the traditional sense. This was illustrated well by the debate in Europe and the United Nations on whether and how they should intervene in the violation of human rights and the 'ethnic cleansing' in former Yugoslavia. The war in Bosnia-Herzegovina and the governments of Serbia and Croatia demonstrated that nation-building is still connected in a fundamental sense with elements of national identity conceived in terms of ethnic identity. Citizenship in this context is not primarily a matter of rights and duties of all who live within the territorial boundaries of the state but of inclusion in and exclusion from the nation on the grounds of blood and homeland. It bears testimony to the fact that the development of citizenship is not an evolutionary process.

This dimension of the development of citizenship is not specific to Yugoslavia, it can be observed in the Balkans and in other countries, as the break-up of Czechoslovakia illustrates. In fact, it may be supposed that one of the causes of the upsurge of nationalism is the transitional process itself. Giddens has pointed out that nationalist sentiments tend to be fairly remote from most of the activities of day-to-day social life, except in fairly unusual conditions. 'In circumstances where the ontological security of individuals is put in jeopardy by the disruption of routines, or by a generalized source of anxiety, regressive forms of object-identification tend to occur.' (Giddens 1985 p. 218) This threat to their ontological security is precisely what the transitional processes are felt to be at the individual level. It explains why, according to a recent survey, 56 per cent of the Bulgarian population says that 'calm and order' should be the primary goal of government policy, with 'fighting rising prices' in second place, mentioned by only 25 per cent. (Genov 1992)

Regressive forms of nationalism are not the inevitable outcome of threats to ontological security. Among other factors the extent to which a civic culture was founded and has historically developed, tends to influence the connection between sovereignty and nationalism. This may be a reason why the break-up of Czechoslovakia may lead to less violence than the dissolution of Yugoslavia. In addition, it will also depend on West European states whether developments in Central and Eastern Europe will 'build on the strand of Enlightenment thought which enshrines the ideal of citizenship' – so that a culture of citizen democracy, of individual rights, of a vigorous civil society can form the new basis of social cohesion – or that 'the atavist return of earlier, exclusionary irrationalist modes of bonding cannot but triumph.' (Howe 1991 p. 125)

West European states should, therefore, make an effort to address fundamentally the question of the present ontological insecurity of the people in Central and Eastern Europe. In this respect, however, Western economic self-interest has been dominant, as may be illustrated by the reservations in granting trading benefits to Central and Eastern European countries. For instance, because of heavy opposition by the French government which wanted to protect its own farmers, the European Community (EC) granted Poland in 1992 an increase of only 10 per cent of the amount of beef which it imports into the EC. Agricultural export facilities are very important, however. In most East European countries a substantial part of the population is dependent on agriculture, as in Poland where 30 per cent of the population work in agriculture. In practice it is Western Europe which has benefited economically from the opening of Europe.

Even more important in terms of ontological security is the approach the European Community takes towards the application for EC membership by states such as Bulgaria, Czechoslovakia, Hungary and Poland. Again, however, the European Community does not appear to have a sense of the vital importance of these applications for the states involved. It is unclear what will happen to these applications and at what time they might possibly result in full membership. The applications seem to be judged in purely economic terms without any awareness of the political and psychological impact of the way in which they are handled. Yet, one can easily imagine that, for instance, the postponement of the procedure of application by Czechoslovakia, because of its break-up, and a renewed application by both new states may contribute to a further sense of ontological insecurity and may have serious political effects.

There is also a second sense to the catchword 'New Europe', however, which may, under certain conditions, be promising to the people in Western and Eastern Europe. This is a 'New Europe' in the sense of extending citizenship rights across the boundaries of the nation-state.

A number of political and social scientists have made a case for global or world citizenship. (Dahrendorf 1988a pp. 45–46; Giddens 1989 pp. 269–270; Heater 1990 pp. 140, 287–288; Held 1989 p. 176) Different arguments are put forward to underpin the case for global citizenship. As long as citizenship is associated with the boundaries of nation-states this entails *ipso facto* a division between insiders and outsiders, between those who are included and those who are excluded. In addition, the dynamics of a world economy, and the threats to humanity of environmental pollution which does not stop at the boundaries of the nation-state (*cf.* Beck 1986) are sound arguments for world citizenship.

One may have doubts as to how compelling these arguments will be for individual citizens. Moreover, the way in which governments go about transnational agreements will contribute to a substantial citizens' resistance to the declining importance of the nation-state. A case in point is the European Community.

The gradual transfer of political powers from the member states to the European Commission has not been coupled with the expansion of political rights of the European Parliament. Whereas there is a certain amount of democratic accountability in the national context, citizens cannot but feel deprived of their political rights *vis-à-vis* the European Commission and the Brussels' bureaucracy. A similar argument holds for social rights. Through the 1950s and 1960s national welfare systems were built with the co-operation of trade unions, which were willing to comply with a low wages policy in return for the extension of a national social security system. Today several member states have launched a policy of 'downward harmonizing' of social security provisions on behalf of the economic integration of the EC. Many citizens cannot but feel robbed without being provided with as much as a Social Charter as a sham of good intentions. In this context a retreat of the nation-state may well contribute, on the part of West European citizens, to a feeling of ontological insecurity rather than be welcomed as an extension of citizenship.

At present the growing importance of the European Community is associated with the loss of citizenship rights, at least by many citizens of welfare states like Denmark, Germany and the Netherlands. Besides, in a growing number of member states feelings of national identity and political autonomy are an important factor in the appreciation of the European integration process, as in the United Kingdom and in France where the EC had a narrow escape from the referendum on the Maastricht treaty concerning the European Monetary and Economic Union and the European Political Union. One may, therefore, wonder whether a 'New Europe' may come to mean anything more than a confederation of nation-states as an appendage to a common economic market.

In our opinion a 'New Europe' might come to mean more, however, if Europe is not conceived in terms of replacing national (or regional) identity, but as another level of citizenship. Social security rights are a good example of what we mean by this.

At present social security rights are part and parcel of citizenship coinciding with membership of a particular nation-state. This implies an exclusionary approach, for all who do not have the particular nationality, such as refugees, will not be entitled to social provisions equal to those of citizens. However, if social rights are not fused with nationality but considered as universal human rights, a new line of thinking opens up. Within the context of the European Community one might imagine universal social security rights replacing economic aid to underdeveloped regions like Spain, Portugal and Greece. At present this kind of economic aid is the result of political compromise, which does neither appeal nor contribute to a sense of being members of a single community. Universal social security rights, on the other hand, may be presented as a principle of social justice translated into terms of equal social rights.

A similar line of reasoning might be adopted regarding economic aid to Central and Eastern Europe. At present the amount of aid is modest, to say the least, with the exception of (West) Germany's share, and it is defensive. West European countries fear a massive migration of citizens of former state socialist countries and this is the main reason for providing aid, despite all kinds of high-spirited declarations. Again an appeal to a principle of social justice might well be made to ask citizens of West European welfare states to extend social rights to the East (and to the South for that matter).

Of course, the problem of financing and redistribution will have to be tackled, as well as taking into account different standards of living in different parts of the world. These are important problems because an acceptable approach towards questions such as these will determine the appeal of the ideal of social justice which is the foundation of the global approach to citizenship. Nevertheless, we will leave these problems unsolved within the context of this introduction.

The attractiveness of this type of approach to citizenship is that important cultural elements of national identity do not have to be given up but may be combined with elements of supranational identity. Universalizing citizenship rights does not have to be understood as a levelling process. Indeed, against the background of globalization 'nationality is a feeling of *relative* cultural homogeneity'. (Heater 1990 p. 188; italics ours) If universalizing specific citizenship rights is an enabling process 'it makes socioeconomic inequalities bearable because it contains them within a common house of entitlements'. (Dahrendorf 1988a p. 158) In the end, the only justification which can be found for the rights citizens enjoy is that they do not infringe on the rights of others. (Held 1987 p. 290; Taylor-Gooby 1991 p. 208) West European citizens may take this to heart.

The Structure of the Book

This book presents original material on the theoretical and empirical questions concerning the relationship between work and citizenship. Some chapters were originally presented as a paper at the International Conference *Quality of Citizenship*, which was held in the Netherlands in 1991. Most of the papers were thoroughly revised and some chapters were commissioned in 1992, and therefore reflect the debate on work and citizenship at that time.

Each chapter does not take up the issue of work and citizenship to its full extent but they all make a substantial contribution to major issues which have been broached or raised in this chapter. An indication of the themes which are covered may be given by the titles of the four parts in which the chapters have been grouped together: the erosion of the welfare state and social citizenship rights, work and citizenship in Central and Eastern Europe, the transformation of work and industrial citizenship, and work, rights and obligations.

This book is not designed to provide detailed statistical information on the political situation, the state of the economy, the labour-market and so on in all countries of the New Europe which are dealt with. Descriptive information is not absent when it is appropriate as empirical documentation or corroboration of a particular thesis. In general our attention has rather focused on the principal qualitative aspects which are essential to understand the evolving relationship between work and citizenship.

Part I is concerned with the erosion of the welfare state and social citizenship rights. The welfare state has been regarded as the institutionalization of social citizenship rights, enabling every citizen to live the life of a civilized being. The Western welfare state has, however, not succeeded in preventing the emergence of poverty and an underclass. Its erosion has led to a renewed emphasis on the obligation to work against the background of a debate about the reciprocity of rights and duties.

Engbersen, in Chapter 2, is concerned with 'modern poverty'. Political debate on the emergence of an underclass in the Netherlands has made the definition of poverty a controversial matter. Engbersen regards poverty as the result of insufficient means, resulting in exclusion from society and implying multiple deprivation. Using these characteristics he gives a qualitative description of modern poverty in the Netherlands. In the second part of his paper Engbersen examines the crucial feature of the permanent dependence of the poor on the care of the state. He indicates that this may partly be explained as a perverse effect of social policy, because some unemployed opt for a life on social security. Another cause of permanent dependence, namely the social selectivity of 'street-level' bureaucrats in their dealings with clients, is also found to be pertinent. As a consequence many welfare recipients are cut off from the dominant institutions of society. They are second-class citizens who no longer seem to be entitled to lead a decent life and to receive fair treatment from the state.

Moore, in Chapter 3, examines the concept of 'underclass'. Analyses of the American underclass cannot simply be applied, Moore argues. Britain has no extensive black ghettoes and has seen the rise of a welfare state. Yet ethnic minorities are being excluded from the full benefit of the welfare state. Under Thatcherism their citizenship status has even been put in question. However, their situation cannot be compared to the social isolation of the underclass in the American inner cities. In fact when the concept is conceived in terms of economic deprivation, an underclass appears to be emerging, comprising long-term unemployed, single-parent families and poor elderly. Besides these approaches to the study of the underclass which are concerned with the process of exclusion, there is another type of approach which is preoccupied with the supposedly immoral behaviour of the underclass. The poor are held responsible for their own poverty. In spite of the differences of approach, the imperfections and the moral connotations of the concept, Moore believes that the term underclass has its uses. He suggests that we use it in combination with a description in terms of the gradations of exclusion from legal, political and social citizenship rights.

There is a historical continuity, as Jacobs shows in Chapter 4, from the earliest welfare policy which viewed claimants as potential scroungers to the tight conditions of unemployment benefits under the Thatcher regime. After the First World War unemployment benefits were introduced, but all claims were subjected to a severe 'genuinely seeking work' test. From 1930 onwards the test was the refusal of an offer of suitable employment. Under Thatcher there were changes in the administration of benefits once more. Claimants had to fill in questionnaires to establish their availability for work. In 1989 conditions were tightened further by introducing the 'actively seeking work' test, which implies that as a rule claimants may not refuse to take any job at any rate of pay. As a result, Jacobs argues, the balance of rights and duties has been disturbed. The onus is on the claimant. At the same time the state has reneged on its obligation to provide work, training and so on. Citizens on benefit deserve better than to be treated as if they were scroungers.

Chapter 5 by van der Veen takes up the issue of the reciprocity of rights and duties in social policy. The effectiveness of social policy has been questioned. Different causes have been indicated such as the theses that people are rationally calculating (Murray) and that social policy undermines the competence of citizens (Mead). Empirical research on the administration of social policy reveals other causes. The increasing complexity and specificity of social policy and the incompleteness and ambiguity of information call for informal norms and strategies of decision-making and can create a retreatist attitude with officials. Research also showed that welfare clients reinterpret their rights and duties, but not related to rational calculations only. These reinterpretations are connected with a reinterpretation of their social position and an acceptance of their unemployment. This is not stopped by the administrative agencies because of the way they function as a result of economic and social conditions. Van der Veen concludes that the theses by Murray and Mead are one-sided. They focus on the individual level of behaviour and on an individualized concept of citizenship. Collective aspects are neglected, that is to say the conditions which the welfare state must create for people to be competent citizens and to live up to their obligations. To increase its effectiveness social policy will have to be directed at creating and redistributing work.

Part II deals with work and citizenship in Central and Eastern Europe. The issues which are dealt with include the right and the obligation to work under really existing socialism and during the actual transition process to a market economy, the changing conception of citizenship and the problems which Western Europe in general and (West) Germany in particular faces if citizenship rights are to be recognized beyond the nation-state.

Andrusz argues in Chapter 6 that social rights were given emphasis in the Constitution of the former USSR and used to offer security to the workers. It is this security which they are losing by attempts at economic reform. Privatization and market economy along the IMF lines inevitably entail unemployment and the curtailing of welfare entitlements. Reactions to these threats intermingle with complex concerns of nationality, which had been ideologically concealed for many years. The desire for sovereignty and economic self-sufficiency form a mixture which may well lead to a further disintegration of the Commonwealth of Independent States. These developments have already led to the migration of ethnic Russians, Armenians and so on, especially from those republics which passed discriminatory laws on citizenship. Andrusz concludes that only if governments of the CIS pay attention to basic needs of the people and pursue a just privatization policy may radical nationalism and virulent 'ethnic cleansing' be avoided.

Dimitrova and Dimitrov open Chapter 7 by examining the fate of civil society in Bulgaria under 45 years of really existing socialism. Their thesis is that civil society was severely affected both by the fact that social rights were granted rather than fought for and that these were extended at the expense of civil and political rights. The enforcement of a one-party system undermined the position of citizens *vis-à-vis* the state. It left them without means of control when the state, or rather the Communist Party, turned social rights into privileges to be distributed according to party interests. Without institutional channels of voice, such as political parties or trade unions, workers reacted by absenteeism, bad performance and so on. This added to the economic inefficiency of the command type of economy. Attempts during the 1980s to raise productivity by introducing workers' participation were in vain. The state was unable to effect a real change because granting a right to property and a real right to work would have undermined the very basis of state ownership and partocracy.

Western Europe takes a rather distant stand to social rights issues in Eastern Europe, regarding these as an internal affair of sovereign states and restricting itself to humanitarian aid. Evidently this cannot be the attitude of West Germany towards the social welfare of citizens of the former East Germany.

Bastian, in Chapter 8, finds that after the political unification the debate is about the prospects and constraints of solidarity within one nation. He contends that equality and efficiency may be incompatible under conditions of system transformation, because securing wealth in the long run demands postponing short-term distributional interests. The harmonization of pay standards and working hours, which trade unions bargained for, may take too long to be achieved from a social justice point of view but still be too quick from an economic recovery point of view. Nevertheless, the actual outcome has caused discontent both among East and West German workers. Bastian suggests that social parliaments at a regional level may help to generate legitimacy and commitment, although they will not be able to put an end to social inequalities.

Part III focuses on the transformation of work and industrial citizenship. It deals to some extent with the process of technological transformation and economic rationalization, which also caused labour shedding and undermined the foundations of the welfare state dealt with in Part I. It also examines the state of industrial citizenship, which has never been adequately elaborated by citizenship theories because of a concentration on the public sphere and a corresponding interest in political rather than industrial democracy, and political rather than economic rights.

Heycock, in Chapter 9, takes up the question why Britain as the oldest industrial society has the least well-developed tradition of workers' participation. He argues that the causes cannot be found with Conservative government only. The virtual absence of workers' participation has much to do with trade union policy itself. Unions saw any form of participation as hampering them in their task of extracting the best wages and working conditions from employers. Participation was regarded as meaningful only in the context of a nationalized economy. However, in the coalmining industry, which was nationalized in 1947, such participation and autonomy at work as existed, were eroded by increasing managerial control of the organization of work through new technologies and flexible working. Heycock also draws attention to the fact that, besides industrial citizenship at work, the political citizenship which traditionally existed in the coalmining communities has been eroded. The decline of working-class communities may be explained as the effect of divisive political and managerial strategies but also as the consequence of the restricted notion of autonomy, participation and industrial citizenship which unions have had.

Chapter 10, by Leisink and Beukema, examines the extent of industrial citizenship in the Netherlands. It is limited by statutory regulations and by practical conditions. The differential distribution of rights to works councils reflects the basic asymmetry of power between capital and labour. Yet, the Netherlands, together with Germany, has the more powerful form of institutional industrial democracy when compared with other European countries. An important condition of industrial democracy is the competence and resources which employees may be able to mobilize. In this respect the Taylorist organization of work has eroded worker autonomy. Changes in the organization of work might enlarge the autonomy of workers and their participatory competence. However, it appears that only a small proportion of highly-skilled employees have seen their autonomy increase; low-skilled workers have hardly benefited so far. This segmentation of employees may even be enhanced by the institutions of industrial democracy themselves. The authors conclude that collective organization of employees at shop-floor level and a trade union policy of non-sectarian solidarity are needed if industrial citizenship is to mean more than a privilege of the core of employees.

Coenen in Chapter 11 analyses the concept of work in the trade union movement. The importance of paying attention to trade unions in this respect is related to the impact they may have on the consolidation of social rights and the future realization of economic rights. Coenen contends that the labour movement was originally ambivalent about the nature of work. Their unreflected adoption of the dominant concept of paid work as a citizen's obligation leaves them ill-equipped to come to grips with fundamental changes of the industrial work-based societies. Moreover, as a consequence of this dominant concept it is accepted that the individual worker must submit himself to the assymetrical relationship between employer and employee. Coenen argues that the twin topics of a right not to work and a basic income should be the central issue of a principal debate by the trade union movement. It may enable unions to develop a broader and differentiated concept of work which they may take up as the core of economic citizenship rights yet to be realized. In addition a right not to work and a basic income may empower individual workers by enabling them not to accept any kind of employment relationship.

Part IV deals with the different options with respect to work and citizenship which are central in the current debate. Broadly speaking one option insists on defending the welfare state by increasing labour participation, whereas the other argues for a citizenship right to a basic income allowing citizens to choose between a job or socially useful activities. Both positions will argue for their own option as well as indicate the shortcomings they perceive in other options.

Chapter 12 assesses the predicament of the welfare state. Adriaansens and Dercksen argue that economic and socio-cultural developments have caused a fast growth in the number of benefit claimants in relation to the number of people having a job. As a consequence the growth of welfare expenditure must be borne by a declining proportion of the population. Their conclusion is that only if more people have a job can we afford a sustainable welfare state. In addition, the functions of work to the individual and to society are arguments for raising labour-force participation. The alternative of a basic income scheme must be rejected, the authors argue, for a number of reasons: it cannot be afforded, it cuts the links between labour and income which may entail social risks such as an increasing number of school drop-outs, and it is principally contestable because it discharges citizens from the duty to take part in the division of labour. The authors conclude by indicating the elements of an active labour market policy, which must lay the foundations for a sustainable welfare state and a serious implementation of social citizenship.

In the Chapter 13 Vilrokx adopts the position that full citizenship is only possible when the link with the labour market is not conditional. The conception of labour market participation in exchange for welfare benefits is rooted in the post-Second World War situation. However, full employment as it existed from the 1950s until the early 1970s was historically unique. Jobloss economic growth is what we face now. Therefore, a totally different line of action must be considered, notably a basic income system.

One argument against a basic income system is that it would erode the integrative function of work. Vilrokx argues, however, that it is doubtful anyhow whether work will continue to integrate individuals in society because of changes in our economic system. Post-industrial society is marked by a different kind of integration pattern which may be called 'selective solidarity'. Along with the transformation of the industrial type of division of labour, the collective interdependencies of collective actors are being replaced by network-like systems of relatively autonomous individuals and small groups. This concept of relative autonomy which characterizes social relations in post-industrial society also offers a new perspective on citizenship. The material independence from work through a basic income system is the next step in the achievement of a fuller citizenship resulting in economic emancipation.

The welfare state, Offe argues in the final chapter, can only safeguard social security through state action, which inevitably raises questions of how much action is required. The effect is that social security and social policy are essentially contested. Yet the potential conflict is contained most of the time, because social policy is embedded in a widely shared set of assumptions concerning social justice and the limits of welfare arrangements. Social and economic changes, however, have rendered the 'productivist' assumptions underpinning the welfare state questionable. These changes concern the traditional family household, full employment and so on. In response to the uncertainties concerning the premises of the welfare state different options can be adopted. Offe prefers the option of citizenship entitlements to a basic income, for which not paid labour but 'useful activities' is the moral justification. His arguments include the disruptive impact of economic growth policies on the natural environment. He concludes with a number of proposals for the politics of a basic income, dealing among other things with the benefits of a basic income scheme both for the individual and for society.

Part I

The Erosion of the Welfare State and Social Citizenship Rights

2. Modern Poverty and Second-Class Citizenship

Godfried Engbersen

> *Through all the stages of industrial economy from the 'take off' to 'mature',*
> *'late', and now 'post' industrialism; through all the phases of an industrial*
> *society, from a vestigial paternalism, to laisser-faireism, to the 'new liberalism'*
> *of social reform, to the welfare state; through all the vicissitudes of an*
> *expanding and contracting empire, of war and peace, depression and prospe-*
> *rity, the poor have remained with us and poverty has continued to be a 'social*
> *problem.' Not, to be sure, the same poor, the same problem, or the same poverty.*
> *(Gertrude Himmelfarb, The Idea of Poverty 1984 p. 532)*

Introduction

On the eve of the nineties, two interesting studies were published, *The Undeserving Poor, from the War on Poverty to the War on Welfare* (1989) by Katz and *Punishing the Poor. Poverty under Thatcher* (1990) by Andrews and Jacobs. Although the books differ greatly, they agree in their condemnation of the social policies implemented in the eighties in America and Great Britain and they note a similar rise in poverty in both countries. The two books are critical of the numerous budget cuts affecting social security and the lack of any truly structural policy to allow the vulnerable groups to participate in society as fully-fledged citizens. A combination of the two titles produces a picture of an internal welfare war, with the poor emerging as the losers. With reference to the Dutch situation, however, warfare metaphors of this kind would seem a bit overdone. And yet a study of the social policies implemented in the Netherlands in the eighties as regards the lowest income groups would produce a comparable picture. The policies geared towards economic recovery more or less overlooked large segments of the population who were involuntarily sentenced to permanent dependence on the state.

In the eighties the number of households who had to make do with the absolute minimum income mushroomed from 313 000 in 1981 to more than 800 000 in 1988 (13 per cent of all Dutch households). This rise had to do with the numbers of long-term unemployed and disabled people, but it also had to do with the growing number of old-age

35

pensioners and the fact that there were more and more single mothers on social security. The permanent dependence on social security of large numbers of people, the absence of an active labour market policy, budget cuts pertaining to such state facilities as public health care, rent subsidies and legal aid, and the loss of purchasing power have once again made poverty an issue. Especially in the period after 1985, various studies were published that made mention of new poverty in the Netherlands.

In this paper, I shall address a number of problems linked to present-day poverty research. I shall also present a picture of the dominant features of modern poverty in the Dutch welfare state. This picture is mainly based on a study of 120 real minimum households. (Engbersen and van der Veen 1987) I will also refer to some of the results of a study of the social consequences of long-term unemployment. (Kroft *et al.* 1989) For this study 271 people were interviewed who had been unemployed for two years or more. Secondly, I shall focus on the role of social policy in the perpetuation of modern poverty and the construction of second-class citizenship.

The Inflation of Poverty

Ever since poverty was first recognized as a social problem the concept of poverty has undergone various transformations. The development of Western social security legislation exhibited a shift from an absolute, physical subsistence level to a relative social subsistence level. Growing prosperity and the development of the welfare state were both instrumental in this connection. Poverty is now viewed in relation to the average living standard of a specific society. Modern poverty is not life-threatening poverty, it is relative poverty.

In order to examine this relative poverty, subjective and objective approaches have both been used. It is striking that the majority of the academic measurements, whether objective or subjective, led to high percentages of poor people. (Durlacher 1973; Hagenaars 1985) In 1985, Berghman *et al.* calculated that 11 per cent of Dutch households were poor 'in strict policy terms' and 17 per cent of Dutch households were subjectively without security in their lives. (Berghman *et al.* 1988) Inspired by Deleeck, I would like to call the phenomenon of large numbers of poor people the law of inflation in poverty research. (Deleeck 1985) Many of the measurements have little credibility, since the final figures are far too large. The Netherlands is one of the richest countries in the world and has one of the most advanced social security systems.

This is why counts that show more than 15 per cent of the Dutch population to be poor should be taken with a grain of salt. However, we also see quite the opposite. Wherever academic researchers present relatively high figures, people with political responsibility tend to play down poverty. The different calculation methods are generated by different definitions of poverty and, even more importantly, different interests.

Six Principles of Poverty

In order to arrive at a realistic notion of relative poverty, based on the work of Ringen, the Norwegian social scientist, and several additions by the Dutch sociologist Schuyt, I would like to discuss six principles of relative poverty. Ringen's point of departure was that as a social phenomenon, poverty really does exist: 'Poverty is real; it is in the life of the poor. If we want to measure poverty, we must believe that there is something real to measure'. (Ringen 1987 p. 126) The measurement of poverty might be a defining problem, but the acknowledgement of the social phenomena that produce poverty certainly is not. Thus the second point Schuyt formulated is that the academic meaning of poverty has to bear a relation to the social meaning of poverty. (Schuyt and Tan 1988 p. 37) If and when the academic interpretation of the concept of poverty fails to be in keeping with common sense, then the concept loses credibility and force. We cannot do much more than shrug our shoulders at poverty measurements that include the majority of a country's university students. (*cf.* Berghman *et al.* 1988 p. 22)

The first three principles pertain to what poverty is *not*:
1. Social inequality does not necessarily result in poverty
Poverty implies the existence of social inequality, though it does not necessarily result from it. Definitions of poverty that classify households that belong to the lowest percentiles of the income distribution as poor tend to overlook this. The citizens of a rich country who belong to the lowest 20 per cent of the income distribution can also be quite prosperous. 'It would be absurd,' Amartya Sen wrote, 'to call someone poor just because he had the means only to buy one Cadillac a day when others in the community could buy two of these cars each day'. (Sen 1983 p. 159)

2. Social problems do not necessarily result in poverty

Such social problems as unemployment, crime, drug abuse and broken families can lead to poverty, but there is not necessarily a link between these phenomena and poverty. Poverty is a separate problem. Unemployment can lead to poverty, for example if the employment benefit is minimal, but it does not necessarily have to be the case. The same holds true of drug use or psychological problems. It is not wise to lump multifarious social problems together.

3. Poverty is not the same as feeling poor

In defining the poverty line, the subjective approach is often used, in other words the 'perception of poverty'. It is the opinion of the individual that plays a central role in the 'Leyden Poverty Line'. (van Praag, Hagenaars, van Weeren 1982) An international comparative study conducted by Hagenaars showed that 16 per cent of the households in the Netherlands viewed themselves as being poor. Hagenaars' study was in 1979, when unemployment was still limited in the Netherlands. (Hagenaars 1985 p. 131) It would seem as if it is not so much poverty that is being measured as income satisfaction or diffuse feelings of insecurity and relative deprivation.

The last three principles pertain to what poverty *is*:

4. Poverty is the result of insufficient means

This rather obvious conclusion brings to mind a dialogue between F. Scott Fitzgerald and Ernest Hemingway. 'The rich are different,' Fitzgerald said. 'Yes,' Hemingway agreed, 'they have more money.' For the present generation of poverty researchers, Hemingway's answer is unsatisfactory. A low income might be a prerequisite, but it is not sufficient to produce poverty. In modern-day society, other resources also play a role: knowledge (cultural capital), durable consumption goods and means of communication (television, car, telephone), social contacts (family, neighbourhood, clubs) and the benefit of state facilities. (*cf.* Sen 1983 p. 162) If we focused solely on income and not on any of the other resources, we would classify certain groups among the poor that do not belong there, for example university students. And then there is the problem that if we take too many resources to be indispensable, we run the chance of taking too many people to be poor.

5. Poverty means exclusion from society

Here we touch upon the core of what modern poverty is, the radical social exclusion of people from dominant institutions of society. (Coser 1965) People are excluded from the dominant societal institutions, the labour market, recreational facilities, community organizations and activities, and included by the Welfare Department, job creation projects, and so forth. Dahrendorf referred to this social exclusion as 'the' social problem of the eighties and nineties. Dahrendorf cited the development of an underclass in Western Europe in danger of being cut off from the mainstream of society in an economic and social sense as well as a geographic one. (Dahrendorf 1988a)

6. Poverty is multiple deprivation

On the basis of principles four and five, it is clear that poverty implies multiple deprivation. For example one social security cheque for a whole household to live on, debts, no work, no prospects for the future, little or no education, poor health, no supportive social network, and so forth. A person with a low score on several of these dimensions is in a situation of poverty.

The six principles that will help us towards a realistic conception of poverty show that it is easier to say what it is not than to say what it is. The terms used to describe the nature of modern poverty are vague and ambiguous. Keeping Ringen's six principles in mind, I should like to give a 'qualitative description' of modern poverty as it occurs in the Netherlands. This description is based on an intensive study of 120 households in Rotterdam. (Engbersen and van der Veen 1987) The households we studied had a weak social position. Two-thirds of the respondents had only attended primary school, if that, and two-thirds had done unskilled labour. Almost 60 per cent of the respondents had been living on an absolute minimum income for more than five years. The study *Moderne armoede* (1987), did not provide any classification instrument to see just exactly how many poor people there were in the Netherlands, but it did give insight into the dominant features of modern poverty in the Dutch welfare state.

The Features of Modern Poverty

Modern poverty can be generally described as 'the structural exclusion of citizens from social participation accompanied by permanent dependence on the state'. The effects of these two interrelated processes are evident in the seven features of poverty.

The first feature of modern poverty is 'very little money'. It is the permanence of having to make do with so little that is so difficult to deal with. Everything a person does is related in some way to making ends meet. A general phenomenon among the modern poor is bargain hunting, spending a lot of time going from one shop to another to buy things at the very lowest price. In particular families with children, whether one-parent or two-parent families, have any number of things to buy. And if they do not have the money to buy what they feel they need, they go into debt. Paying the instalments often leads in turn to new problems. The result is that half the 800 000 minimum-income households are prone to a process of increasing indebtedness. (Oude Engberink 1984; Engbersen and van der Veen 1987)

The second feature of modern poverty is the 'social isolation' many of the poor are gradually faced with. The loss of work and the lack of funds combine to make their social network shrink. People cut down on social activities, they no longer subscribe to a newspaper, they have their telephone cut off. For instance only 16 per cent of the respondents of the study *Moderne armoede* (1987) were members of a club or did voluntary work, while the average national participation figure is about 60 per cent. To many people, though not to everyone, their relatives are the last source of social contact. In the past few decades, family relations have altered considerably. Not only in a financial sense, but in an emotional one as well. Many people can no longer count on the unconditional support of their relatives. Growing geographic mobility has also affected traditional family structures. If one's relatives do not live in the neighbourhood, then maintaining contact with them costs money. A lot of poor people simply cannot afford it. The isolation resulting from the household budget has a self-reinforcing element. If you lose touch with other people, you also lose your informal sources of care and your informal channels of information. The fact that people on a minimum income are so inaccessible also makes it difficult for public or private job placement offices to reach them, for example, almost a third of the long-term unemployed in *Een tijd zonder werk.* (Kroft *et al.* 1989) Since the long-term unemployed are so difficult to reach, these offices are not so quick to help them, even if they could. Thus the long-term unemployed do not get any working experience and their chances on the labour market become slimmer and slimmer.

The third feature of poverty is the 'lack of benefit from some public facilities'. The modern poor do take advantage of the social security system, but they barely make use of the other facilities provided by the state. The field of education is the best example. In the course of three generations, there was a rise in the educational level of the Rotterdam respondents, but it did not lead to a good position on the labour market. (Engbersen and van der Veen 1987 pp. 72–76) The insecure and unstable position on the labour market of the lower income groups is passed on from one generation to the next.

The fourth way that modern poverty manifests itself is in the 'officialization of care'. Permanent dependence on the state is often a crucial feature of modern poverty. In many facets of their lives, the modern poor have come to rely on the authorities (income, housing, health, legal aid). The care they receive has become something they have a right to, and this is the way most of the people who live on a minimum income perceive it. Anyone faced with unusual problems of any kind, for example due to debts or ill health, is soon embraced by the bureaucracy – only to discover that the state has no compunctions about intervening in the most private aspects of life. (Engbersen 1990 pp. 135–139)

The fifth point is that the modern poor constitute an extremely 'heterogeneous group'. Group distinctions are based on the type of benefit they receive, their ethnic descent and family structure. The increase of these group distinctions leads individuals to compare themselves with others, which only intensifies their feeling of dissatisfaction with their situation. In part, people on the minimum income level blame each other for their poor situation. Scapegoat groups are created, mainly consisting of people of foreign descent. A feeling of relative deprivation is constantly experienced.

The sixth point is that modern poverty can be 'geographically localized'. Particularly in the old inner cities, a concentration can be observed of people who receive social security and people who have been out of work for long periods of time. In these neighbourhoods, a cumulation of problems can be observed. These problems not only pertain to long-term unemployment and permanent dependence on social security, but also to petty crime, poor housing, pauperization and a concentration of people of foreign descent. In fact very few of the schoolchildren in these districts are of Dutch descent. In inner districts of the major cities in the Netherlands (Amsterdam, Rotterdam and The Hague), there is a growing number of primary schools where 80 per cent of the pupils are of foreign descent. (de Jong 1989 pp. 61–73) Although it would not be fair to describe the old inner cities solely in negative terms, we do see a concentration of people there who barely participate in the dominant societal institutions such as the labour market, education and recreational activities.

The seventh feature of modern poverty has to do with the 'cultural adaptations' of people in reaction to their limited opportunities. In this connection, Lewis once introduced the term 'culture of poverty'. (Lewis 1968) He developed the culture of poverty concept on the basis of various studies conducted among the urban poor in Mexico and Puerto Rico. In an effort to cope with social insecurity, the poor develop adapted values, aspirations and local institutions. In the course of time, they acquire relative autonomy *vis-à-vis* the societal conditions that produced them. An elimination of these conditions does not necessarily imply the immediate disappearance of certain cultural patterns. In the Netherlands, the culture of poverty is mainly a culture in care of the state. For some people on social security, long-term unemployment and dependence on benefits lead to severe financial problems, exclusion from the social circles they would like to belong to, and complete dependence on the state. The dependence on the care of the state gradually comes to be perceived as natural and normal. However, the culture of dependence should not be viewed as the cause of poverty, but mainly as a realistic adaptation to limited opportunities. (*cf.* Wilson 1987 and 1989)

The Poverty of Social Policy

A closer examination of the features of modern poverty shows that, although multiple deprivation is definitely involved, the emphasis has clearly shifted from the material dimensions to the social ones. This is particularly evident if we compare today's situation with the results of older studies, as conducted by Mayhew, Booth and Rowntree in the nineteenth century. (Himmelfarb 1984) A crucial feature of modern poverty is permanent dependence on the care of the state. This feature is a reflection of the profit-and-loss account of the welfare state. In the one column, there is the automatic right to benefits, in the other there is the reduction of independence due to the permanent intervention of the state in the lives of the people who receive them. Continuing along the lines sketched by Murray and Lipsky, I would like to further examine the relation between the policies of the state and its citizens. Murray and Lipsky both devoted attention to the role of social policy in the 'creation' and the 'perpetuation' of poverty.

A Leisure Class?

In *Losing Ground* (1984), Murray elaborated upon the thesis that the social security system in America had not alleviated the problems of the poor in America, it had reinforced them. He did not seek the cause of the perpetuation of poverty in the culture of the poor or in the socio-economic structure, but in the perverse effects of social policy developed with the best of intentions in the sixties. The system of social security benefits led to a 'leisure class'. Not of the rich, but of the poor. The crux of Murray's contention was that the poor made cost–profit analyses, and then opted for a life on social security. There were more advantages to this kind of life than to getting married, for example, or working for a minimum wage. There are many objections that could be raised to Murray's analysis, which stressed the strategic conduct of people on social security, in particular to the selective and rather shaky empirical foundation. I shall not go into this here, and refer the reader to the criticism formulated by Wilson (1987) and Katz (1989).

In *Een tijd zonder werk* (1989) an effort was made to examine Murray's thesis. It should be noted here that Murray's analysis mainly pertained to the American AFDC programme (Aid to Families with Dependent Children), with a strong over-representation of 'welfare mothers', whereas the Dutch study mainly pertained to unemployed men who had to remain available for employment. The Dutch study showed that 30 per cent of the respondents had more or less voluntarily opted for a life on social security: 10 per cent of the respondents viewed their benefits as a permanent basic income that enabled them to live more or less as they pleased, 10 per cent had regular, unofficial earnings on the side and 10 per cent manipulated the social security system, for example by living together and receiving two benefits, although only eligible for one family benefit. More than 35 per cent of the respondents did honestly try to get out of the dependency situation by continuing to look for a new job. And another 35 per cent had, by necessity, become resigned to the unemployment situation and accepted it. In these two last groups, considerations played a role that were not related to the immediate usefulness of the social security system. (Engbersen 1990 pp. 235–237)

These results partially confirm Murray's thesis. Especially the young respondents who lived in Amsterdam and Rotterdam tended to permanently or temporarily arrange their lives around the fact that social security benefits were available to them. However, their strategic behaviour led more to an acceptance of their dependence on the care of the state than it did to an actual perpetuation of modern poverty. In fact for these respondents, earning an extra income as they did and certainly not living isolated lives, the term modern poverty was not applicable.

The Poverty Industry

A second relevant theory was formulated by Lipsky in *Street-level Bureaucracy*. (1980) The term street-level bureaucracy referred to public service organizations employing the officials who had face-to-face contact with citizens, such as the Welfare Department, local police stations and employment bureaux. These street-level bureaucrats were responsible for the concrete implementation of the centrally-formulated social policies. In the course of this implementation, however, underprivileged clients were at an institutionalized disadvantage, which served to perpetuate their situation of poverty and dependence. Lipsky accounted for this institutionalized disadvantage by citing the limited funds of these institutions. The influx of clients and their restricted capacities forced them to make choices, and they often chose to help their relatively more privileged clients. (Lipsky 1980 pp. 105–111) Comparable mechanisms can be observed in the Netherlands. Anyone who studies the actual practice at the Welfare Department, by far the most important institution in the lives of people who are dependent on the social security system as a whole, observes the favouring of certain clients above others. The social workers there have a preference for clients of a certain minimum social standing, clients who would benefit from specific forms of assistance such as debt arrangements or job counselling. (Engbersen 1990 pp. 166–173) The same social selectivity was evident in the joint efforts of the local Welfare Departments and Employment Offices, which called in a total of 150 000 long-term unemployed people for 'reorientation talks' in the 1988–1990 period. On the basis of these talks, action plans were drawn up that could result in a training place, a job experience place or a job. However, the clients who were too old, had been unemployed for too long or had too poor a command of the Dutch language had very little chance of being helped by these efforts. (Engbersen 1990 p. 222) This creaming process is stimulated by the pressure not to fall below the target figures. (*cf.* Mead 1989)

In the way officials implement the social security and labour market policies, the poverty of these policies can be discerned. There are too few job experience and training places and there are insufficient funds to solve the financial problems of the modern poor, for example by radically settling their debts. Due to the scarcity of resources, selections have to be made and in the course of this selection process, the weakest groups least able to stand up for themselves tend to fall by the wayside. The intended and unintended selection processes that take place are an interesting addition to what Deleeck referred to as the 'Matthew effect' of social policy. In Deleeck's own words, 'there are certain mechanisms in society that cause the advantages of social policies, proportionally and directionally, to work more in favour of the higher social groups than the lower ones'. (Deleeck 1977) Deleeck was referring to the negligible effectiveness of the redistributive efforts of the government in such fields as housing and education. The prosperous seem to benefit more from the government than the less privileged. However, we can take Deleeck's thesis one step further. There are differences in the extent to which equivalent categories of people receiving social security benefits do indeed benefit from the social security and labour market policies. This takes us to the following thesis: in the implementation of social policies for citizens dependent on the Welfare Department, there are certain mechanisms in society that cause the advantages of the social policies, proportionally and directionally, to work more in favour of the people within this category who have higher social standing and are relatively more privileged.

Herbert Gans once drew attention to an important function of poverty. Poverty supplies work – and not only for social science researchers. (Gans 1973) In the Netherlands, there has been a sharp rise in the number of job placement and training programmes, but so far the effects of this new poverty industry on the position of the people receiving social security benefits and on the long-term unemployed have been negligible. (WRR 1987 pp. 75–76) The consequence of the ineffectiveness of the policies on unemployment has been that a sizeable segment of the population will remain permanently dependent on the care of the state. The social repercussions are already visible in the inner cities where many welfare recipients live, partly Dutch and partly of foreign descent, people who are economically, socially and geographically cut off from the dominant institutions of society. This Dutch underclass is in danger of becoming unreachable for the official policy.

Modern Poverty and Second-Class Citizenship

Social science research into poverty brings to mind the myth of Sisyphus. Like Sisyphus rolling his stone to the top of the hill, only to watch it tumbling down and then starting all over again, the poverty researcher finds his subject constantly slipping out of his grip. (Seabrook 1985 p.

16) Poverty, linked as it is to a specific time and place, is thus constantly conceptualized anew. The recurrent rediscovery of poverty in its various metamorphoses bears witness to this. That makes the concept difficult to get a grip on and forever subject to contemporary dispute.

In *The Idea of Poverty*, Himmelfarb wrote: 'Even the "hard facts" about poverty – about wages and prices, employment and unemployment, living and working conditions – appeared to contemporaries as facts and functioned as such only as they were mediated by the structure of ideas, values, opinions, beliefs, attitudes, perceptions, and images'. (Himmelfarb 1984 p. 8) The perspective from which poverty is examined in the post-war welfare state has a lot to do with the concept of citizenship. People who cannot participate in society on an equal level with the rest of the population are poor because they are excluded from important societal institutions. The modern poor are secondclass citizens who cannot take full advantage of their basic social rights. I would like to reserve the term modern poverty for the category of citizens who exhibit the various features of modern poverty and who have become unreachable for 'activating' forms of social policy (for example, active labour market policy). However, it would be unrealistic to assume that all the 800 000 households living on the absolute minimum income level should be classified as the modern poor, although modern poverty does exist among them. The underlying idea here is that some citizens no longer seem to be entitled to lead a decent life and to receive fair treatment from the institutions of the state and are thus trapped in a marginal position as second-class citizens. (Katz 1989 pp. 179–184; Turner 1986 p. 108)

The after-war welfare state arrangements have been seen as the accomplishment of the social rights of all citizens, as described by T.H. Marshall. Growing problems of modern poverty, long-term unemployment, non-participation of welfare recipients in mainstream-institutions and selective treatment of poor citizens by state agencies, show, however, that the citizenship-building process is stagnating or even reversing. There is a growing divide between first-class citizens with stable and decent jobs protected by social security arrangements and second-class citizens who are permanently dependent on public assistance. Even a rather comprehensive welfare state like the Netherlands, has turned into an exclusive society. (Lister 1990) For many long-term unemployed citizenship is not a universal status, but an exclusive status preserved for certain privileged groups.

It is evident that the structure of the Dutch welfare state has prevented the emergence of extreme forms of social exclusion. On the other hand the Dutch welfare regime is rather ineffective with regard to long-term unemployment and has put a premium on the non-participation of groups of citizens. Besides, it has produced some side effects, especially the coming into existence of autonomous and calculating unemployed. The Dutch welfare state subsidizes the 'exit' from the labour market and blocks the 'entry' of citizens (mainly women) on the labour market. (Esping-Andersen 1990; de Wachter and Somers 1989) The Dutch welfare regime compensates the loss of income or the absence of a job, but is not able to conduct an effective employment strategy. So, the Dutch welfare state produces a specific archetype of modern poverty: the permanent non-working 'welfare client'. As most research demonstrates permanent welfare dependency brings to most of the welfare recipients no long-term security and no peace of mind, but leads to growing financial insecurity and social isolation.

3. Citizenship and the Underclass

Robert Moore

Introductory Comments

Much of the first day of the Pan European Congress of Migrant Workers in Wageningen in 1972 was taken up with a debate concerning the admission to the Congress of an official of IG-Metall. Should he be admitted as an observer or a delegate? Advocates of observer status argued that migrant workers were victims of exploitation in Europe, in which the native working classes took an active part often through the agency of their trades unions. European working classes were direct beneficiaries of the exploitation of migrants. A union boss was not therefore 'one of us', but part of the problem. Others argued for delegate status because whilst they agreed on the question of exploitation they believed that native and migrant workers were nonetheless all members of a working class which must not stand divided. The outcome of this apparently theoretical argument had direct consequences for the conference, for migrants workers' action, and for the man waiting outside the door with a speech in his pocket.

The difficulties arose because minorities are situated at the intersection of two systems of domination; class and colonial. Women, who form a high proportion of migrant workers, are at the intersection of three systems of domination. The issue for an observing sociologist was the extent to which immigrants, migrants and ethnic minorities are part of the class structure of European societies and the extent to which they occupy uniquely and separately subordinate positions. In writing about this debate in the late 1970s and more recently I suggested that the argument in Wageningen was not about the 'exclusion' of minorities but about their 'integration' into the subordinated and marginal roles occupied by what has increasingly been come to be called the underclass. (Moore 1977)

The Underclass in Sociology

The earliest post-war reference by a social scientist to the idea of an underclass is in Gunnar Myrdal's *Challenge to Affluence,* in 1964.

(Myrdal 1964) Looking at the booming American economy he saw unemployment as no longer cyclical or amenable to demand stimulation. New technical developments were eliminating altogether the need for wide categories of labour. This was creating an underclass

> of unemployed and, gradually, unemployable persons and families at the bottom of a society in which, for the majority of people above that level the increasingly democratic structure of the educational system creates more and more liberty - real liberty – and equality of opportunity ... Opening up more opportunities to more people has closed some opportunities for some. And now in the end it threatens to split off a true 'underclass' – not really an integrated part of the nation at all but a useless and miserable substratum. (Myrdal 1964 pp. 40–41)

None of the institutions intended to protect the poor and poorest actually helped the underclass; benefits and protection stopped at the stratum above. In addition the underclass did not vote or participate in politics and there were no movements of protest on their behalf.

The term underclass has been more recently developed by William Julius Wilson, notably in his book *The Truly Disadvantaged*, which addresses problems of inner city dislocation, such as joblessness, teenage pregnancy, welfare dependency and serious crime. (Wilson 1987)

The 1965 Moynihan Report (Moynihan 1965) was said to have blamed the black family for the poverty and exclusion of the black population from the American society. The reaction to it created an intolerant climate in which sociologists in the USA and Europe became reluctant to conduct research that might be thought to be unflattering to the black population. One result was that conservative commentators came to dominate the field. They elaborated analyses that stressed individual responsibility and then, increasingly, identified the level of social welfare benefits as the cause of social dislocation. (*cf.* Auletta 1981)

Wilson dealt with the welfare argument quite simply by pointing out that without welfare there would have been even more in poverty. Nonetheless the dislocation of the ghetto areas had to be explained.

Wilson argued firstly that young black males were concentrated in the educational categories for whom employment opportunities were declining the fastest. Secondly, the Civil Rights campaigns of the 1960s had enabled the black professionals who had previously been held in the ghetto areas by discrimination to move out. This not only residualized the inner city population but it removed from ghetto areas models of black success that could serve to motivate and encourage others to strive. Furthermore it removed those key members of the local community who managed the voluntary associations that sustained the vitality of the community.

An effect of these changes was that the young literally did not see the value of work, nor the connection between education and employment, nor did they see many families not living on welfare. Furthermore the areas in which the ghetto poor live are avoided by others and so they become more isolated – and more isolated from what Wilson calls 'the mainstream patterns of behaviour'. Wilson was not arguing that the poor live in a 'culture of poverty' but were suffering the effects of social isolation. The isolation of the poor amplifies their problems.

The ghetto underclass is, according to Wilson, the product of the organization of the American economy in conditions where the history of discrimination and deprivation has disadvantaged the black population. We are seeing the effects of the decline of smokestack industries and the flight of blue-collar jobs from the centre of large cities, in conditions where historically most of the black working class was confined to those jobs.

If we were simply to import Wilson's idea of underclass and apply it to British society we would encounter problems. Firstly, the extensive ghettoes of the Northern American cities in which large black populations have lived for generations are not a feature of British society. Secondly, when Wilson refers to 'the mainstream patterns of behaviour' he refers to conventional behaviour as worker, consumer and parent. Working and spending in the markets for labour and goods are central values in the dominant North American culture. The open and competitive society, with values of openness and competition implied by Myrdal is not found in the United Kingdom. Britain (like many European countries) has in the twentieth century, however, seen the rise of a welfare state based upon an implied contract between capital and important sections of organized labour. This contract was gendered and racially constructed from its beginning, as Fiona Williams and Ruth Lister have recently reminded us. (Lister 1990) With this serious proviso we can say that belonging to the mainstream of British society entailed fully participating in the rights and benefits of the welfare state and enjoying the security that citizenship (in T.H. Marshall's sense) confers. The working classes enjoyed a measure of industrial power, the benefits of full employment policies, support in unemployment, health care and education. The first they secured by industrial organization in trades unions and the other benefits as part of the near-universal provision for the whole population.

Rex and Moore writing in the late 1960s showed how the Birmingham City Council systematically excluded immigrants (as they then were) from public housing and punished and stigmatized them for the alternatives they were forced to adopt. (Rex and Moore 1967) It was suggested that immigrants were being excluded from the full benefit of the welfare state to which they were entitled by virtue of nationality and were not therefore realizing their full citizenship. Minorities would become a part of the mainstream when they shared those rights. We did not use the term underclass.

John Rex adopted the term in his second Birmingham study, with Sally Tomlinson, in the late 1970s. (Rex and Tomlinson 1979 p. 275) They said that Britain had a working class in a secure contractual relationship with those who run the economy and an underclass which enjoys no security. They describe minorities as: 'systematically at a disadvantage compared with working class whites ... a separate underprivileged class.'(*ibid*. p. 275)

It would be possible to elaborate this analysis by reference to a number of recent changes; the increasing concentration of the black and Asian populations in the United Kingdom; the loss of rights to family life and now, effectively, freedom of movement in Europe; the *de facto* denial of access to many welfare state services through the extension of surveillance to all non-white people; harassment by the police and the relative lack of protection afforded the non-white community by the police. As in the case of the European migrant workers so we might argue that incremental exclusions and deprivations eventually puts British ethnic minorities over a threshold into a qualitatively different position from the white population, where they do have separate and at times conflicting interests.

The Thatcher years have seen a very substantial decline in the citizenship rights of all British subjects; the erosion of political rights, reduction in the rights of trades unions, the reduction of local government powers and the disenfranchisement of people employed by local government. There have been limitations on rights of assembly and increased powers given to the police (largely to legitimize previous abuses). There have also been very substantial reductions in social security, health and education provision, all resulting in very considerable hardship for those without the means to provide through the market.

The deterioration of the situation of ethnic minorities is both relative and absolute because whilst the post-war contract has now been broken, their basic citizenship (nationality) status has additionally been put in question and reinforced by legal restrictions. Their needs have largely disappeared from the social agenda and their presence has moved to the law and order agenda. In Europe, immigration is on the same agenda as international terrorism and drug trafficking and the member states of the European Community are taking steps to ensure the full exchange of information necessary to ensure that a person denied entry to one state is not admitted to another.

It would be hard nonetheless to sustain the argument that the black British population is downtrodden into isolation, apathy and despair. I have seen no research which says that this is the case. Work in Liverpool suggests, for example, that young blacks display a range of attitudes towards their employment chances, from despair to high aspirations. (Connolly, Parsell and Roberts 1990) Minorities in Britain are actively involved in trade union and political life. Furthermore in areas like Brixton young black people can see others going to work every day, many in suits and carrying briefcases. In the evenings they can see black people dressed and leaving home for an evening out. In minority communities we also find thriving political, cultural and religious life. We also find successful entrepreneurship even though this may be precarious when it is situated in a niche created by the flight of capital and the abandonment of the inner city.

So far we have equated the underclass with ethnic minorities. Rather than starting with a consideration of ethnic minorities we might, like Halsey and Dahrendorf, observe how people in general are now becoming surplus to the requirements of the home European labour market. This approach to the underclass stresses general rather than ethnic or 'racial' recruitment to its ranks. Thus A.H. Halsey once asserted in a newspaper article:

> The class structure of industrial societies, including Britain, is developing an underclass of those who can not be placed in the stable workforce of the formerly employed .... They suffer a cumulation of social pathologies – educational failure, illiteracy, broken families, high crime rates, poor housing, and spatial concentration in the inner city. They are disproportionately recruited from the young and the ethnic minorities, and they lead a ghetto existence outside of the normal social contract of citizenship and with little or no stake in official society.

The term underclass also appeared in the subtitle of Frank Field's book *Losing out: the Emergence of Britain's Underclass.* (Field 1989) Field sees the underclass mainly in terms of economic deprivation. He is less concerned with the position of ethnic minorities than with the condition of the very poorest whom he suggests have been separated from other low-income groups and from the working class in general. His underclass comprise the long-term unemployed, single-parent families and the poor elderly.

We should note that British poor have been excluded from rising living standards, even if they are employed. Male manual workers in the lowest decile of income now earn a lower percentage of average earnings than they did in 1886 when the first records were kept. The protection traditionally afforded the lowest paid workers has been removed, the powers of Wages Councils restricted and employers are subsidized to employ low-paid young workers. The number of part-time workers doubled from 1961 to 1981 and the United Kingdom now employs 40 per cent of all part-time workers in the European Community. It is not surprising that the British government is so hostile to the European Social Charter when it contains provisions to protect workers' rights – a contradiction in terms for British Conservatives.

Field concentrates on the unemployed. 41 per cent of them are long-term unemployed. Long-term unemployment prevents the accumulation of savings either through owner-occupation or the acquisition of pension rights. The sale of council houses in conditions where allocations were already stratified re-enforces the isolation of the 'sink' estates, thus further cutting the underclass off from employment and other opportunities. Long-term unemployment also exhausts rights to insurance benefits and makes the unemployed person dependent upon means-tested benefits, which heightens the feelings of dependency and loss of personal worth.

Field and others suggest that the burden of the poll-tax is now constraining some of the poorest to avoid registration as voters, thus cutting them off from the political rights of citizenship. (Field 1989; Esam and Oppenheime 1989) Field argues that common citizenship is breaking up, and attitudes towards the poor are changing with the rise of a 'drawbridge' mentality amongst the employed.

We can see in these contrasting but complementary views of the underclass that there are important issues about, for example, how important the difference between the employed and unemployed is as a criterion defining an underclass, and the relative importance of ethnicity and poverty in creating and perpetuating conditions of exclusion and isolation.

Recent discussion of the underclass in Britain has moved however from academic publications into the arena of colour supplements and tabloid newspapers. The term has been applied to meths drinkers and homosexuals, to people sleeping rough, to beggars and to football hooligans. In this public discourse the idea of the underclass has taken on an older meaning conjuring up the drunks, idlers and degenerates who were thought to threaten late nineteenth-century society.

The Underclass in History

At the turn of the century, concern was expressed at the degeneration of the national or 'racial' stock. It was a concern with social inefficiency and national decline, not structural inequality. What we would today call a 'moral panic' sprang in large part from the apprehension felt by middle-class people on encountering teeming inner city populations, slum-dwellers and the beggars who reached out to touch them on the pavements. With the extension of the franchise there was also a feeling of alarm that those seeking election would increasingly appeal to the 'pauper vote' with promises to be redeemed by taxes on a working population who would be impoverished thereby. (Armstrong 1929)

The panic was amplified by the decline of what were thought to be the better classes. Mary Drew commented to her father William Gladstone in 1886 on the small families of aristocrats married in the past fifteen years and wrote to her sister in 1911:

> Really it is a tremendous and awe inspiring fact that since 1875, the educated and aristocratic classes have more than halved their families, so that the fittest are rapidly declining while the less fit, the feeble minded, the unhealthy alone increase (except in the case of Jews, R.C.'s and the clergy, blessings be on them). (quoted in Jalland and Hooper 1986)

Marie Stopes would not have agreed entirely, her study of the 1911 census suggested that ministers of religion were by far the most success-ful family limiters – exceeded only by teachers and professors. (Jalland and Hooper 1986 pp. 273-274) But we see here alarm at the fecundity of what Karl Pearson thought of as the least useful members of society. The poor physical condition of men volunteering for the Anglo-Boer wars heightened the panic.

One direction in which these panics and the possible inheritance of underclass characteristics led was to enquiries into mental deficiency. Thus the inter-war years saw the establishment of the Wood Committee on Mental Deficiency (of which Cyril Burt was a member). The Eugenics Society also sponsored research into the 'social qualities and health of a sample of our population'. Professor Caradog Jones who became Director of the Merseyside social survey in 1929 (Macnicol 1987 p. 311) believed: 'that in any large centre there exists a social problem group, the source from which the majority of criminals and paupers, unemployables and defectives of all kinds are recruited.' (*ibid.* p. 311)

According to Macnicol he made constant reference to the Wood and Brock Reports but was never able either to enumerate the problem group or separate hereditary from environmental factors. (*ibid.* p. 312) In general all research on the question of heritability was (and remains) methodologically weak and the results inconclusive.

Because the 'social problem group' was believed to be more prolific than the more valuable members of society prominent members of the Eugenics Society advocated voluntary sterilization. Proponents of voluntary sterilization saw it as a step towards compulsion. Compulsion was adopted in some states of the United States, where on the flimsiest of grounds (including truanting) about 43 000 young women are believed to have been sterilized in state institutions between Buck *versus* Bell (decided on the basis of an IQ-test) in 1927 and 1944. (Kevles 1986 p. 116; Trombley 1988 p. 114) We cannot know the total number of sterilizations achieved because many were carried out after pressure had been exerted to obtain the consent of the subject or their kin. It was to the United States that Hitler's government sent observers to see how such a policy was implemented.

Some members of the British *Interdepartmental Committee on Sterilisation* (the Brock Committee) approved the wide-ranging powers of Nazi laws on sterilization. This committee was established after the failure of the eugenics lobby to get a sterilization bill through Parliament. It recommended extending what it called 'the right to sterilization' to, in effect, 3.5 million people.

Many eugenic views were quite benign by the standards of the Brock Report. Eugenic assumptions were part of the common currency of debates on social issues and they were accepted across the political spectrum. Eleanor Rathbone, for example, wanted an income tax regime that would facilitate larger middle-class families. The assumptions, debates and policies seem extraordinary to us today. But they were entirely congruent with more populist notions dividing the rough from the respectable and the deserving from the undeserving poor. Only with the quite recent establishment of the science of genetics and the discrediting of Burtian ideas of IQ did such arguments cease to be common currency in reformist debate. But they did not entirely die. Eugenic ideas and concern with national deterioration were closely entwined in both the United States and the United Kingdom with the arguments for immigration control which did much to fuel beliefs about the inferiority of non-white immigrants. Debates about the underclass have therefore been racialized from the beginning. Eugenically-based control of fertility has not ceased to be an issue as evidenced by debates on the use of Depo Provera amongst ethnic minority women in the United Kingdom. (Brent Community Health Council 1981)

The New Populism

In popular thought today there is one new villain, and it is her fertility too that is cause for concern. As the *Today* newspaper put it, 'Single Mums Wreck Society'. *Today* was responding to a lecture by Charles Murray now published as *The Emerging British Underclass.* (Murray 1990)

Contemporary sociologists are discussing the underclass in terms of people who have been excluded from mainstream society or the welfare state. They are concerned with the process of exclusion and explanations of why certain people are more likely to be excluded than others. Murray, by contrast, is concerned with behaviour and wishes to distinguish between the worthy and the unworthy, the deserving and the undeserving poor, for him 'underclass' does not refer to a degree of poverty, but to a type of poverty. (*ibid.* p.1)

The vocabulary of the social sciences is replaced by the language of disease. Murray describes himself as 'a visitor from a plague area come to see whether the disease is spreading' and later asks 'how contagious is this disease?'.

Murray admits his ignorance of British society (and shows rather more than he admits) but he has no compunction about transferring ideas based on the American experience directly to the United Kingdom. His evidence is anecdotal, fragmentary and speculative. Nonetheless he is able to conclude that: 'Britain does have an underclass ... out of sight. But it is growing rapidly.' (*ibid.* p. 3) Murray suggests that the underclass may be identified in various ways but he chooses illegitimacy, violent crime and labour force drop-out; we recognize these as key issues addressed by Wilson in the United States. According to Murray the 1980s saw a rise of illegitimacy. This was abolished as a legal category in 1987 but by using it Murray is able to discount the circumstances of children born in stable unions, or registered by both parents. Fifteen years ago, Murray argues, poor neighbourhoods had plentiful examples of good fathers but 'today the balance has already shifted ... in a few years the situation will be much worse, for this is a problem that nurtures itself.' (*ibid.* p. 1)

Most importantly little boys lack role models, they do not know about getting up and going to work every morning and do not 'become adolescents naturally wanting to refrain from sex, just as little girls don't become adolescents naturally wanting to refrain from having babies'. (*ibid.* p. 3)

Murray has no idea what proportion of lower-class people are indifferent to work, perhaps not even 20 per cent he suggests, arbitrarily. They acquire this indifference by growing up without a clear picture of the meaning and necessity of work, young men cannot picture themselves in their fathers' jobs. Murray collected his British evidence on Clydeside and in Birkenhead and it is surprising that he did not notice the extent to which fathers' jobs no longer exist in these areas.

Indifference to work leads to the community around the work-shy breaking down.

> Men who do not have to support families find other ways to prove that they are men, which tend to take various destructive forms ... (*ibid.* p. 22)
>
> Marriage is an indispensable civilising force ... young men who don't work don't make good marriage material. Often they don't get married at all ... too many of them remain barbarians. (*ibid.* p. 23)

The reasons for these developments are, according to Murray, that illegitimacy and single parenthood are no longer stigmatized. Furthermore, the level of benefit available to a poor woman and the provisions of the 1977 Homeless Persons Act makes being a single mother 'not so bad' rather than 'extremely punishing'. Thus having and keeping a baby becomes economically feasible and if a woman does not need a man then there is less incentive for a man to plug away at a menial job to support her. It is important to note that it is in making this kind of point that Murray offers no evidence. He is drawing on the work of George Gilder and others who argue that the extension of women's rights has created independent women who emasculate men for whom the necessity of supporting a family is an essential civilizing force. Curiously Gilder seems to be arguing the innate superiority of women who must be dominated by men to ensure the latter's good behaviour.

Murray suborned what could have been an important debate about poverty and people excluded from the mainstream, or the underclass as understood by sociologists. Murray's underclass are the undeserving poor. He has little to say about the deserving poor who, for example, have to suffer the impact of the declining value of child benefit.

All significant arguments in the social sciences are grounded in social and political experience. The question of the position of migrants and other minorities in Europe, for example, has direct implications for political action on their part. Murray's work is politically grounded also. Most importantly it uncouples the plight of the poor from the effects of social policy and makes them responsible for their own poverty.

The Future of the Idea

What then shall we do about the term underclass? Shall we defend it as a useful and illuminating concept or drop it because of the connotations it has accumulated? Since Murray's visit there has been renewed pressure to stop using the term in Britain.

There are good sociological reasons for dropping the term quite apart from its historical accretions. As a blanket term it does less than justice to the wide variety of conditions, experiences and responses of the people to whom it applies and for whose problems quite diverse policies might be appropriate. The work of Engbersen and his colleagues in the Netherlands is in sharp contrast to Murray's generalizations and notable for its attempts to tease out the variety of conditions of the poor and the attitudes and strategies they adopt. (Engbersen, Schuyt and Timmer 1991) Poor people do not refer to themselves as a class and the poor seldom refer to poverty, only to their difficulty in making ends meet or finding the money for the poll-tax. Making ends meet is the day-to-day reality, not an abstract idea of poverty. The term underclass treats members as objects of study and perhaps gives an impression of homogeneity, passivity and resignation that does much less than justice to the culture of the poor and excluded.

There is also a danger of reification: newspaper readers and the public at large can begin to believe that there is actually a body of people 'out there' who constitute a threat to society and its values. Then people showing what are believed to be underclass characteristics or having an address in an underclass area are excluded from employment and other opportunities.

Politically the use of the term may have the effect of amplifying stigma. It may be thought we are researching people less deserving of consideration as fellow human beings. Those included in the underclass, usually on administrative terms which include dependency and violation of middle-class norms of behaviour, become more isolated and exposed to hostile policy and administration in the field of social security. We know as a matter of historical fact such political stigmatization has led to deportation, sterilization and murder. This process of amplification is especially dangerous when the term underclass is a thinly disguised proxy for non-white.

We may, as Herbert Gans suggests, risk actually creating an underclass. (Gans 1990) First through intensification of zoning policies, and then through exclusion and control – exemplified by the proliferation of entry-phones, closed circuit TV and the security guards who keep undesirables (for example poor people) out of shopping malls. European visitors to the United States will already be familiar with the next step, equipping private estates with chain-link fencing and guards.

The term also suffers from its flexibility. We have seen how Myrdal used the term for people excluded from the labour market by structural change. I (almost) used the concept for migrants politically excluded but *in* the labour market in subordinate roles, Rex and Wilson restore Myrdal's usage of exclusion, the latter adding political exclusion. Field deploys the terms to describe what he sees as the victims of social policy changes.

The term 'underclass' has its uses. There *are* people deprived and excluded from the full benefits of their citizenship. We need some way to talk about them. So we do need a collective term. But we also need to be clear about the subjects of our discourse – marginalized migrant workers and refugees and asylum seekers throughout Europe (for whom I believe we do need a further separate term, anyhow, so dire is their exclusion), ethnic minority populations of inner cities, the very poor, or particular sections of the very poor. When we wish to underline the common features of their situations we need a term. That they share common elements of their life-situation suggests that the term class might appropriately be applied. By class I mean all persons in the same class position, so it is possible to define an underclass as comprising those who typically have little or no control over goods and skills either within or outside a given economic order. To underline the importance of the external and constraining conditions that create this class I would add that what deprives an underclass of access to or control over goods and skills are the characteristics ascribed to them by others. In other words their class position is increasingly derived from their social status.

The term also invites us to think of the overclass which in the United Kingdom has recently engaged in a massive experiment in social engineering resulting in what Frank Field described as 'the most significant redistribution of income to the rich since the dissolution of the monasteries'. What did he mean? In 1988 90 per cent of those in full-time employment earned less than £350 a week. In that year income tax cuts gave the richest one per cent £436 per week extra income. Part-time women workers in the top ten percentile of female part-time earnings (that is above the Council of Europe's decency threshold) would have needed to work between 87 and 121 hours to earn a wage equal to the *extra* income given to top earners.

Although sociologists have been careful enough in defining what they mean by underclass when they are using the term there will always be the problem of saying what we mean in a way that cannot be turned against a section or sections of the public. Perhaps the problem is insoluble so long as it is important to certain interests to marginalize and stigmatize others. In so far as this is the case then we also have a responsibility to study the interests served by the definitions of terms.

Any terms we use could be abused and I would suggest that the use to which others put them is more important than the specific words we use. Wilson ended his Presidential Address to the ASA by saying that:

> Researchers have to recognise that they have the political and social responsibility as social scientists to insure that their findings and theories are interpreted accurately by those in the public who use their ideas ... They have to provide intellectual leadership with arguments based on systematic research and theoretical analyses that confront ideologically driven and short-sighted public views. (Wilson 1990)

This is a tall order in the United Kingdom, precisely because we are a much less open society than the United States and intellectuals occupy an extremely low position in popular esteem. Ruth Lister is more blunt and pragmatic than Wilson: 'Those who invoke the development of an underclass to make the case for the restoration of full citizenship rights to the poor are playing with fire.' (Lister *op.cit.* p. 26)

At the end of the Utrecht conference Wilson suggested that the term "underclass" should no longer be used in Europe. In Europe the term's historical antecedents and current usage overload it with threatening meanings that are much less apparent in North America.

Lister refers to Marshall's idea of citizenship. The idea's critical power remains undiminished and is perhaps enhanced by the conditions of the 1990s. Such is its critical force that citizenship has already re-emerged both explicitly and implicitly as a powerful focus of debate in both academic and political circles. By contrast, the idea of an underclass has, in Europe at least, accumulated a set of connotations that may make it an impossible term to use. But the need for such a term derives from the long and possibly permanent exclusion of sections of the population of European and North American societies from the labour market. Rather than seeking a term that embraces what are, in fact, a range of socially excluded groups we should perhaps use terms derived from Marshall. Exclusion from legal, political and social rights places an individual or a section of a population at a disadvantage. We may think in terms of gradations of exclusion according to the extent to which citizenship rights are unobtainable or unavailable. Where the exclusion is based on juridical concepts of nationality we cross a threshold from a simple system of exclusion based on gradations of negative esteem to institutionalized exclusion. But this too comprises gradations; legal exclusion ranging from the trivial requirements laid upon a person from another European Community country to the uncertain and marginal position of clandestine workers and refugees and asylum seekers. We increasingly need to recognize the twin base of exclusion based on social status and legal status.

Thus we can locate members of what we have hitherto called an underclass at the intersection of two gradations, one is social, based upon negative esteem and including negatively valued life-style (unemployment, single-parenthood, etcetera), skin colour and culture. The other comprises formal grades of legal 'belonging' and exclusion, increasingly defined at a transnational, European level.

4. Welfare, Work and Training for the Unemployed in Britain: a Historical Review

John Jacobs

Built into the 1911 unemployment insurance scheme were two conditions designed to safeguard against abuse. One was that claimants had to be 'available for work', to ensure that only those genuinely unemployed and wishing to return to the labour market would receive benefits, and to underline the obligation that those who can are expected to work; the other was that, once in work, the worker must not leave employment 'without good cause'. This was to safeguard against frivolous claims, and once more to underpin the expectation that citizens should work. There were also, of course, penalties for fraudulent claims, with prosecution as the ultimate weapon. It is hard to argue against these safeguards, since any scheme based on the giving of public money is obliged, for the credibility on which it depends for continued political support, to prevent abuse. If it is right that these policies exist, it must also be right that they should be properly enforced. Why is it then, that when these three conditions have been strengthened under the Thatcher regime we nevertheless feel that the rules have been changed, gone too far, and become oppressive?

The answer is to be found by looking at the concept of 'citizenship', and in particular at the balance between rights and obligations. This is neatly expressed by Ruth Lister: 'Few would deny that citizenship involves obligations as well as rights. But the two must be in balance. What is happening today is that obligations are being emphasized at the expense of rights.' (Lister 1990 p. 68)

The obligation on the citizen enshrined in these policies is the obligation to find work and then to keep it, in return for which he or she will be given benefit while looking for it and wages once it is found. A related issue is whether the state also has the obligation to 'provide' work for the unemployed, or, if not work, then training, and whether it also has the obligation to ensure that wages are at a reasonable level. These are the basic ingredients in the citizenship contract.

From a brief look at welfare policy for the unemployed in Britain we can see that, while the balance has shifted from time to time, there has been a persistent theme running throughout which, apart from one short period, has viewed the claimant as a potential loafer or scrounger to be coerced into work by a variety of deterrent means. This fear of the scrounger has been the motivation driving policies for the unemployed.

The New Poor Law

The most famous and far-reaching statement of this ideology was the 1834 Poor Law Amendment Act, built upon the twin notions of less-eligibility and the workhouse test, self-regulating devices for sorting the loafer from the genuinely destitute. So much has been written about the effects of these penal policies that we need not dwell on them here, but there is one point that does need emphasizing to illustrate the extraordinarily punitive lengths to which these policies were taken.

The Poor Law and Work

At the heart of the deterrent system of the new poor law was not just work, but punitive work. It was one of the essential consequences of embarking upon a scheme based upon the principle that destitution could only be tested by an offer of the House. In order for the workhouse test to be discriminating conditions in the workhouse had to be worse than the worst conditions outside, therefore work in the workhouse had necessarily to be arduous and unpleasant, in short, punitive. The parish was to be, in the words of the Poor Law Commissioners, 'the hardest taskmaster and the worst paymaster.' (Poor Law Commissioners 1836 p. 46)

It is important to note that more productive and more satisfying work was specifically ruled out. It could have been made available but, on principle, was not. By 1843 the central authorities insisted that the work provided must be hard, not of a kind usually performed by independent labourers or competing with them, nor 'much regarded as to profitable results', strictly supervised, 'of a laborious and undesirable nature in itself', and 'of such a nature as to discourage applications from all who are not really necessitous.' (S. and B. Webb 1910 p. 28)

By 1842 the tasks recommended by the central authority as most likely to meet these conditions were stone-breaking, grinding corn and oakum-picking, which became the standard tasks for the next fifty years.

Finding that the ordinary general mixed workhouse was not deterring applicants to a sufficient degree, some unions set up test workhouses which were intended to be so punitive that only those for whom starvation was the alternative would contemplate entry. In 1871 the first test house was established in Poplar, soon to be followed by others. The tasks were exceptionally hard and the regimes severe. As the 1909 Royal Commission commented: 'The character and amount of the work exacted from these merely destitute persons will, we think, surprise some prison administrators.' (*Royal Commission on the Poor Laws and Relief of Distress* 1909, Separate (Minority) Report (hereafter Minority Report) Pt. 2, ch. 1, D (V) p. 1073)

The comparison was apt; we know from the Gladstone Committee, which enquired into labour in prisons in 1895, that the policies pursued by the Local Government Board in relation to paupers were, on paper at least, harsher than those in prisons.

The Committee reported that almost all labour in prisons, both the local prisons and the hard labour convict prisons, was, unlike workhouse labour, productive and had long been so. Prisoners were either engaged on large-scale public works, (indeed, they were known as Public Works Prisons) such as building dockyards or they were engaged in prison industries such as mat-making. One of the recommendations of the Committee was that productive prison industries should be increased as much as possible. (*Report of the Departmental Committee on Prisons* 1895) Stone-breaking and oakum-picking were the recommended routine tasks of the workhouse, yet in prisons stone-breaking was classed as grade one hard labour, to be given only to those sentenced to a term of imprisonment which had a term of hard labour specifically attached to it. In local prisons stone-breaking was hardly ever used as a task; in 1893/4, out of a total of 18 438 prisoners in local prisons, only 101 had been employed breaking stones. (*Ibid.* App. IV (iv)) Even the Governor of Dartmoor told the Committee that he only made the men break stones when the weather was too bad for other outside work. (*Ibid.* Minutes of Evidence) The weekly amount of stone to be broken was less than that required in the test workhouses. (*Ibid.* App. IV, Weekly Tasks) Oakum-picking was universally condemned by all who gave evidence to the Committee as degrading and unsuitable even for convicts. Such was the unanimity of the condemnation that the Committee recommended that 'oakum-picking should be discontinued as much as possible except for penal purposes' and by 1897 it had been discontinued by the Prison Commissioners. (*Statement by Prison Commissioners* 1898) Again, the actual amount of work required was harder for paupers than for prisoners, and both stone-breaking and oakum-picking continued to be set as tasks for paupers long after they were abandoned in prisons. Hence the force of Disraeli's famous remark, following the passing of the 1834 Act, that 'in England, poverty is a crime'. (Disraeli 1839)

What is important about these houses of penal servitude is that from the 1870s onwards they were expressly encouraged and urged on unions by the central authorities; they were official policy, not the hard-hearted aberrations of local Guardians. In his evidence to the 1909 Royal Commission J.S. Davy, the head of the Poor Law Division of the Local Government Board, told the Commission that he 'most strongly advocates a Test house in all large urban communities'. (Minority Report, Pt. 2, ch. 1, D (vii) p. 1075)

Summarizing their views on the test houses the writers of the Minority Report concluded that 'When the power of compulsory detention is used in such a "testing" establishment ... it seems to us that it amounts to a week's imprisonment with hard labour, under conditions actually more severe than those in gaol'. (*Ibid.* p. 1075)

It is essential to understand that such punishment of paupers was no accident; it was the deliberate, considered policy of the architects and implementers of the poor law throughout the whole of the nineteenth century and well into the twentieth. If the able-bodied would-be pauper did not like it, he was free to go and find work in the market.

Labour Yards

From 1834 onwards, until well into the twentieth century, the poor law authorities realized that insisting on the abolition of all outdoor relief for the able-bodied was not only impractical, as not every union would have sufficient space in its workhouse to house all those who might need relief, but was also likely to lead to trouble, especially in the larger towns. They nevertheless stood firm on the principle that relief should only be given in return for work, and, of equal importance, that in return for work those who relied upon the poor law should be given relief, not wages. They therefore allowed most of the more populous urban unions to substitute an outdoor labour test for the offer of the workhouse. What this meant in most places was that a stoneyard was opened and the men were sent there to perform a task of work, usually stone-breaking or crushing, though other tasks such as wood chopping or oakum-picking might also be set. The actual tasks set varied considerably from union to union, from breaking 5 cwt. of stone to 20 cwt., similarly, the amounts of oakum to be picked varied between 2lb. and 6lb. As with the workhouse, an important ideological principle of the labour yards was that they should not provide useful work. What the authorities wanted to avoid at all costs was that the Guardians should come to be seen as providers of employment when times were hard. Work was purely a test of destitution, and as such was only successful if it deterred men from claiming, not attracted them.

The Unemployed Workmen Act 1905

In an attempt to provide for the unemployed outside the punitive poor laws local authorities were urged from 1886 to provide municipal relief works. This culminated in the Unemployed Workmen Act (1905) designed to provide work for the 'elite' of the unemployed. It was a half-baked idea, since the Distress Committees which operated the Act had to beg work from local authorities, who might or might not provide it, while the men could not be paid wages out of the rates by the local authorities for whom they did the work but had, originally at least, to rely on local charities, so the number of men helped depended on the success of the Mayor's appeals for contributions. This caused such an outcry that the Exchequer was forced to provide a small amount of money directly to finance some work, which was the beginning of state responsibility for unemployment.

Of interest here is the attempt to ensure that only the elite of the unemployed were helped, which once again meant weeding out the loafers. Regulations accompanying the Act stated that applicants had to be 'of good character' and 'honestly desirous of obtaining work'. To ensure that they were, anyone who had been in receipt of poor law relief in the previous year was disqualified, and applicants had to fill in a record paper which asked 18 questions, the prototype of all subsequent unemployment benefit claims forms. (In the first year they even had to supply names of two referees.) (Local Government Board *Annual Report* 1906, App. pt. 3 pp. 417 and 433)

Enquiries into the applicant's character were extensive. In Brighton for example, every applicant was visited at home by an Inquiry Officer, every application was vetted by the Poor Law Relieving Officer and in some cases enquiries were made of the police. In Brighton in 1905 this elaborate machinery yielded only 31 men out of 2050 who were considered 'bad characters'. Of the remaining 2019 who were given some work that year, only 25 were deemed not to have worked satisfactorily. The men were desperate for any work, even the odd one or two weeks that the Distress Committee could supply, but the regulations demanded that they all be treated as potential loafers. (Brighton Distress Committee 1906)

The failure of this Act gave municipal works a bad name. It was condemned in both the Majority and Minority Reports of 1909 as being wasteful, uneconomic, useless to the men taken on for only a week or so at a time and harmful to those who were laid off as a result of the work done by those employed under the Act. Nevertheless, municipal works re-appeared between the wars as one of the ways in which the state sought to provide for the unemployed. The nearest we have come to them in post-war Britain is on the short-lived Community Programme, a frankly workfare scheme of the mid-1980s for giving the long-term unemployed work, though in return not for wages but for slightly enhanced benefit.

The 'Genuinely Seeking Work' Test

After the Great War, when it became politically impossible to throw millions of unemployed ex-soldiers and civilian war workers on to the poor law, unemployment benefit was made available even where this had not been earned by contributions. Once again the spectre of the scrounger loomed; this time the remedy was to insert in the conditions for benefit in 1921 the requirement that the claimant be 'genuinely seeking whole-time employment', to which was added in 1924 the condition that they were 'making all reasonable efforts to secure employment'. In 1925 the return of the Baldwin administration led to the establishment of a Committee on Unemployment Insurance Administration whose brief can be guessed from its semi-official Whitehall name, the Tightening-up Committee. The effect was to subject all claims to even closer scrutiny, with a view to making the 'genuinely seeking work' test bite even harder.

In 1926 the test took on a new character when an Umpire, the forerunner of a Social Security Commissioner, declared that 'In considering whether a person is genuinely seeking work the most important fact to be ascertained is the state of the applicant's mind', which opened the way for the unfettered use of discretion, whim, prejudice, etcetera, on the part of benefit officers.

The effect of the 'genuinely seeking work' test was to put the onus of proof squarely on to the claimant. It was enforced with devastating effect throughout the 1920s, a period of exceptionally high and enduring unemployment. In 1929 the TUC claimed that the test 'has probably caused more friction and injustice than anything else in the administration of Unemployment Benefit', and the attempt to enforce it 'has resulted in the undeserved penalisation of thousands of decent people'. (TUC 1929 paras 10 and 26)

The 'genuinely seeking work' test led to the disallowance of almost three million claims. In the judgement of Alan Deacon:

> The seeking work test was as pernicious as it was unnecessary. It led to hundreds of thousands of unemployed men and women being arbitrarily deprived of benefits which they desperately needed, and forced many more to make repeated journeys in search of jobs which they knew did not exist. The operation of the test required the Exchanges to enforce the very 'hawking of labour' they had been established to prevent. (Deacon 1976 p. 89)

The test was finally removed in March 1930; the test of availability from 1930 onwards was the refusal of an offer of suitable employment, which it remained until the 1989 Social Security Act reinstated the discredited 'actively seeking work' condition, once more putting the onus of proof back on to the claimant, and once more sending men and women chasing illusory jobs.

Post-War Policy

After the Second World War the combination of full employment and the comprehensive insurance system which followed the Beveridge report meant that policies to weed out the scrounger became less salient. They re-emerged between 1966 and 1975, when for a brief period the 'wage-stop' rule limited the amount of benefit to that which the unemployed would have earned in their normal weekly employment, thus reinstating the poor law principle of less-eligibility. This rule mostly applied to those whose normal earnings were very low because they were disadvantaged in the labour market, usually with some form of disability. In 1968 the 'four week rule' was introduced for a brief period, which was an administrative device for chasing up suspected scroungers, which, whatever its official justification, was seen by claimants as a means of chasing them off benefit. And throughout the whole period until the Social Security Act 1986 the unemployed were always disadvantaged in the social assistance schemes because their level of benefit was kept below that of other claimants by exclusion from the higher long-term rate which, for other claimants, came into effect after being on benefit for a year. Again, the justification was pure 1834 less-eligibility.

Thatcherism

Under Thatcher the policies aimed at the unemployed had a coherence about them which made their overall intention unmistakable. Benefit levels have been systematically cut, resulting in a shift away from insurance benefits and towards means-tested benefits; the qualifying conditions for unemployment benefit have been made harder, and the period of disqualification from receiving benefit for leaving a job without 'just cause' has increased fourfold. The administration of benefits has been tightened up considerably in the attempt to prevent the unemployed from claiming; special fraud squads have been introduced to frighten people off benefit; and at the same time the rights of low-paid employees have been eroded both in respect of wages and job security. The cumulative effect of all these changes has been to lower the living standards of almost all unemployed claimants, to deprive many of benefits altogether, and to drive others into either very low-paid jobs or Government training schemes, which in turn help to reinforce a low wage economy. Once in such work, employees are often forced to remain there or risk being disqualified from benefit.

In a review of the effects of Government cuts in benefits for the unemployed from 1979 to 1988, aptly titled *Turning The Screw*, Atkinson and Micklewright list no fewer than 27 separate cuts in benefits that have worsened the lot of the unemployed, in contrast to four which have benefited them and seven which had some positive and some negative effects. They summarize the changes:

> Although many of the measures are limited in their individual impact, the great majority have made the system less generous and have weakened the role of unemployment *insurance* as opposed to unemployment *assistance*. The total effect of the Conservative Government's actions is such that the structure of benefits for the unemployed in 1988 is quite different from that in 1979. ... Moreover, the extent of income support for the unemployed has become markedly less generous at a time when it is most needed. (Atkinson and Micklewright 1988 p. 2)

The rich, meanwhile, and those in employment, have done well, thus widening the gap between those in work and out. The significance of this in terms of the ability of the unemployed to share fully in the life of the community, one of the acid tests of citizenship, is clear. Unemployment has increasingly come to mean poverty, stigmatization, reliance not only on means-tested benefits such as income support but through that also on the iniquitous social fund, where there are virtually no entitlements, only discretion, and no independent appeal.

But the unemployed have been attacked not only through policy changes but also through changes in the administration of benefits. There have been three main arenas where the latter day equivalent of the 'tightening-up' committee have been hard at work. Space does not permit a full account of all three; I shall therefore use one as an example.

Availability for Work; Guilty until Proved Innocent

Stricter availability testing came out of Sir Derek Rayner's review of the operation of unemployment benefits in 1981. The intention of the test is nowhere more starkly revealed than in the chapter heading in the report which recommended it, *Policing The Workshy*. (Rayner 1981) Until 1982 claimants' availability for work had been tested by asking them if they were available for work whenever they made a new claim for benefit. If they said they were that was generally accepted and payment of benefit would follow. If subsequently that availability was called into doubt, either because they refused to follow up reasonable job offers or were suspected of being involved in activities incompatible with work, for example childminding or taking a course of full-time study, it was always open to staff at the job centres or benefit offices to call the claimant in for interview and, where appropriate, to stop payment.

Throughout the 1980s this procedure was progressively tightened. Now, every new claimant for unemployment benefit is required to fill in a special questionnaire designed specifically to probe the claimant's availability for work. By 1988, after several revisions, the questionnaire comprised 18 separate questions, a 'wrong' answer to any one of which could and usually did result in the claimant's benefit being immediately suspended. Once benefit was suspended further action within the department would be taken which would either result in the claimant's being deemed to be unavailable for work and therefore ineligible for unemployment benefit, or would result in a decision in the claimant's favour, in which case benefit would be restored and backdated, though often not until weeks or months later. In the meantime no benefit would have been in payment, often causing considerable hardship and distress. Since benefit would only be paid when it had been established that the claimant was available for work, the delay in payment would have been for no good reason; a clear case of the claimant being considered guilty until proved innocent.

The Department of Employment issued a circular in December 1987 to all benefit managers setting out in minute detail the steps to be taken when administering the form. This begins by setting out the basic policy to be pursued:

> A claimant must be able to accept at once (or at 24 hours notice in certain specified circumstances) any opportunity of suitable employment. This also means not just being ready to take a job, but taking active steps to draw attention to their availability for work.
>
> A claimant must not place restrictions on the nature and conditions (such as pay, hours of work, locality, etc.) they are prepared to accept which would prevent them from having reasonable prospects of getting work. (Department of Employment Circular 1987)

Not placing restrictions on the nature and conditions of work is another way of saying that claimants must be prepared to work for rock bottom wages, for any hours, however unsociable, and at considerable distances from their homes.

Moreover, managers of benefit offices are under instructions to ensure that these policies are followed to the letter; they were told to monitor the 'availability awareness' of their staff and to see that the procedures were being properly applied, and to make daily quality control checks on all decisions where benefit has not been suspended. There can be no doubt that the tightening of these administrative procedures are part of a concerted plan to squeeze claimants off the register, and so bring down the monthly unemployment statistics and to underpin a low wage economy.

Availability for work testing does not apply only to new claimants. Under the euphemism *Restart*, the same test was also introduced for the long-term unemployed in 1986. Anyone who had been drawing benefit for a year, which was later reduced to six months, was called in for interview to have their availability for work questioned. Repeated failure to attend the interview could result in loss of benefit.

What this means in practice can be judged by the cases which began to come to the notice of advice bureaux for help; for example the following cases known to the Citizens' Advice Bureaux were all suspended during 1987; a man who had been unemployed for three years who refused to take a job which paid less than his supplementary benefit and which would not have covered his weekly expenditure; a man who had recently had a heart attack and was only prepared to work from 10.00 a.m. to 4.00 p.m.; three young mothers who, whilst being prepared to work from 8.30 to 5.00 p.m., were not prepared to travel more than 10 miles to work.

For every claimant disallowed benefit there are more who are temporarily suspended while their claim is investigated, but whose claims are subsequently judged to be in order. In the last two months of 1986 nearly 30 000 claimants were suspended from benefit after Restart interviews because their availability was thought to be in doubt; of these only 10 000 were disallowed. (Hansard 28 October 1986 and 22 July 1987) All those claimants who were suspended but who were not subsequently disallowed benefit nevertheless had to go without any benefit until their cases were decided; suspension from unemployment benefit automatically suspends supplementary benefit or income support also.

Faced with the evidence that the new tests were causing thousands of claimants considerable hardship, far from relaxing the measures in any way, the Government reversed its usual trend of cutting civil servants and took on an extra 1400, specifically for availability testing.

The 1989 Social Security Act continued this tightening-up process with the introduction of the requirement that claimants be not only available for work but also actively seeking work, with accompanying procedural hoops to jump through. Just as importantly, claimants are no longer able to claim that their refusal to take certain jobs is justified by reference to the level of wages; the defence of being able to refuse a job because the conditions and wages are not reasonable has been specifically removed. After a short 'permitted period', which for the most highly qualified people is a maximum of thirteen weeks, but in practice for most claimants is about two weeks, claimants may not refuse to take any job at any rates of pay, subject only to very few limitations.

Disqualification and Fraud Control

Similar developments have occurred with regard to policies and administration of disqualification for leaving a job without good cause and in fraud control. The period of disqualification, after staying at six weeks for 75 years, has been quadrupled to six months, leading Michael Meacher, the Opposition spokesman in the relevant debate, to call the new measures 'penal, harsh and unreasonable.' Peter Barclay, chairman of the Social Security Advisory Committee, called them 'the English version of workfare', since the threat of disqualification forces many people to remain in jobs where, as a report from the Low Pay Unit showed, they may be subjected to health hazards, racial abuse, very low levels of pay and appalling working conditions. (Barclay 1988; Byrne and Jacobs 1988)

Fraud control too has been tightened up, by the use of extra staff organized into hit-squads both in the DSS and the DE, and by the occasional spectacular media event such as Operation Major, where the DHSS preferred knowingly to allow abuse to take place so that they could swoop and catch the claimants publicly rather than head it off by preventive action.

The Balance of Rights and Obligations

Returning to the theme of citizenship, we can see that the onus is now very firmly on the claimant, both to find work and to keep it. At the same time, the state has reneged on its obligation to ensure that work is available by retreating from policies of full employment, and by using unemployment as a key part of its economic strategy. Nor does it undertake to provide work, either directly or by guaranteeing the offer of a job from the private sector, nor does it, except for 16 and 17 year olds, provide training as of right, and even that training is obligatory, whatever the quality, since the vast majority of this age group are not entitled to any benefits.

Where claimants can find work they will find that the state has also reneged on its duty to see that the pay and conditions are adequate. It was entirely predictable that Britain would refuse to adopt the European Social Charter, with its attempt to regularize the conditions of labour, as this would have gone completely against Thatcherite policies. In 1982 the Fair Wages resolution which had ensured that local authorities could insist on fair wages clauses in contracts for privatized public services was scrapped, and in 1986 the Wages Act drastically curtailed the effectiveness of Wages Councils, the regulating body for non-unionized low-paid industries comprising about three million workers. Cuts in the numbers of wages inspectors and health and safety inspectors had already contributed to lower standards of employment conditions. Protection against unfair dismissal has also been considerably weakened, especially for those in low-paid, insecure employment.

As the workplace has become increasingly deregulated so the claimant has been increasingly forced to take and keep jobs on pain of loss of benefit. Therein lies the imbalance in the rights and obligations of citizenship. Any system of state welfare is probably going to have to insist that claimants take steps to support themselves in work, but in order to balance that obligation the state must similarly undertake to regulate the workplace, and, as far as possible, ensure that work and or high quality training is available, and that the well-known obstacles to their being taken up, such as inadequate child care facilities, and practices which discriminate against the disabled and other groups are eliminated. Until then, the traditional British pastime of 'policing the workshy' will once again, as it did in the 1920s, result in the 'undeserved penalisation of thousands of decent people', and, by treating all claimants as if they were scroungers, stigmatize millions of men and women and rob them of their self-respect. Citizens deserve better.

5. Citizenship and the Modern Welfare State. Social Integration, Competence and the Reciprocity of Rights and Duties in Social Policy

Romke van der Veen

Introduction

In this paper I will discuss problems of social policy and citizenship in the modern welfare state. The European and North American welfare states are confronted with a number of social and economic problems which call into question the premises of the welfare state. First I will pay some attention to the concept of citizenship in relation to the welfare state and to problems of social policy. I will concentrate on the Dutch welfare state.

Then, two different criticisms of social policy in the welfare state will be discussed. In the first the 'adverse effects' (contrary to the intended effects) of social policy are stressed. The second criticism concentrates on the 'permissiveness of social policy': rights are stressed and duties are neglected. This permissiveness leads to ineffective social policies. Both criticisms are related to the central features of modern citizenship. Having reviewed these criticisms I will give an empirical analysis of the effectiveness of social policy. Social security and social welfare policy in the Netherlands will be discussed in particular.

In the concluding paragraph I will first confront this empirical analysis of the effectiveness of social policy with the aforementioned criticisms and, second, bring the discussion back to the notion of citizenship in the modern welfare state.

The Development of Citizenship

In *Citizenship and Capitalism* (1986) Turner states that the conditions which define modernity simultaneously define citizenship: 'The development of citizenship seems inextricably bound up with the development of modern social conditions.' (Turner 1986 pp. 17–18) This

77

development is characterized by the emergence of egalitarian horizontal relationships between people defined in universalistic terms; a secular environment; a growing freedom of exchange, belief and choice; and the growth of formal rational law. (Turner 1986 p. 18) These characteristics of modern social conditions have consequences for the concept of citizenship. Citizenship revolves around three issues: *social inclusion and participation* (who belongs to the group and has the right to participate in the community and who does not?), *civic competence* (in the modern concept of citizenship, the classical interpretation of 'capacity' is transformed into the concept of autonomy, which is almost universally ascribed to the members of a community) and *reciprocity of rights and duties* (being a member of a community does confer certain benefits; traditionally there are corresponding duties of the citizen in public life). Under modern social conditions, the status of citizen as well as the scope of the rights and duties of citizenship have expanded and became more universal. As a consequence of this, more and more members of Western, democratic societies received the status of citizen. Secondly, the rights of citizenship expanded from civic via political to social rights. (Marshall 1973) The development of civil and political rights, although they were based upon the idea of equality, did not undermine capitalism, because they did not undermine the principle of 'work' as a distributive mechanism. In a way they even strengthened the functioning of the capitalist economy (which requires laws of contract, fair exchange, and so on). Social rights, however, are more or less in contradiction with the capitalist principles. They are not based on work but on 'need' as a distributive mechanism. This opens up a constant struggle about the boundaries of both systems of distribution. (*cf.* Stone 1984) So the modern aspects of the concept of citizenship are the increasing universality of citizenship (in the nation-state) and a new interpretation of participation, competence and reciprocity expressed in social rights. These social rights stress the 'duties of the community' towards the individual.

The modern welfare state is the product of this development of social conditions and citizenship. It is a constitutional state in which the civil rights of citizens are guaranteed. It is also a democratic state in which the political rights of citizens are guaranteed. And, finally, it encompasses a system which guarantees the social rights of citizens. With the guarantee of the social rights of citizens the welfare state performs four functions which are inextricably linked to the modern concept of citizenship:

- **Guarantee:** It guarantees the rights of citizens. Social rights are guaranteed by social security, education, health care, etcetera.
- **Redistribution:** By guaranteeing the social rights of citizens the welfare state also performs a redistributive function. 'Social security' is redistributed from the haves to the have-nots.
- **Social Control:** The welfare state is a complex system of rights and duties. A certain amount of social solidarity but also a certain amount of social control is necessary for the enforcement of these rights and duties.
- **Integration:** The former three functions enable citizens to participate fully in the community. The integrative function of the welfare state is built upon a successful realization of the guarantee of social security, of redistribution and social control.

Through the discharge of these four functions modern citizenship in terms of social inclusion, civic competence and reciprocity of rights and duties has to be realized. It is with these four functions that I will later confront the effectiveness of welfare state policies.

The Modern Social Conflict

Marshall – and many with him (for example, Bell 1976) – saw contemporary capitalism as a contradictory system. The contradiction is between the political sphere which is relatively democratic and egalitarian and which enabled different social groups to acquire civil, political and social rights, and the economic sphere, which tends to generate inequalities. (*cf.* Turner 1986 p. 6) This contradiction is incorporated in the modern concept of citizenship (in the tension between civil and political rights on the one hand and social rights on the other) and in the structure of the modern welfare state. For some time this contradiction could easily be overcome because of an almost constant economic growth in the Western world which made reduction of economic inequality possible. Some ongoing socio-economic developments, however (such as internationalization, growth of labour-extensive production methods and of the service sector) have put this contradiction again at the top of the political agenda. In the Netherlands these developments have generated a growing discrepancy between supply and demand on the labour market. The demand has diminished and the educational level required of workers has risen. The decline of the demand of labour in the industrial sector was temporarily compensated by a growth of the employment in the public sector. Since 1975–1980, however, there has been a drop in the number of jobs in the public sector as well. This led to an extensive exit from the labour market. This resulted in large numbers of long-term unemployed people and a high percentage of occupational disability. Because of this extensive exit from the labour market, economic inequality increased again. The way people left the labour market was highly dependent on the structure of the social security regulations in the different welfare states. (*cf.* de Vroom 1988) In the Netherlands the exit manifested itself first in a growth of occupational disability (1975–1980) but later in a growth of early retirement and unemployment. Table 8.1 gives some data for the Netherlands:

Table 5.1
Development of the Volume of Social Security Claims
1970–1989 (x 1000 benefit years)

	1970	1975	1980	1985	1989
benefit years for:					
old-age pensions	1028	1159	1280	1781	1929
widows/orphans	151	162	168	171	195
disability	196	312	608	740	744
sickness	234	280	306	257	307
unemployment	58	197	235	650	583
national assistance	70	117	117	183	178
total	1737	2227	2714	3740	3945
index (1980=100)	63	82	100	122	127
ratio of active to inactive*	9.9	5.5	4.3	2.7	2.9

* excl. old-age pensions
Based on: SCP 1991 p. 110

The ratio of active to inactive people in the working population has declined sharply since 1960.[1] (in 1960 the ratio was 12.6 : 1). It is this ratio which indicates most prominently the socio-economic 'revolution' taking place in the Dutch welfare state. This revolution has led to a radical shift in the importance of the two distributive mechanisms mentioned before: work and needs. The mechanism of need has grown in importance whereas the mechanism of work has sharply declined in importance. It is this contradiction between two different distributive mechanisms which Dahrendorf called 'the modern social conflict'. He points out a tension in modern societies between 'the provisions party', which stresses the necessity of economic growth for the realization of rights (and therefore the mechanism of work), and the 'entitlement party' which demands rights and redistribution (and thus stresses the mechanism of need). (Dahrendorf 1988a p. 13) This shift in importance between the distributive principles of work and need has increased the above-mentioned contradiction in the modern concept of citizenship.

A second development which has undermined the stability of the welfare state as a compromise between contradictory concepts of citizenship and thus between contradictory ideologies is the process of 'individualization', which has accelerated sharply in the last two decades. Some simple figures can illustrate this development. Between 1960 and 1989 the number of people in an average household in the Netherlands declined from almost 4 to 2.4. Between 1975 and 1989 the number of one-person households more than doubled, and now one-third of all households consists of only one person. This purely demographic individualization is accompanied by a process of socio-cultural individualization. The wish to be independent and autonomous, in which this socio-cultural individualization is expressed, manifests itself in a growth of the one-person households, in a sharp increase in the number of married women looking for jobs (the Netherlands traditionally have a low level of participation of married women in the labour market), in a decline of the status of traditional marriage and an increase of alternative household forms. The most important consequences these processes of demographic, economic and socio-cultural individualization have for welfare state policies are:

- The increasing socio-cultural 'diversity' which is a result of these processes of individualization diminishes the effectiveness of social policies;
- Social reality is becoming increasingly 'opaque' for policy-makers. This frustrates the process of policy-making as well as the administration of policy.

Both developments (structural socio-economic changes and individualization) combined have undermined the foundations of the post-war welfare state. In the first place social policy in the post-war welfare state was based on the assumption of near-total employment. Secondly, social rights and duties (such as insurances and premiums) were derived from someone's position on the labour market. Thirdly, income and social security policies were based on the needs of a traditional household, consisting of a working man, a non-working woman who took care of the household and dependent children. None of these three foundations of the post-war welfare state is self-evident anymore. (*cf.* Engbersen *et al.* 1991)

To conclude, the modern social conflict is a resurrection of a more fundamental contradiction in the concept of citizenship and in the structure of the modern welfare state. It manifests itself in a massive process of exclusion from the labour market and in an increasing difficulty to define and implement social rights. Both manifestations of this social conflict threaten the modern concept of citizenship because social participation (on the labour market) is threatened and the guarantee and reciprocity of (social) rights and duties are undermined because of the consequences socio-economic and socio-cultural developments have for social policy.

The Ineffectiveness of Social Policy: Adverse Effects and Permissiveness

Having defined the concept of citizenship and reviewed its relation to welfare state policies, I will now concentrate on issues concerning social policy in the modern welfare state. The leading question in this and the next paragraph is to what extent social policies contribute to full citizenship (in terms of integration, competence and reciprocity).

The welfare state and its social policies have been under constant attack since the mid-seventies. These attacks are inspired by an (assumed) ineffectiveness of welfare state policies. In this paragraph I will sketch two 'archetypes of critique' on welfare state policies.[2] Both types of criticism are linked to the concept of citizenship. In the first it is suggested that social policy undermines citizenship by weakening social integration and the reciprocity of rights and duties. In the second type of critique it is suggested that social policy undermines the civic competence of citizens.

a. Adverse Effects

In the first type of critique the unintended and adverse (contrary to the intended effects) effects of social policies are stressed. The emphasis is placed on the contradictory rationality of social policy and of citizens. A well-known example of this approach is *Losing Ground, American Social Policy 1950–1980* by Charles Murray (1984) . Murray's argument is simple and straightforward: contemporary social welfare policy harms the poor because it rewards being poor and jobless. Social welfare policy must therefore be stripped of much unnecessary or counter-productive programmes and must emphasize the stick rather than the carrot.

Murray's thesis can be summed up in the following six points (Katz 1989 p. 153):
- Despite massively swollen spending on social welfare after 1965, the incidence of both poverty and antisocial behaviour increased.
- Neither the growth of poverty nor of antisocial behaviour were the result of economic conditions, which were improving.
- Black unemployment increased during the period because young blacks voluntarily withdrew from the labour market.
- Female-headed black families increased because young men and women were less disposed towards marriage.
- Labour market and family behaviour (also criminal behaviour) reflected rational short-term responses to economic incentives.
- These incentives were the adverse result of federal social policy after 1965.

All these assumptions have been heavily attacked and shown to be wrong or incomplete. (Katz 1989 pp. 153–156) The first fundamental premise of Murray's argument, that the rise of poverty and unemployment is not the result of economic developments, is weakened. His second and more fundamental premise, that men are rationally calculating and oriented on the maximization of short-term gains, which undermines the effectiveness of social policy, has survived better, however, and plays an important role in the approach which stresses the permissiveness of social policy.

On the basis of his analysis of American social policy from 1950 to 1980, Murray formulates three laws of social programmes:
- The law of imperfect selection: any objective rule that defines eligibility for a social transfer programme will irrationally exclude some people. (Murray 1984 p. 211) In everyday reality the law of imperfect selection leads to programmes with constantly broadening target populations. (Murray 1984 p. 212)
- The law of unintended rewards: any social transfer increases the net value of being in the condition that prompted the transfer. (Murray 1984 p. 212) All social programmes provide an unintended reward for being in the condition that the programme is trying to change or

make more tolerable, which also leads to a growth of entitlement. Only 'persons who are in the unwanted condition "completely un-voluntarily" are not affected by the existence of the reward'. (Murray 1984 p. 213)

- The law of net harm: the less likely it is that the unwanted behaviour will change voluntarily, the more likely it is that a programme to induce change will cause net harm. (Murray 1984 p. 216) 'any program that mounts an intervention with sufficient rewards to sustain participation and an effective result will generate so much of the unwanted behaviour (in order to become eligible for the pro-gram's rewards) that the net effect will be to increase the incidence of the unwanted behaviour. In practice, the programs that deal with the most intractable behaviour problems have included a package of rewards large enough to induce participation, but not large enough to produce the desired result'. (Murray 1984 p. 217)

Murray's conclusion is obvious and simple: reduce social welfare policy to a minimum and use sticks instead of carrots. Important in Murray's analysis – even though his argument has been seriously weakened by criticism – is his emphasis on the fact that social programmes create a strategic environment (*cf.* de Swaan 1988) and on the fact that people are not passive consumers of social programmes. His treatment of these phenomena, however, is very one-sided: the environment is reduced to a purely economic environment and people are seen as purely economic cost-reducers and reward-maximizers. I will return later to this.

Although Murray's thesis has been heavily attacked (mainly on em-pirical grounds) his line of thinking is very persistent, as is illustrated by Katz in his book *The Undeserving Poor* (1989). In recent discussions in the Netherlands about the functioning of the welfare state, ideas which resemble Murray's arguments also play an important role.

b. The Permissive Welfare State

Mead's analysis of the welfare state in his book *Beyond Entitlement* (1986) echoes Murray's analysis. His question is also why federal programmes have coped so poorly with the social problems that afflict American society. Mead believes that the competence of the American citizen to function has declined during the last two decades. Competence is measured by Mead in the proportion of the population dependent on welfare, the unemployment rate, the amount of serious crime, etcetera. Like Murray, Mead believes the cause of this not to lie in the socio-economic development of American society.

Mead's answer to the question of the cause of the 'declining competence' of American citizens, however, is radically different from Murray's answer. The major problem of the American welfare state, according to Mead, is its permissiveness: welfare programmes award benefits as entitlements, expecting little in return from the beneficiaries. This permissiveness has negative effects on the individual will: apathy and incompetence are promoted. So Mead concludes: 'Unemployment has more to do with functioning problems of the jobless than with economic conditions.'

Mead's remedy for the problems of the American welfare state is an authoritative social policy, in which social obligations are enforced. Citizenship, according to Mead, implies mutual responsibilities. Where benefits are granted, obligations have to be imposed and enforced in return.

Critique can be levelled against Mead's arguments on several points:
- The empirical argument of Mead, that labour supply does not exceed demand, is unconvincing and is for example extensively criticized by Wilson. (Katz 1989 pp. 162–163)
- Mead's historical analysis of American social reform – which, according to Mead, assumed the competence of American citizens only until 1960 – is criticized by Katz. (1989 pp. 159–162)
- Mead's moral or philosophical analysis of the concept of citizenship and rights and duties (entitlements and obligations) is one-sided. Whereas such concepts as competence and reciprocity always have two sides, collective and individual, Mead consistently focuses on the individual side. I will later return to this argument.

Mead distinguishes two fundamental dimensions in politics: the competence and the collectivist dimension. The competence dimension has to do with ideas about people in terms of autonomy and civility. The collectivist dimension has to do with ideas about the state in terms of a large or small state or an authoritative or a permissive government. Mead defines his own views on social policy as 'civic conservatism' (Mead 1986 p. 251), thereby choosing for a large and authoritative state and for individual autonomy.

According to Murray and Mead, social policy (social security and employment policies) does not contribute to the realization of citizenship. This is due to the fact that social policy, in their view, weakens the competence and social integration of people that are dependent on these policies. In the next paragraph I will analyse Dutch social policy, and again the leading question is to what extent these policies contribute to full citizenship.

The Effectiveness of Social Policy

The preceding criticisms of social policy raise some fundamental issues concerning the functioning and effectiveness of social policy. The first issue concerns the attitude of people dependent on social security and the way they perceive and act upon their rights and duties as defined in social policy programmes. The second is the question how socio-economic conditions interact with social policy. The third issue concerns problems of categorization in social policy and the consequences of legal categorization. The fourth issue, finally, concerns the effectiveness of social policy in terms of administering and enforcing rights and duties. I will discuss these four issues on the basis of recent research into the development and administration of social security policy in the Netherlands. (*cf.* van der Veen 1990) The starting-point of this research was the idea that we can only gain further insight in the functioning and effectiveness of social policy by precise and intensive study of the process of administration and of the recipients, instead of focusing too much on the structure of social policy and on aggregate data. I will give a short review of this research and return to the above-mentioned issues from time to time.

a. The Administration of Social Policy

Three agencies and their clients were studied in detail. First, a public welfare agency which administers unemployment provisions and public services. Second, an agency which judges the rate of occupational disability for the disability insurances. And third, an agency which administers unemployment insurances. Three subjects were studied at the agencies: first the process of decision-making, second the distribution of rights and duties, and third the way in which social policy influences the behaviour of clients.

The three agencies that were studied represent three different forms of bureaucratic organization. The public welfare agency is to a certain extent based on the discretion of its officials. The enacted laws are broad and vague and the problems of the public the officials have to solve are complex and various. This calls for individualized treatment and hence for a certain amount of discretion. (*cf.* Handler and Hollingsworth 1971 p. 209) The agency judging the rate of occupational disability is a professional bureaucracy. Professionals (such as medical doctors) have a high amount of discretion. Professional knowledge and professional decision-making cannot be caught in legal rules. Professionals and professional knowledge therefore 'define and legitimate the actions of (the agency) rather than the other way round'. (Mashaw 1983 p. 32) The third agency is the most bureaucratic. Unemployment insurance in the Netherlands is very detailed and complex. The agency tries to structure the decisions of officials as much as possible, hence the discretion of officials is low.

Problems of Categorization and Opacity

Each agency encounters different problems. The public welfare agency is confronted with two main problems. First, it is very difficult for officials to collect all the necessary information about their clients. The structure of the household and the financial situation of clients are very important data for the decisions taken by officials. As he or she collects this information, the official will soon be confronted with the opacity of social reality (what kind of relationship do people have?) and with problems of privacy. The development of the laws on public provision (towards more specificity and selectivity) and the social developments concerning household structure and income (towards increasing diversity) during the last fifteen years have complicated these problems enormously. Secondly, the official is confronted with ambiguous goals. On the one hand he or she is a bureaucrat who has to enact a law, on the other hand he or she is a social worker who has to give clients individual treatment and is allowed to deviate from the rules. The medical service judging occupational disability is confronted with the insufficiency of professional knowledge for reaching a decision. Occupational disability is not a purely medical phenomenon. It also depends on the psychological status of clients, on their age, and on their opportunities on the labour market. The agency that administers the unemployment insurances, finally, is mainly confronted with the increasing complexity of the laws that have to be enacted and with the discrepancies that exist between the structure of the law and the situation of clients.

All the above-mentioned (administrative) problems are typical for social policy in a modern welfare state. They are related to the two fundamental problems of social policy mentioned before. The first is the problem of categorization and the related problem of enforcing entitlements and obligations. In a society with an increasing socio-cultural diversity and an increasing complexity and specificity of social policy (both are more or less autonomous processes; Goodin 1982) the formulation of unambiguous categories is becoming more and more difficult. Therefore the match between social and legal reality is always partial and incomplete, not in the least because each new category in social policy creates new 'boundary problems'. This impedes a just and efficient enforcement of rights and duties. The second issue is what I have called the increasing opacity of social reality. More specific categorizations in social policy require transparency and unambiguity. More specific categorizations, however, create more boundary problems and therefore decrease transparency and increase ambiguity. This is again reinforced by the increasing socio-cultural diversity.

Informal Norms and Strategies
All three agencies are therefore confronted with problems of incomplete information and ambiguity. The officials have to find solutions to these problems to be able to make decisions. The solutions officials have found to the problems they encounter in their daily decision-making can be observed in the informal strategies and norms they use. The informal norms employed by the officials of the public welfare agency are based on a judgement of the needs and the behaviour of clients (Do they provide all the necessary information? Can their behaviour be called responsible?). This generates client typifications: elderly people and single-parent families will be helped more readily than other clients. The informal norms applied by professionals correspond more or less with those of the public welfare officials. Elderly people (with few opportunities on the labour market) and the disabled will get an occupational disability pension more easily than others. Norms of responsibility and client behaviour can also be observed in the decision-making process of professionals. Clients demonstrating a work ethic, which means they want (at least partially) to earn their own income or to be retrained, will get a (partial) disability pension more easily and be helped with retraining and finding a new place on the labour market. At the unemployment insurance agency, client typifications manifest themselves mainly in the way officials control clients, which Lipsky (1980) calls 'processing the client'. The problems the officials have with the enactment of the laws cause over-concentration on the administrative aspects of the administration and create strategies to keep the client at a distance.

To conclude: in the daily administration of social security regulations a number of problems manifest themselves. Firstly, the problem of the discrepancy between legal categorizations and the social situation of clients promotes the use of informal norms and strategies of decision-making. These informal strategies and norms can lead to a distribution of rights and duties which deviates from the official rules: they favour clients who conform to the informal norms of need and responsibility (like elderly people, female-headed households, and so on). Secondly, problems with categorization and administration can create a retreatist or fatalist attitude with the officials: they neglect the rules and aims of the policy they have to administer. (*cf.* Kagan 1978) The consequence of this attitude is often that the duties of clients are hardly enforced. For example, the enactment of the duty to do everything possible to find a job and earn one's own income is often slack and merely symbolic. Officials justify their behaviour by pointing out that their clients have few opportunities on the labour market, so why should they be severe?

b. The Perception of Rights and Duties
The way in which clients experience their rights and duties and their behaviour in relation to their duties was the second topic of the study. The way beneficiaries experienced their rights and duties was highly dependent on their perception of the way they had been treated by the administrative agencies. This perception was often couched in terms of justice-arguments. (*cf.* Mathiessen 1965)

Reinterpretation of Rights and Duties
The clients of the unemployment insurance agency and the clients with a (partial) disability pension expressed very often that they had been confronted with injustice or unjust treatment. The administrative problems which the unemployment agency encountered during the enactment of the unemployment insurance were the main cause of these perceptions. Because of administrative problems clients had to wait a long time before they received their benefits, and the relations between officials and clients were detached and problematic. The majority of the clients nevertheless accepted the duties the unemployment insurance placed on them. Perceptions of injustice by clients with a (partial) disability pension were also related to an estimate of their occupational disability which, as these clients felt, was too low. This illustrates the strategic element in the way clients experience their rights and duties. A higher estimate of occupational disability leads to a higher pension. The majority of these clients neglected their duty to do everything possible to find a suitable place on the labour market. Apart from their perception of injustice, the fact that most people with a disability pension had

already been dependent on a social security benefit for a long period also caused this attitude. This effect of the duration of dependence on a social security benefit on the interpretation of rights and duties was also found with the clients of the public welfare agency. Most clients of the public welfare agency had already been dependent on this agency for their income for many years. They had little hope of finding a place on the labour market. Because of this they started to interpret their provision as a guaranteed minimum income scheme (free of duties) instead of a temporary provision. This led to many deviations of the rules the law imposed on them.

In the way clients experience their rights and duties, processes of 'reinterpretation' can be observed. All the observed reinterpretations strengthened the dependence on social security benefits, because one way or the other the reinterpretations reinforced resignation. The question is what incited this reinterpretation.

Rational Calculation?

Two alternative ways to explain the reinterpretation processes by clients can be followed. In the first, rational calculation by the client is emphasized. In the second, emphasis is put on moral evaluations by citizens and on processes of social comparison and evaluations of justice. (*cf.* Schuyt 1983) I will use a combination of both explanations. Processes of reinterpretation of rights and duties are related to rational calculations as well as to moral evaluations. This implies that rational calculations can be more complex than Murray for example suggests. It can be rational for long-term unemployed to neglect their duties, not because of the economic reward, but because it is psychologically rewarding to do so. If they accept their position of unemployment (and thus neglect their duties and reinterpret their rights more in terms of a guaranteed minimum income scheme) the frustrating effect of unemployment diminishes. It is in this relation between the social position of clients (being dependent, long-term unemployed, with little prospect of re-entering the labour market) and the way they experience their rights and duties, that an explanation for their behaviour can be found. The consequence of the resulting reinterpretations is that people accept their unemployment and dependence.

To conclude, the process of reinterpretation of rights and duties is the result of the social and economic position of beneficiaries of social security. Their opportunities on the labour market are few and they have often been dependent on social security benefits for long periods of time.

Because of the characteristics of the process of administration, as illustrated in the previous paragraph, this process of reinterpretation is hardly or not at all stopped or controlled by the administrative agencies.

c. Social Policy: Adverse or Permissive?

It must be admitted that social policy in the modern welfare state does have adverse effects (social policy does to some extent increase dependence and resignation) and is to a certain extent permissive (for example, symbolic or slack enforcement of duties, officials with a retreatist attitude). In this way it can be said that social policy does not contribute to full citizenship because it weakens social integration, competence and reciprocity of rights and duties. The causes of these adverse effects and this permissiveness, however, are different from the ones suggested by Murray or Mead. Murray perceives people as purely economic cost-reducers and reward-maximizers and interprets social policy solely as a strategic environment for the reward-maximizing behaviour of beneficiaries. Mead sketches social policy as permissive in its structure and it is this permissiveness which promotes apathy and incompetence. The problem with both views is their one-sidedness. Social policy does indeed create a 'strategic environment' and this can stimulate rational calculation, meaning that some people prefer being dependent on social security benefits. This calculation, however, is more socio-psychological than economically inspired. It is the social position of beneficiaries (being dependent, long-term unemployed, with little prospect of re-entering the labour market) that stimulates this process. Social policy can also stimulate the neglect of duties, or as Mead terms it: 'apathy and incompetence'. This, however, has little to do with functioning problems of the jobless, as Mead suggests; it is the social- and economic position of clients, the problems encountered in the implementation of social policy, and the problems with enforcing duties that make people neglect their duties.

So the problems which social policy is said to create are not the result of social policy *per se*, they are mainly the result of the social and economic conditions under which these policies operate. In other words, the causes of these problems are not primarily internal to social policy, as Mead and Murray suggest, but mainly external to social policy.

Conclusion: Realizing Citizenship in the Modern Welfare State

What I have tried to do is to show to what extent the effectiveness of social policy is dependent upon social and economic conditions. These conditions influence the effectiveness and administration of social policy to a high degree, as well as the attitude and the behaviour of beneficiaries. This sheds a light on problems of social policy in the modern welfare state as well as on problems of citizenship which is different from that suggested by the two archetypes of criticism I reviewed before. Both types of criticism are one-sided in that they focus mainly on the individual level of behaviour (the social and economic dimension of attitudes and behaviour is neglected) or on an individualized concept of citizenship.

Duties of the Collectivity

Mead's analysis of the concept of civic competence and reciprocity of rights and duties emphasizes the individual aspects of competence and reciprocity (the obligations of beneficiaries) and neglects the collective (social and economic) aspects of competence and reciprocity. As Katz writes: '... obligation implies mutual responsibilities, and Mead fails to ask what we in our organized capacity as government ... owe in return'. (Katz 1989 p. 164) As I have tried to illustrate, the fundamental problem with civic competence and reciprocity of rights and duties is not to be found on the individual level (the neglect of duties, the permissiveness of social policy) but on a more collective level. The problem is that modern society does not provide the prerequisites of competence to a large category of citizens. This prerequisite is social integration and participation. A massive process of social exclusion is taking place or has taken place, which undermines the foundations of modern citizenship defined in terms of social inclusion or participation. Because of problems of long-term unemployment and social exclusion, for example, people can hardly be expected to live up to their obligations. The possibilities for people to be competent citizens have to be created first. Formulated in terms of the functions of the welfare state distinguished above: the integrative function of the welfare system is severely weakened.

Analysing problems of competence and reciprocity of rights and duties on a collective level instead of an individual level redirects the evaluation of social policy from problems of permissiveness and unbalanced rights and duties to the 'conditions' necessary for civic competence and reciprocity. This raises the question what the duties of the collectivity are towards the individual instead of the other way round. In the remainder of this article I will try to give an answer to this question.

Vulnerabilities and Secondary Responsibilities

A first attempt to answer the former question can be found in Goodin's *Protecting the Vulnerable, a Re-Analysis of our Social Responsibilities.* (1985) The central concept in his definition of responsibility is 'vulnerability'. We are responsible for people who are vulnerable to our actions. Vulnerability is defined in terms of dependence and autonomy. People are vulnerable to our actions when they are dependent on us and are not autonomous individuals (for example, children). Because of social, technological and economic changes the consequences of action reach further (*cf.* Jonas 1984; de Swaan 1988) and therefore people have become more dependent on each other. In other words, dependence relations are generalized and have become more abstract and distant. The category of what Goodin calls 'secondary responsibilities' (responsibilities towards others not directly dependent upon us) has therefore increased. These secondary responsibilities are discharged by the welfare state. Our definition of the tasks of the welfare state (the duties of the collectivity) is therefore dependent on the question who are vulnerable to our actions – which is dependent on social and economic developments – and to whom and how far our secondary responsibilities extend.

Goodin's definition of the tasks of the welfare state embraces more, however, than just 'protecting the vulnerable'. In relation to the welfare state he defines vulnerability also in terms of participation. He writes:

> If full participation in our societies is conditional upon a person's being a minimally independent agent, then morally we must not only serve the needs of those who are dependent upon us but also do what we can to render those persons independent. ... (The welfare state) secures for them the sort of minimal independence that is required for them to participate in the other market and quasi-market sectors of their society. (Goodin 1988 p. 183)

So the task of the welfare state is two-fold: protecting the vulnerable and preventing people from becoming vulnerable. This definition fits in with the concept of citizenship that I have described. The duties of the collectivity towards the individual can now be defined in terms of the concept of citizenship as guaranteeing social integration and the prerequisites of civic competence. These are the mirror-image of the rights and duties of the individual.

As we have seen in the last paragraph, the guarantee of an adequate minimum-income level for people dependent on social security (which is the cornerstone of the Dutch social security system) is insufficient to guarantee full citizenship. Processes of massive exclusion from the labour market can lead to social exclusion and thus to a weakening of social integration and civic competence which cannot be countered by a simple income-guarantee. Following Goodin's definition of the tasks of the welfare state, a 'reanalysis of social policy' therefore has to be directed at the possibilities of guaranteeing social integration and the prerequisites of civic competence, thereby preventing people from becoming vulnerable. Now, as we have seen, social policy too often reinforces the dependence of beneficiaries and gives them few or no alternatives to being long-term dependent on social security benefits. By changing social policy in this direction, the adverse effects and the permissive character of social policy can be diminished.

With Dahrendorf I do not think this has to lead us to 'a right to work'. This is either an empty phrase when it cannot be met, or a misuse of the word right when it cannot be guaranteed. (*cf.* Dahrendorf 1988a p. 148) The significance of work as a key to social participation and self-esteem, however, makes full employment still a desirable objective. It is a short-term objective, 'but under given social conditions, it is a prerequisite of a society of citizens which helps make entitlements real'. (Dahrendorf 1988a pp. 176–177) Because the modern labour market can achieve full employment only at a high price, the American price of poverty, social policy has to be directed at creating and redistributing work. Increasing the 'life-chances' of people in this way, will also increase the effectiveness of social policy.

Notes

1. This ratio is flattered. Early exit from the labour market through semi-collective or private arrangements is not taken into account.
2. These archetypes can be found in the discussion about the effectiveness of social policy in every modern welfare state. Although the examples I will use are North American, the same criticism (though in a more friendly form) can be heard in the Netherlands and other European countries. I have dubbed the criticisms 'archetypes' because these types of criticism have a rhetorical and political function which are hardly influenced by empirical evidence for or against their central theses. Both are very 'persistent': since the eighteenth century they figure predominantly in 'reactionary rhetoric'. (*cf.* Hirschman 1991) The fact that the same type of

discussion can be found in North America as well as in the Netherlands (with a completely different structure of welfare state policies and a rather different socio-economic situation) illustrates this.

Part II

Work and Citizenship in Central and Eastern Europe

6. Citizenship and the Organization of Work under 'Perestroika'

Gregory Andrusz

Introduction

On 1 June 1992 the Danish electorate voted on the Maastricht agreement about the European Monetary and Political Union. Their negative decision expressed the first nationwide anxiety within the expanded European Community over policies adopted by politicians and officials in Brussels. In this context the term 'anxiety' may be appositely employed in its Kierkegaardian sense of 'a feeling that has no definite object'. It is a universally felt emotion which settles around words, and inadequately understood concepts, such as sovereignty and national identity. The perception of overcentralization overrides political and bureaucratic talk of 'subsidiarity'.

For the purposes of this chapter, the significant issue is that the anxieties manifested in the outcome of the Danish referendum are remarkably similar to those being revealed at different levels in the member states of the Commonwealth of Independent States (CIS). Ironically, these analogous feelings are being generated by opposite processes. For instance, whereas in the European Community, citizens of individual states are being granted citizenship of a supra-national European territorial community, in the CIS, individuals who, as Soviet citizens, were members of a large, federal, political entity, are now becoming citizens of much smaller states.

Secondly, as the European Parliament discusses how 'to secure the effective operation of the Internal Market across the whole Community', members of the CIS and other former members of the USSR are erecting trade barriers, introducing their own tax regimes and laws governing investment, commerce and trade. Thirdly, whilst the European Community moves towards monetary union and a single currency and one Central Bank, the newly independent states in the former Soviet Union rush headlong to create their own separate Central Banks and own currencies.[1] (Burakovsky 1992) Finally, whereas the Delors Plan aims to 'harmonize' working conditions throughout the Community, on the basis of the Social Contract, and the Commission pursues its objectives of ensuring the equal rights of citizens throughout the Community,[2] across the River Bug each state is beginning to 'improvise' its own laws and regulations to protect its citizens. These trends might come to a halt, or even go into reverse. In the foreseeable future, however, it seems likely that in the former Soviet Union the nation-building process will lead to new forms of discrimination based on citizenship.

From the standpoint of today (July 1992), the CIS may best be regarded as an unstable political arrangement. The *modus operandi* which has been reached between the republics of the former Soviet Union (FSU) evolved out of policies devised in the heartland of the state – European Russia. Moscow, the capital of all the Russians, of the USSR and now the Russian Federation, imposed its concept of citizenship and understanding of Constitution on the other republics. Should any of the republics with predominantly Muslim populations adopt Islamic law and should older, non-European cultural traditions re-emerge, not only might definitions of citizenship and rights to work and rights at the work-place change, but socially sanctioned infringements of formal rights might become widespread.

This essay takes as its problematic the interplay between (a) the changing world of work and employment-based provision of welfare benefits, (b) the disintegration of a unified citizenship into different citizenships associated with the nation-building process, and (c) the sanctioning of discrimination through the exclusionary device of citizenship.

Citizenship and Property

In contemporary Russia the relationship between property and the middle classes is complex and contradictory. This is because of the basic division within the 'middle class' between the new entrepreneurs who want to own property outright (in the classical nineteenth-century sense) and the old middle-class functionaries who enjoy enormous property rights which grant them privileged access to goods and services. Political support for the unreconstructed conservative elite comes from large sections of the working class, for state property has offered that which people seek in property, namely security. The guaranteed security in property has long ceased to be a plot of land on which the family might be sustained; it is work itself. Constant assured employment is precisely that which both the well-off and the ordinary person stand to lose if privatization occurs.

Today, the advanced industrial, affluent societies of the West are witnessing the appearance of a poorly articulated demand for 'consumer citizenship' (Young 1992): in a world where political rights and social welfare entitlements have been largely won,[3] new expectations have been born. In failing to meet these needs, the 'society of contentment' (Galbraith 1992) engenders feelings of deprivation and of exclusion from society among those who do not have cars and designer clothes. In Russia and other members of the CIS, however, the claims of citizens are essentially for a variety of welfare entitlements, those needed in order to survive and to progress.

Citizenship in the USSR

The USSR came into existence on the basis of a treaty concluded in December 1922 between the RSFSR, Belorussian, Ukrainian and Trans-caucasian republics. Other republics joined later. Before the October Revolution, only the smallest fraction of the population were citizens in a formal, political sense. The founders of the Soviet state, while regarding universal suffrage and the issue of citizenship as a *sine qua non*, nonetheless regarded enfranchisement as a 'formality'.

Soviet constitutions contain 30 articles defining the rights and duties of citizens and are distinguished from the Constitutions of most other countries in the emphasis which they place on economic and social rights, such as the right to work, to leisure, to material provision in old age, to medical care, to education and housing.[4] (Wolf-Phillips 1968) This range of entitlements, in preceding the listing of political rights in the Constitution, reflected the belief that equality before the law and universal adult suffrage do not in themselves ensure rights to 'life, liberty and the pursuit of happiness'. The attainment of the latter demands an economic and social underpinning which is provided by decent housing, good health and education. People lacking in literacy and numeracy, living in debilitating conditions and unemployed or unemployable do not become freer because of a Constitutional declaration of the political right to vote. Put in another way, the devisors of the Soviet Constitution realized that the equal right and opportunity to housing, health care and education – social justice – were prerequisites for meaningful citizenship.[5] Attention to 'rights' has as a corollary an attention to duties. Hence the Soviet Constitution has always placed on the citizen a duty to work, to adhere to labour discipline and to take care of public property.

For the population both before and after 1917 the important issue was the state's responsibility – and if not the state then the factory or landowner – to provide work and subsistence for the worker and his family.

This attitude is far from disappearing. The threat of widespread unemployment is reviving demands for 'social protection' and 'social guarantees' by the state. These demands are arising under circumstances where the new political climate has cast on to the public stage concerns which for decades had been ideologically concealed and denied a place in the forum, but which were simmering in the private domain. For better or worse, nationality (and its constituent components – identity, language, history, international status) has come to the fore. This is radically effecting reactions to the threat of unemployment, as it becomes associated with immigration and national minorities. This correlation has catapulted the subject of citizenship into the public imagination and politics.

The World of Work in the USSR

It has frequently been said that Russia's history is more relevant than Marxism in order to understand Soviet economic and political structures, for, despite the use of a Marxist vocabulary, the one-party state and multifarious, interlocking informal dependencies have very little to do with Marx. (Nove 1979 p. 42)

Similarly, Soviet labour law is as much Russian as it is socialist. Under Peter the Great the State was directly responsible for the employment of industrial labour. State-owned serfs were assigned to manufacturing establishments. Children were bonded to the workplaces of their parents. The legacy of serfdom is traceable to regulations instituted firstly during War Communism (1918–1921) and then more systematically by Stalin when labour was actually 'tied' to the workplace.

Discipline and control over mobility were exercised through the internal passport system which was reintroduced in 1932, essentially to limit the geographical mobility of farm workers who were denied passports. Restrictions on the rural population remained until the introduction of a new passport law in 1974 when all Soviet citizens were granted passports. Apart from personal data the passport records information on marriage, divorce, dependent children, military service, place of residence and nationality, which is determined by either of the parents and is difficult to change.[6]

Another device for limiting labour mobility is the system of compulsory residence registration; a residence permit is obligatory for residing anywhere for more than six weeks. It is issued by the passport department of the local militia who can refuse to register applicants, especially those wanting to move into the capital and other large cities.[7] The promise of a permanent residential permit in Moscow attracted workers to accept temporary permits for decades. Many were never converted into permanent permits. In this way large industrial employers such as the ZIL plant in Moscow created a tied labour force: a worker on a temporary permit dismissed from his job was not allowed to take up another in Moscow. Employers provided their workers with jobs and not only with the obligatory residential permit but also accommodation. The hope of improved living conditions (and perhaps permanent residential status) led to the creation of an enserfed population (*krepostnye lyudi*). Although the Constitutional Committee of the Supreme Soviet declared the residence permit (*propiska*) illegal two years ago, in many republics it remains in operation. Although theoretically abolished in the Russian Federation it continues in force in Moscow and will operate in Alma Ata until (at least) 1993.

Contemporary Russian scholars speak of workers as still being serfs because of the way in which they are tied to their workplaces through a variety of employer-provided welfare and social benefits. Trade unions and management agree on the allocation to housing, child care and medical and leisure facilities of funds from the central state budget and from their own profits. (Andrusz 1992) The provision of social benefits did not prevent high labour turnover, walk-outs, absenteeism and breach of contract which are more and more a reaction to the organization of work. (Grancelli 1988 p. 135) Workers have been masterful in regulating their work speeds and disrupting production by, literally, 'putting a spanner in the works', or less consciously through negligence. The tactics employed by both labour and management to counter and accommodate such behaviour had to be tackled. Andropov sought to do so in the traditional Russian manner by using the disciplinary fist of the commanding political authority. Gorbachev, his aides and successors preferred the equally traditional capitalist way of using the discipline of the impersonal market and unemployment. If unemployment, through redundancy, became accepted as 'inevitable', then the Russian state might overcome the most frequent cause of labour disputes – dismissal by the employer for indiscipline. The problem has been that, because 'indiscipline' (in one of its many guises) was so widespread, management's action could be said to bear the stamp of arbitrariness and therefore was unjust and unacceptable. The economic reforms that comprise 'perestroika' required the laying off of manpower for 'sound economic reasons'. Reform was justified by the promise of a higher standard of living resulting from greater efficiency. Redundancies caused by bankruptcies and restructuring could be portrayed as being the consequence of 'objective forces' (*zakonnomernosti*) – the iron laws of supply and demand and competition in the market-place – and therefore, possibly, less open to challenge by the workforce.

In addition, in order to achieve a more efficient industry, Gorbachev opened the challenge to the state's monopoly over the ownership of property and championed the establishment of different property forms. Co-operatives were the first to be created. Their outputs were higher as were the wages of members and 'employees'. They also used less labour.

Instead of members of the CIS moving directly from feudalistic patron–client relationships to a system based on the association of freely contracting individuals, it is possible that sections of the population will be 'protected' by new patron–client relations, no less exploitative than those that they are replacing. Because not all plants will be able to modernize rapidly, they will wish to continue to draw upon sources of cheap labour. Those most vulnerable to exploitation are the Soviet functional equivalents of 'Gastarbeiter' and people from small provincial towns. All the republics employ immigrant labour.[8] Refugees from areas of ethnic conflict already numbering over one million in July 1991 comprise another exploitable and vulnerable population. (*Veteran* 29 July 1991)

Restructuring: Implementation

The inauguration in 1987 of 'perestroika' heralded a new Enlightenment and the first Russian Reformation: in official rhetoric 'the human factor' was to be released so that the economy could grow. The 'individual' was for the first time in Russian history to be given precedence over the collective. Simultaneously, the administrative-command economy came to be described as less efficacious than the market as a means of allocating resources. The monopolist powers exercised by state enterprises, wholly indifferent to consumer needs and costs, came under criticism. Competition was declared the *sine qua non* for economic success. The ideas of Adam Smith and the nineteenth-century liberals were invoked: to criticize the all-pervasiveness of the state and the privileges enjoyed by social groups in positions of power (the *nomen-klatura*); and to demonstrate the benefits to be gained from competition in the political and economic market-place. As early as 1989 some free market liberals in the Soviet Union were advocating the market as the panacea for the economic and social ills of the society. Initially, the Government maintained that weaker, vulnerable social groups in society would have to be protected from the vicissitudes of the market by a comprehensive system of 'social guarantees'. Yet, by late 1990 the Government was disingenuously employing a market rhetoric to justify decreases in living standards. The Government's prevarication on the issue of widespread social distress did not dilute the torrent of criticism from economic radicals throughout 1991 that the reforms were failing to create an optimal environment for entrepreneurship and technical innovation. As inflation increased and confidence in the rouble declined and foreign debts multiplied, the Government began to beat a retreat from market reforms. In the summer of 1992 there is doubt whether the ascent of Yeltsin following the attempted coup in August 1991 has witnessed significant changes in the general economic environment.

The decision to encourage greater economic efficiency by granting state enterprises more independence and by introducing different forms of property ownership was to have wide-ranging implications. The first two years of 'perestroika' saw a compromise between two sets of social forces, neither of which could be said to be homogenous and without internal conflicts and contradictions. One was concerned to enhance collective control in the workplace, while the other focused on individual control over the distribution of resources. These developments, though distinctive, were related in that they both fractured the ferro-concrete monopolies and generated new property forms.

The 1987 Law on State Enterprises (Associations) laid down that enterprise managers were to be elected by their workers who would also elect a works council to determine the enterprise's plans. The Law on Individual Labour Activity passed in the same year was a harbinger of the Law on Co-operatives enacted in 1988, which allowed the formation of self-financing, profit- and market-oriented co-opera'ives which would be owned by the membership. (*Pravda* 8 June 1988) Laws enacted in the first years of 'perestroika' were concerned to radically reform the 'old' system while creating new forms of 'collective' ownership and control. The challenge to outright private ownership of the means of production and land was vehemently maintained within the CPSU leadership by Likhachev. Even today opposition to the 'principle' of private ownership remains strong. As late as autumn 1990 there was still strong support for a system of leasing state property which, 'given an almost complete state monopoly, offers the most efficient and fair chance for working people to control ownership and to end that form of exploitation practised by the bureaucratic system'. (Bunich 1990 p. 10)

This trend towards developing the private sector was taken a step further with the publication in July 1990 of new regulations 'On Joint Stock Companies and Associations with Limited Liability' and 'On Securities'. A council, established to look after the interests of the shareholders, was weakened by regulations strengthening the power of the management and work collectives over that of the shareholders. Later in 1990 entrepreneurs were given the right to hire and fire workers. At the same time they had to assume responsibility for the social, medical and 'other types of compulsory insurance' of the workforce employed (*Argumenty i Fakty* No. 43, 1990 p. 8). In other words, a set of norms found under tsarism and Sovietism were being prescribed for the dawning era of liberalism.

The nature of the conflict in society then (1990) as compared to now (1992) is revealed in this and in a comment by one economist who, while approving of work collectives having a seat on the company's management board in order to protect the interests of the workers, emphasized that it was essential that we 'avoid a repeat of the Yugoslav experience [*sic*], whereby the work collective was given a disproportionate say in economic management, enabling it to block moves towards an effective market economy'. (Grigoriev 1990 p. 10) On the other hand, some stalwart protagonists of privatization, including advisors to Boris Yeltsin, regard the new bankruptcy laws as an opportunity for the issuing of a Presidential Edict transferring property to 'workers' collectives' on a long-term credit basis. (Fedorov 1992)[9]

When the Government embarked on its path of economic and political reform, opposition in the upper echelons retaliated. Within a very short period of time, questions began to be posed on, for instance, whether people working in the 'private' or co-operative sectors qualified for pensions, or whether they had the same rights as those guaranteed by trade unions, and even whether they were entitled to a state apartment. This led to the creation of a trade union for members of co-operatives and other types of business enterprise in the 'non-state sector'. (*Argumenty i Fakty* No. 38, 1990 p. 8)[10]

The importance of this questioning of the entitlement to pensions by those who left the state sector should not be neglected. First of all, like other welfare entitlements, pensions form part of a 'universalistic' value system which allows the individual to feel integrated in the society. Secondly, in the above case, it was the conservatives who were insisting on excluding people from benefits because they were not in the public domain (and therefore 'not deserving' of public entitlements).

Restructuring: the Price

A tragic irony of the 'real existing socialism' found in the former Soviet Union was that while the levels of economic productivity were far lower than those found in Western Europe, their levels of social provision were commensurate. It would be surprising if CIS citizens would be willing to see these standards fall. Yet, price liberalization, currency stabilization and industrial restructuring are probably incompatible with the maintenance of existing levels of expenditure on welfare. The economic policies being demanded by the World Bank, the IMF and the members of G7 imply a reduction in this provision, a sharp decline in private consumption and an increase in unemployment.

Since the earliest days of 'perestroika' wide sections of the population have communicated genuine fears of the negative impact that 'market relations' will have on their lives. Surveys have consistently shown that the greatest anxieties surround inflation, followed by increased crime, social chaos, falls in real income and loss of social guarantees. These fears and anxieties are not misplaced. Possibly the greatest underestimated, and still largely unrealized cost of reform is unemployment. This subject is among the most difficult for the majority of the population and government to accept. The rescinding of the fundamental premise and promise of socialism, the right to work, has been traumatic for governments and people, leaving the former to prevaricate and the latter to contemplate and deal with the reality. The disintegration of the Union has left each of the fifteen republics and all the fledgling republics pirouetting on the topic.

Already the privatization of industry is creating unemployment. According to the Director of the Institute for Unemployment Problems in Moscow, 'the real level of unemployment will reach 10–12 million people [8 per cent of the working population]'. (*Argumenty i Fakty* No.

24, 1991) A year earlier the estimate was that 16 million people would be 'displaced' from their jobs by the year 2000. It was estimated that by the end of 1991 the Moscow Labour Exchange would be catering for 300 000 jobless. (Davydova 1991) By 1992, while still speaking of the threat of unemployment, a well-informed source estimated that the number of registered job-seekers would reach 6.3 million by the end of 1992, of whom only 3.8 million would *not* find work. (Shmelev 1992)[11] A survey conducted by the ILO, covering 500 plants in all manufacturing sectors in Moscow and St. Petersburg, yielded a figure of 10–11 million unemployed by the end of 1992. According to another source, unemployment was already affecting the most vulnerable and low paid, predominantly women (who comprise 40 per cent of the manufacturing labour force) and the handicapped. (Ustinov 1992 p. 11) The incidence of unemployment fluctuates by region as well as social characteristics. In the northern Caucasus generally, for instance, it is one-and-a-half times higher than the Russian average, and is four times higher in the Chechen-Ingush autonomous republic. (*Rossiya* No. 22, 1992 p. 6)

The advocates of marketization have almost certainly underestimated the level of unemployment that is likely to occur, for political motives. A bias is equally present in the forecast of one of the members of the Parliamentary opposition, *Russian Unity* (*Rossiiskoe edinstvo*). One of its members cites mathematical modelling by 'independent economists' as showing that privatization of 70 per cent of industry by the end of 1993 will lead to 25–30 million unemployed. (Pavlov 1992 p. 2) The $1 billion loan made available by the IMF on 7 July 1992 is in part a recognition that the Russian government has to continue subsidizing inefficient industrial enterprises.

Citizenship in the CIS: a Defensive Mechanism

Managing the restructuring of the economy is extremely difficult and the common experience of the process exceedingly painful. A crucial component in the compact between the Party and people, under the old regime, and between the government and the people in the emerging democratic polities, is observance of the entitlements of citizenship. This comprises one of the weakest links in the modernizing and democratizing chain. The plurality of demands, ranging from higher levels of personal consumption than those provided under the *ancien régime* to an insistence on maintaining the same level of welfare provision, cannot all be met. Most importantly, the latter cannot be universally sustained.

Ideally, the introduction of a more sophisticated system of subsidies, based on criteria of selectivity, could be defended on moral grounds.

The population might acquiesce to an appeal for a restructuring of the welfare system on the grounds of social justice. They would be less tolerant of a restructuring of benefits, long accepted as entitlements as part of the social compact, in the name of economic necessity or retrenchment. However, such is the level of poverty that only a relatively small proportion of the population would not be recipients of some degree of subsidy from the central state or local budget. During the recent strike by employees in the health service explicit reference was made to the inability of the mass of the population to pay for medical services. In fact, despite the firm stipulation by the IMF on the conditions under which the loan would be made available, on the last day of the summer recess, conservatives within the Russian Parliament succeeded in increasing the 1992 budget deficit by 150 billion roubles more than that promised to the IMF by the Russian Prime Minister.

The cuts in public expenditure required by the logic of conventional 'Bretton Woods' wisdom may only be made politically acceptable if some people are excluded from entitlements. If this were done, the same amount of money could be available to provide the same level of service, but for a smaller number of people. The fracturing and fractionalizing experienced by the former Soviet Union and which is being replicated in the Russian Federation and elsewhere, might permit this to happen.

For instance, Yakutia, in the far north-east, whilst declaring that it does not want to leave the Russian Federation, nonetheless wants a 'federal treaty' on the sale of the gold, diamonds and other precious metals and stones that are mined on the territory. In another case, the former autonomous republic of Bashkiria has renamed itself the republic of Bashkortostan and wishes to 'conclude an equal treaty on interstate relations between the Russian Federation and Bashkortostan'. Once again political sovereignty is associated with a degree of economic independence, with the Supreme Soviet complaining that 'despite an agreement with Russia to allow Bashkortostan to control 30 per cent of all oil and gas produced and processed on its territory there are still obstacles to its doing so'. (*Postfactum* 26 February 1992) However, as one quite penetrating recent newspaper article observed:

although much has been said about the national composition of different regions and the role of "local tyrants" within the Russian Federation, their capacity to be economically self-sufficient may be more important in determining their decisions on sovereignty. (*Rossiya* No. 22, 1992 p. 6)

The disintegration of the USSR and the abandonment of Soviet citizenship is an awesome prelude to the internal fragmentation of the individual member states and the creation of still more citizenships.

In these circumstances, sophists posing as pragmatists might well persuade electorates on the morality and efficacy of excluding as ineligible for entitlements individuals who are not citizens living within a republic. Since non-indigenes comprise over one-third of the population in ten of the fifteen Union republics, the social welfare aspect of the citizenship–ethnicity nexus could be significant. (Sheehy 1991 p. 58)[12] In 1991, over 70 million Soviet citizens lived outside their national territories or had none. (*Der Spiegel* No. 13, 1991 p. 174; Sheehy 1991 p. 85) Those republics where the ethnic population is in a minority (or nearly so) – Kazakhstan, Latvia, Kyrghizstan, Bashkortostan – are faced with particularly difficult choices. The increase in ethnic conflict and nationalistic sentiments more generally is leading to an exodus from 'war zones', especially in the Caucasus and Central Asia. Already in spring 1991 there were an estimated 800 000 refugees from inter-ethnic violence. (*Trud* No. 110, 1991 p. 2)

The individual sovereign states are treading this path very warily. In the main the principal of reciprocity applies; entitlements, such as retirement pensions, are transferable across state boundaries and citizens of one republic are able to claim medical assistance in another. Continuities in provision are to be expected, since there are mutual benefits to be gained. Apart from reciprocity, another factor militating against 'repatriation' of non-indigenes, especially Russians, is that the latter provide a skilled workforce for the local economy.

The out-migration of ethnic Russians is now occurring on a very large scale. The process has been accelerated by the discriminatory laws on citizenship passed in some former republics, especially the Baltic states. Those returning to Russia from the CIS are not so much migrants and refugees. By spring 1992, their number had reached 800 000, of which 230 000 were Russian-language migrants within the Russian Federation.[13] Thus, in scale they exceed the number of migrating ethnic Germans, Armenians and Jews. (*Rossiya* No. 22, 1992) While this could be a serious loss to certain republics, some writers regard it as a necessary loss in order to stimulate the nation to produce its own qualified workforce and increase the number of important posts occupied by the indigenous population. (*cf.* Tazhin and Tazhimbetov 1991)

In this latter case, Russians might face a fate similar to that of Asians forced to leave Central and East Africa during the 1960s. Like them, on leaving they lose their homes, property, jobs and 'lacking the means to exist, are deprived of rights and security'. (*Rossiya* No. 22, 1992) In Estonia those denied citizenship (for failing to meet the qualifications for citizenship) 'forgo the right to residency, accommodation, property and work'. (Perushkin 1992 p. 4) Equally, when they arrive in the country where they possess formal citizenship, they are met with hostility, as is illustrated by the experience of one Russian family which left Uzbekistan 'after well-known events' and emigrated to a Russian village:

> We were ordinary people who worked, earned money and tried to create a decent life by accumulating furniture and other things...When our container was unloaded, the local people flew into a rage, denouncing us as 'kulaks' who lived well off stolen property and adding that it was not for nothing that we had been thrown out. Since these 'well-wishing people' promised to burn our house down, we were forced to go back. (*Argumenty i Fakty* No. 24, 1992)

To date the predicaments of these migrants, rejected by the country in which they lived and unwanted in their 'mother country', have not been fully recognized by public, parliament or government. The latter have failed to devise an employment or resettlement policy for these immigrant specialists. One recommendation is that ways should be examined of financing the cost of immigration from the state budgets of the CIS in the form of deductions and payments proportionate to the number and level of qualification of the specialists who are emigrating. These payments would contribute towards compensating them for their lost homes, property, jobs and social welfare. (*Rossiya* No. 22, 1992)

Already, the Law on Property (*Ugolovnoe delo*, Nos 5–6, 1992) and the Land Code of the Ukraine do differentiate between the rights of citizens and non-citizens. The land cannot be transferred to foreign citizens and persons without citizenship. (*Pravda Ukrainy* 7 May 1992) Section 2 of the 1991 Kazakhstan Law on De-nationalization and Privatization states that 'participation in the auctioning of privatized property is open to citizens who qualify after having lived permanently in Kazakhstan for at least five years'. In October 1991 the Ukrainian Supreme Soviet accepted the notion of de-nationalization and privatization of enterprises, land and accommodation on the assumption that 'every citizen of the Ukraine has a right to state property'. (Burakovsky 1992) The exact meaning of this is unclear and will almost certainly remain unclear for some time. For instance, it cannot be 'beyond doubt' that a person who has lived for many years in the Ukraine but who held Russian nationality and has decided to retain his Russian connection by not becoming a Ukrainian citizen will be able to enjoy all the rights of Ukrainian citizenship. On the other hand, at present, the new, comprehensive, state-financed social security scheme covering retirement and disability pensions, unemployment and sickness benefit, training programmes, maternity leave and family allowances is, apparently, available to non-Ukrainian citizens (members of the FSU). Possibly, as nationals return to their 'homelands' so that the republics become more 'ethnically' homogeneous, bilateral, reciprocal agreements will be made between individual states.

Yet, there are already signs that the new Constitutions and rules governing citizenship will lead to discriminatory practices. In the case of Estonia, the referendum on the new post-Soviet Constitution indicated that the electorate was against extending voting rights to Russian-speakers (that is, those with Russian nationality) living in Estonia and who comprise almost 40 per cent of the population. Since achieving independence, the three Baltic states have drawn up citizenship laws which restrict admission to citizenship to native speakers and to direct descendants of people who lived in the republics before they were incorporated into the Soviet Union in 1940. The Law on the Restoration of Property Rights of Citizens of the Latvian Republic, enacted in October 1991, states that:

> Persons who were citizens of the Latvian Republic before 17 June 1940 and their successors shall be issued passports as citizens of the [new] Latvian Republic. All other residents can be regarded as Latvian citizens if they know the Latvian language [which is to be certified by a special examination], and have a record of having lived in Latvia for at least 16 years.

These decisions, whilst understandable in the context of nation-building, are nonetheless uncondonable in terms of political ethics and human rights. Discrimination in admitting people to citizenship could be a pacific stage in the 'ethnic cleansing' process. At present, the outcome of the Estonian referendum does not mean that people living in Estonia who are not citizens will be deprived of social welfare and other rights. Although this might happen in the future, it is not a necessary consequence; residential qualifications and employment may confer rights associated with citizenship.

Still the justification for this policy merits serious attention. According to an authoritative Estonian account, the creation of the 'new Soviet person' meant the dissolving of the 'different Soviet nations into a new Russian-speaking nation with a denationalized cultural identity and a new national awareness'. (Hint 1991 p. 111) The doyen of Soviet anthropology, Yuri Bromlei, considered that this might be achieved by: territorial mingling of nationalities; large-scale migrations and ethnic deconcentration; the formation of multi-national work teams; mixed ethnic marriages; bilingualism (of non-Russians); and the cultural integration of Soviet peoples on the basis of Marxist–Leninist ideology. (Bromlei 1983) From Hint's point of view, this doctrine

> meant the suppression of those aspects of the individual's identity which arise from one's ethnic and national belonging. De-nationalisation of the ethnic environment deprived the members of numerous national minorities of full self-realisation in social life as their vernacular cultural environment and economic activity in the vernacular were only of marginal importance. (Hint 1989)

Although the criticism raised by Balts could be invoked by Kazakhs, the government in Kazakhstan has acted differently. There a new Law on Citizenship was adopted in January 1992 which conferred Kazakhstan citizenship on everyone living on Kazakhstan territory on 20 March 1992. New Kazakh passports will be available from July 1992. At the same time, Kazakhs living outside the republic may hold dual citizenship and also benefit from an active policy to encourage their return to the country by offering them a variety of incentives, including higher incomes and privileged access to accommodation.

Conclusion

The exclusion of immigrants and those living in the state but of a different nationality from citizenship means that they are deprived of direct representation in the political process. Their interests do not have to be taken into account by legislators. Failure to grant citizenship to sections of the population provides the ground for actual and perceived injustice and for civil disobedience and forms scar tissue on the body of the *Rechtsstaat*.

De-nationalization and privatization of state enterprises may be necessary in order to modernize industry and raise productivity levels. A network of financial institutions has to be established and the communications' infrastructure radically improved. This, however, should not occur at the expense of the whole array of welfare entitlements which should continue to be provided at low, subsidized prices. Secondly, the social and political atmosphere must generate feelings of security amongst the population generally and among investors. The important value of security has to be recognized and balanced against the goal of efficiency. That the transition to a 'market economy' could be achieved quickly with a burst of short, sharp *laissez-faire* therapy and that the haemophiliac's needs could be met by an armful of blood were always blissful illusions. The historical conditions will not allow another exhortation to sacrifice.

If, as is thought, the size of the state sector in Hungary will ensure the perpetuation of a dual economy for a further 20 years (Kornai 1990), then there is a high probability that privatization will proceed much more slowly than predicted and promised by the Russian, Ukrainian and Kazakh governments. In May 1992 the Deputy Chairman of the Supreme Soviet of the Russian Federation declared that 'it would take at least ten years for the situation to be reached where fifty per cent of enterprises had been privatised'. (Shumeiko 1992) Even so, in the eyes of some, the Law on Privatization is an irrelevance for the mass of the population since only the very rich and foreigners can afford to buy it. (Fedorov 1992)

Despite the rhetoric on de-nationalization and privatization and ingenious coupon systems for disposing of state property, it is likely that a combination of pressures from ministries, local authorities, trade unions and other labour organizations will slow the movement towards the marketization of the economy and society. The description of the system and prescription offered by Fedorov is another instance of the polarized and rainbow views of Russia's past and its future trajectory:

> We have been living in an economic Buchenwald for 75 years and have accumulated nothing other than sickness and fatigue from the regime. Therefore property must be transferred to the people immediately and, if they agree to take it then we should thank them.

In July 1992 an organization called the *All-Union Communists Committee* (the 'Skvortsov Group') summoned the XXIX Congress of the CPSU. It claimed to represent thousands of rank and file communists who want to rebuild the Communist Party from below. According to

Academician Alexander Yakovlev it is not the Communists who present a real threat but the neo-fascists who are 'boosted by our traditional intolerance, as well as chauvinism, radical nationalism, economic dislocation, social instability and impoverishment of the society'. (Yakovlev 1992)

For this to be avoided, and to ameliorate feelings of anomie and alienation, the governments of the CIS might be advised to pay attention to the workplace and pursue a policy of empowering the many by a just distribution of the accumulated wealth. The coupon scheme and Yeltsin's decision to give each Russian citizen 10 000 roubles to purchase state property are 'individualist' alternatives to co-operatives and collectives as ways of de-nationalization. Despite the antipathy that seems to be felt by broad sections of the population to the very notion of planning, the State should continue to intervene to meet the basic needs of the population. Ironically, this suggests greater concentration than hitherto existed, since economic reform demands that enterprises begin to concentrate on their primary objectives and cease to act like miniature welfare states and serf owners.

Certainly greater attention should be devoted to the development of the social infrastructure so that people feel that they are all, *qua* citizens, benefiting from the changes which they are being urged to accept. It is not at all surprising that a session of the Council of Europe in Strasburg in July 1992 discussed the problem of protecting the social rights of the 'citizen of Europe'. It is a grand idea and the citizens of the former Soviet Union should bear in mind the direction in which the West is moving and learn a salutary lesson from the situation that is being created in the CIS, illustrated in the following tale:

> I was a citizen of the former Soviet Union and now live in Estonia, where I cannot receive citizenship. Only those who lived here before 1940 and their descendants are eligible. The remaining inhabitants must take their citizenship from the place where they have their roots. The USSR has disintegrated into sovereign states and I do not know in which of them to search for my roots. My ancestors emigrated in the seventeenth century from Germany and Holland to the Ukraine, where I was born. In 1941 we were sent, as Germans, to Siberia and then to North Kazakhstan. I only returned to the Ukraine in 1978. The district in which we lived was within the Chernobyl radiation fallout zone, so I went to live with my sons who live in Estonia. I speak Russian, Ukrainian, German and Dutch and understand Kazakh and Polish. I would with pleasure learn Estonian, but my memory is no longer up to it. So where am I to live – in the Ukraine, in Russia or Kazakhstan? Perhaps I could return to Germany or Holland? (Burtseva 1992)

Notes

1. According to one author, a separate Ukrainian currency is being introduced because: it will strengthen a sense of independent national identity and statehood; 'economic integration among the former Soviet republics is not strong enough to ensure the further usage of a single currency'; 'of difficulties in cooperating with the Russian Federation in the sphere of monetary and financial policy'.

2. In July 1992 a landmark ruling by the European Court of Justice allows European Community citizens who are working in the UK and on low incomes and with families living abroad, to encourage their partner to apply for British social security benefits. The implications of this ruling for granting citizenship to East Europeans are considerable. See: 'Court allows cross border benefit claims', *The Independent*, 22 July 1992, p. 1

3. Despite declarations on 'rolling back the state' and an avowed policy to reduce Government expenditure, in June 1992 the British Government consumed 48.5 per cent of GDP.

4. Although at the time of writing, new Constitutions are in the course of preparation or adoption, it is still advisable to use the present tense in referring to the Constitution of the former Soviet Union. On 29 June 1992 Estonia became the first former Soviet republic to vote in a referendum to adopt a new Constitution since the disintegration of the Soviet Union in October 1991. It is instructive to remember that the 1918 Weimar Constitution also contained a clause on the 'right to work', stipulating that 'every German was to be given his chance to earn his livelihood through work in the national economy'.

5. In the 1990s this prescription provides a foundation stone of the Delors 'Social Charter'.

6. Besides having a passport each person has a document showing where s/he works, a military credential indicating that military service has been performed, an 'order' from the local soviet or a 'house book' (depending on whether the accommodation was in the public or private sector) indicating place of residence.

7. Someone moving to Kiev to work, for instance, would be given a temporary permit for one year, which would be renewable annually. After five years he could apply for a permanent permit. In Dnepropetrovsk a newcomer would have to be a resident for two years before becoming eligible for a permanent permit. The system did not work perfectly; people did manage to 'seep' into the urban environment, largely because of the perpetual demand for unskilled labour. As far as these 'illegal immigrants' were concerned, however, they forfeited a number of their citizen's rights.

8. Bulgarians and Vietnamese in Russia, and Chinese and Koreans in Kazakhstan, for instance.

9. The author of these views is widely considered to be a possible future Prime Minister of Russia, but who could only do so if Parliament conceded the basic right of the individual to own land (*kusok zemli*). He somewhat naively proposed that, if the first collective failed to make the enterprise operate profitably it should pass to some other collective. In this way 'property passes from hand to hand until it comes to rest in the hands of the most intelligent owners'.

10. This was 'The All-Union Confederation of Workers in Co-operatives and other forms of Free Enterprise'. See: *Argumenty i Fakty* No. 38, 1990 p. 8.

11. See: *Moscow News*, No. 27, 5–12 July 1992, pp. 10–11. It should be noted that the figures cited by Shmelev only refer to the Russian Federation.
12. According to the 1989 Census:

Table 6.1
National Composition of the Population of the USSR

Union Republic Nationalities	Absolute numbers in USSR	Per cent of Population	
		of USSR	of own territory
(Total population)	285.76		
Russians	145.16	50.80	81.5
Ukrainians	44.19	15.46	72.7
Uzbeks	16.70	5.84	71.4
Belorussians	10.04	3.51	77.9
Kazakhs	8.14	2.85	39.7
Azerbaidzhanis	6.77	2.37	82.7
Armenians	4.62	1.62	93.3
Tajiks	4.22	1.48	62.3
Georgians	3.98	1.39	70.1
Moldavians	3.35	1.17	64.5
Lithuanians	3.07	1.07	79.6
Turkmen	2.73	0.95	72.0
Kirgiz	2.53	0.88	52.4
Latvians	1.46	0.51	52.0
Estonians	1.03	0.36	61.5
Autonomous Republic nationalities			
Bashkirs	1.45	0.51	21.9
Udmurts	0.75	0.26	30.9

Source: Sheehy 1991, p. 58

13. The figure of 800 000 refugees cited above refers to Russian and non-Russian-speaking migrants (refugees).

7. Citizenship and the Right to Work in Bulgaria

Dimitrina Dimitrova and Stefan Dimitrov

The Fate of Civil Society in Bulgaria

The necessity to look for its own road to salvation from the deep economic and political crisis which has overwhelmed Bulgarian society today demands an analysis of the reasons for the fiasco of the historical experiment, called 'socialism'. This analysis refers to the fate of civil society in Bulgaria. Its goal is to elucidate the way in which the new political power, which came into being with the revolution of 1944 in the name of freedom and prosperity of the people, finally brought those same people to a state of deprivation.

Our thesis is that under 'real socialism' the expansion of social rights – including the right to work – was achieved at the expense of the civil and political rights of the individual. The fate of civil society was in practice determined by the revolutionary way of enlarging the entitlements. In the countries of Western Europe social rights appeared at a comparatively late stage and were the result of a step-by-step enlargement of entitlements. (Marshall 1950) By contrast Bulgarian social rights were offered with the revolutionary act itself. This is not a unique, Bulgarian phenomenon but it deserves consideration in view of the concrete historical process through which it became reality.

A Short History of Civil Society in Bulgaria

The revolution of 1944 was based on a wide, anti-fascist movement within the country and the decisive help of the Soviet Army. It found a comparatively underdeveloped capitalist society in Bulgaria. Capitalism had been slow in its development due to five centuries of Turkish yoke of the country which lasted from 1396 until 1878. After 70 years of capitalist development the country was only beginning the process of industrialization. In 1946 there were 506 183 wage-earners employed in industry and agriculture, only 115 000 of which were industrial workers. (Genchev 1987 pp. 105–107) In their social and economic struggle they lagged far behind their West European counterparts. The economic profile of the country was agrarian, based on small family ownership and traditional, primitive means of processing the land. Of a total population of seven million, 75 per cent was agrarian. (*Demographic and Socio-Economic Characteristics of the Population* 1988 p. 8) The vast majority of the population lived in poverty. With such a background of poverty, socialism became an attractive alternative for large parts of the population. It offered to the traditional proletariat and the agricultural workers a guaranteed right to work, free education and health care, which had not been provided before.

Social rights were given to the masses rather than fought for and this was connected with their deprivation of political rights. A one-party system was enforced in the country after the elimination of the rest of the political parties and movements in 1948. This party, the Bulgarian Communist Party, claimed to represent the interests of all social groups in the society. This was a precondition for the destruction of all civil rights. All possibilities for a political choice were destroyed – and thus all mechanisms for effective parliamentary control were destroyed. The Bolshevik principle, the so-called principle of democratic centralism on the basis of which the Bulgarian Communist Party existed, did not allow internal mechanisms for controlling the party elite. The fusion between party and state and the formation of the *nomenklatura* brought about the domination of the state over civil society. The mechanism for this was founded in economic planning of the collective type.

Central planning implies legislation different from that of the market economy. In the latter, 'the government is restricted to enforcing rules as to how to employ the existing resources leaving it to the individual to decide on the final aims'. (Hayek 1990 p. 124) Rules are formulated beforehand in the form of formal prescriptions and are not related to the interests and aims of concrete individuals. Their importance is that they should be instruments for achieving individual aims. (Hayek 1990 p. 124)

In a planned economy, the government is burdened with managing all economic processes, including the means of production and their concrete application. The enormous complexity of planning everything for everyone in constantly changing conditions does not permit common and lasting formal rules. In this situation, governing is not based on the demands of formal legislation but rather on decrees and other temporal acts which are specified in connection with every separate case. This leads ultimately to the *de facto* subordination of legislative to executive power. The planning subject is the one to decide which social groups' interests are a priority at a certain moment. These decisions depend not only on the aims of the act of planning, as emphasizing for example industrial workers' interests at the expense of agricultural workers and the intelligentsia, but also on corporate party interests. This type of legislation inherently contains the tendency to biased legislature.

All this resulted in a system of privileges in Bulgarian society which harmed civil rights, in particular the principle of formal equality of all before the law. Moreover, as the opportunity to exercise a right depends not only on entitlements but also on provisions (Dahrendorf 1988a), the incapability of centrally-planned economies to provide for sustainable growth affected social rights. Through the system of privileges, the party elite assured itself a legal access to the decreasing provisions. Individuals did not fight for their rights because they did not dispose of institutional channels to exercise their political rights. Finally they turned to the tactics of adaptation and passive resistance. Indeed, the Bulgarian case shows that the condition for exercising social rights lies in enjoying civil and political rights. If the latter are absent and if the state is the only guarantor for social rights, citizens become loyal subjects. As a reaction to this kind of state dependency, however, many individuals responded by disregarding their duties. This was most obvious in the sphere of labour.

Barriers to Labour Mobility

If people were deprived of political rights by the lack of political choice, so labour rights were restricted by the limited number of job opportunities. The right to work was paralleled by an obligation to work. However, the obligation came to dominate the right due to a number of factors: first of all because of the limited number of job opportunities; second, the absence of the right to private ownership prevented citizens from starting a firm by themselves -- the state was the sole owner of material wealth; third, the mechanism of central planning and the absence of a free labour market contributed to the dominance of the obligation to work over the right to work.

The result of having a macro-economic centre in conditions of a total lack of market mechanisms was a dictate placing every separate enterprise in the position of simply implementing ideas and decisions sent from above. This 'macro-centre' decided what was to be produced and by whom; who was to bring in supplies and at what price the products should be sold. The idea was to constantly produce more and this was to be achieved by material incentives in case the plans were fullfilled. As a system, however, this made the directors of plants and other institutions hide the actual results and their real economic capabilities. They kept a workforce which was larger than necessary not because, or not only because, they expected larger government orders for the next year, but because interrupted supplies of raw materials and spare parts created periods of production halts. Efforts were made to speed up the technological progress in industry, but they failed. The main barrier against technological progress was the lack of financial independence of industrial enterprises, which were forced to hand over the greater part of their profits to the central state. This was deemed indispensable for the functioning of the system of centralized planning, because it gave the government the opportunity to redistribute profits among branches in the economy which were making losses. Had the latter been permitted to go bankrupt, the immediate consequence would have been unemployment. Consequently, profitable enterprises were not able to renew their investments in machinery. The machinery grew old and outdated, and was in constant need of maintenance, which on its part demanded more work-hands. Moreover, the transmission of economic decisions from above to the level of plants demanded additional 'intermediate' administrative staff, which grew to impressive dimensions.

Under these circumstances the right to work was guaranteed by creating full employment – something contradicting the very basis of economic efficiency. The price for the guaranteed right to work was the lack of choice for the individual. In exchange for free public education everybody was obliged to take a job in an enterprise selected by the government. All college graduates were centrally allocated according to government regulation.

The right of the individual to change his place of work was fixed in labour legislation. (*Labour Code* of 1951 and *Labour Code* of 1986) However, many decrees contradicted the law and in practice this right of the individual depended on the interests of the enterprise which employed him or her. Moving from one enterprise to another (turnover) was considered anomalous and dangerous to the planned economy. Labour legislation had a fixed law considering cases of a worker changing his place of work without the permission of his employer. Sanctions, including deprivation of annual leave and bonus, were supposed to prevent turnover. The culmination in the attempt to restrict horizontal labour mobility came in 1987 when a decree was issued, defining penalties against enterprises hiring workers not officially dismissed by their former employer. According to the same decree, such an enterprise had to pay a fine of eight salaries to the former employer. This was a way to grant absolute priority to the interests of the enterprise over those of the individual.

Job changes involving change of place of residence were an even graver situation. The individual was confronted with the so-called 'residency problem'. This phenomenon is unknown to countries with market economies. A vast number of restrictive legislative acts were passed in this connection, in spite of the constitutional right to choose one's own place of residence. They were intended to curtail the immigration to big cities resulting from the rapid industrialization of the country. Their consequence was that a person had the right to work and the right to a home in any town only after acquiring the official right of 'resident', a special status of a permanent resident of a particular town. At the same time – and depending on the need for labour – the state turned this barrier into a privilege and offered it when and where extra workforce was needed. These administrative restrictions over labour mobility often led to breaking the law, corruption and nepotism. In short, they undermined the legal order.

Another typical aspect of barriers to labour mobility had to do with the subordination of workers' competence to party loyalty. To explain this relationship we must first turn our attention to the insufficiencies of the pay system.

The absence of real market mechanisms and the absolute monopoly of the government over property (about 92 per cent of the GNP was produced in the state sector) impeded the implementation of the principle of 'equal pay for equal work'. (*Statistical Yearbook of the Peoples Republic of Bulgaria* 1988) In setting the price of labour – just like all other commodities – the state followed bureaucratic principles.

The system of payment, which set fixed wages for certain types of labour according only to the level of qualification, could not differentiate between labour input of different individuals. With no market mechanisms and, hence, no criteria, the result was equal pay for all irrespective of contribution. Those who worked better were robbed of their wages. This deficiency of the system was tackled by administrative measures without any results. For example, in 1979 a new system of payment called 'Unified Staff Table' was introduced. Its purpose was to introduce a 'system of points', reflecting to a greater degree the individual contribution – the so-called 'co-efficient of labour participation'. This co-efficient was supposed to measure more precisely the individual labour contribution through indicators such as labour, technological discipline and quality of the product. Subjectivities in assessment of the individual labour contribution as well as egalitarian attitudes of the workers undermined this attempt to eliminate wage levelling.

Another way in which the principle of 'equal pay for equal work' was violated was the practice of distinguishing priority branches and enterprises in the economy – depending on the view of the government as to which were most important at a given moment. In this case workers in a priority enterprise were given higher salaries, often much higher, than workers with the same qualifications and in the same occupation, but employed in branches or enterprises which were not considered a priority.

The individual promotion opportunities in an occupation on the grounds of occupational skills and good performance, which were formally guaranteed by the labour legislation, depended in fact to a great extent on party membership and loyalty. Communist party membership was a prerequisite for promotions. The impossibility of climbing the occupational ladder by being a competent worker forced people to accommodate themselves by becoming party members.

On the one hand, this undermined the very motive for acquiring professional competence and organizational skills which resulted in low job satisfaction. On the other hand, it also led to a situation where those who became managers were utterly incompetent, with all its negative consequences, most notably in the sphere of industry.

In these conditions, the increase of nepotism was dramatic. Climbing the ladder of hierarchy and working in prestigious jobs depended very often on personal and family relations. This was possible because of the lack of correspondence between the quality of the product and its realization on the market. The market was guaranteed. As a result enterprise managers had nothing to lose. They surrounded themselves with loyal people. The gratitude to the employer–benefactor was expressed in 'favours' to him or her.

Barriers to labour mobility were one aspect of deprivation at work. Another aspect was the exclusion of workers from decision-making, which we will deal with in the next paragraph.

Ownership and Participation

Under socialism the right of the individual to participate in decision-making stemmed from the ruling ideology's thesis of the basic role of the property relationships in the whole system of the social relations. The political dictate of the Bulgarian Communist Party and its partocracy in particular, led between 1944 and 1946 to the elimination of the rights to private ownership of all means of production.

The party-state became the sole owner of all means of production. Until 1989 the state owned 97 per cent of the means of production. Being absolute owner the state had all possible rights in and over things. This allowed the party-state to impose models of labour relations and participation in accordance with its own interests at any given moment. The managers of the enterprises which were representatives of the owner-state were given the right to organize and control the process of production. The lowest level, the workers, were excluded from the process of decision-making. To put it briefly, deprivation of a basic citizen right – the property right – led to the exclusion of the workers of decision-making. The owner-state usurped the right to decide on behalf of the individual. The latter was allowed to accept decisions sent from above. He was 'entitled' to implement them. Subordination and obedience were indispensable prerequisites for the functioning of central planning in which fulfilling the plan was a top priority.

There used to be a right of the individual to participate in trade unions in Bulgaria. However, the existence of a single trade union which, in addition, was controlled by the party-state made this union unsuited for defending the rights of the workers. The trade union itself was part of the system of management. Under centralized planning the union's role was reduced to two functions: productive and social. The former involved emulation and dissemination of the experience of 'front rankers' (workers showing the best performance of their work tasks) and collecting workers' proposals aiming mainly at improvements of work performance. In practice, this function was an extension of management aimed at increasing labour productivity. The social function of trade unions did not involve more than a concern with holidays, housing and, to some extent, physical conditions of work.

Full employment formally being effected, the state did not offer unemployment benefits in case of temporary unemployment. Unemployment mainly took the form of hidden unemployment. The individual did not have the right to strike or any other form of collective protest. Trade unions did not take part in setting the length of the working day and the wages.

Being alienated from the property, the individuals gradually turned into 'industrial serfs'. They were forced to sell their labour power at a price fixed by the supreme owner - the state. (Dimitrov 1991 p. 63) The guaranteed right to work turned into a duty. As a consequence, this undermined work motivation and finally affected the obligation to work itself. The fact that work was not an entry ticket for acquiring provisions such as free education, health care, etcetera, further undermined the obligation to work. Passive resistance, bad performance, absenteeism, sabotage and theft of state property became common. These phenomena could continue to exist for a long time because of the ineffective control over labour processes.

Late Attempts at Reform and their Inherent Failure

Against this background, at the beginning of the eighties the government attempted to overcome low productivity by rationalizing and reforming the organization of work. This attempt was supposed to give the individual enterprise some measure of autonomy in organizing its fulfilment of the plan. Allocation of work tasks and the ways in which these were executed, were new at the discretion of the brigades. For the first time, the right of the individual to participate in decision-making was considered a means to achieve higher productivity.

These ideas laid the foundation of the *Labour Code* of 1986. The most important idea in the *Labour Code* was the priority given to the role of the brigade, the so-called primary collective. Many of the decisions concerning the personnel policy of the enterprise were to be taken at the level of the brigades and their collective bodies – the general assembly of the brigade and the council of the brigade. At shop-floor level, the workers received the right to elect the brigade leader and to admit new members. At company level – the level of the main collective, which consists of all primary collectives in the enterprise – the workers received the right to make proposals for improving the organization of work, and the right to acquire and employ information. (*Labour Code* 1986, arts. 20, 125, 126) The initiative to introduce workers' participation once more came from above. It was again 'offered' rather than fought for in the name of prolonging the life of the system.

According to the Code, the state was to continue taking the role of a single owner and the main collective of the enterprise was to become *stopanin*. The latter was supposed to possess and use the property (here we mean the classical legal roman distinction between the rights to own, to possess and to use the property). The individual could exercise his or her right to use the property only as a member of the main collective.

This legal paradox was another ideologem of the party-elite. Its aim was to hand over the responsibility from the top to the bottom in the conditions of a deterioration of the economic situation rather than offering rights of full ownership. Practically it failed, because enterprises did not have any independence from the state. Realizing this fact, in 1989 the authorities allowed individual enterprises to become companies with financial independence and self-management. The state was given the role of a regulator. For the first time individuals had the right to organize their own firms as long as they employed their own labour power. No hiring of labour was allowed. This was the first attempt to change the subject of ownership and to make the individual less dependent on state institutions.

The attempt to replace the system of centralized planning with state regulation of the economy was not successful, because the functioning and self-management of firms depended on the mechanisms of political power. Political power not only offered the right to self-management, defining its parameters, but it also defined the conditions under which self-management was to be realized. The Party continued to be a 'level' in the management of the industry. For this reason the formally granted rights, with the exception of the election of leaders of the brigade, collective bodies and directors of the enterprise, could not become reality. In both 1986 and 1989 the attempts to change property relations and introduce industrial democracy did not succeed. They were pseudo-changes.

Under socialism a real expansion of the right to work would have undermined the very basis of state ownership, that means would have threatened the power of the partocracy. The outcome was paradoxical. The guaranteed right to work, being considered as one of the major achievements of socialism, contributed to the undermining of the system. Our recent history has shown that no social rights, a right to work included, are possible without civil and political rights.

8. Unification, Solidarity and Equality. Dilemmas of Trade Union Strategies in Germany

Jens Bastian

Introduction

In terms of establishing civil and political citizenship, the German unification process[1] was finalized in October 1990 when the German Democratic Republic (GDR) dissolved itself as an independent political entity, and the five new states[2] became members of the Federal Republic of Germany. Whilst the East German population is now learning to adapt to a new currency and has made its first infantile attempts to walk the thin ice of democratic participation, it simultaneously witnesses the institutional recasting of society with a mixture of amazement and relief. By the same token, however, preoccupation among the 'Ossies' – as they are being labelled by the 'Wessies' – is growing regarding the third element of citizenship: the social dimension, or the social rights of citizenship.

As Marshall (1973 p. 72) remarked, the social element incorporates 'the whole range from the right to a modicum of economic welfare and security to the right to share to the full in the social heritage and to live the life of a civilized being according to the standards prevailing in the society'. With regard to German unification, Marshall's definition of social citizenship impels us to elaborate the means and constraints of establishing equal and just living standards between two populations, among whom the members of the joining side – the respective five new states – have very little experience with a free market economy, and even less with social inequality in the context of political and democratic citizenship.

The following text tries to shed some light upon some rather dark fields of the social dimension of German unification, though, admittedly, the problem posed (still) involves a high degree of speculation. German unification did not only come unexpectedly for virtually all in society and the political system, but also took legal experts, economists and political sociologists completely by surprise. Given this, I shall be obliged to confine my endeavour to a few tentative observations. These are made in an attempt to elaborate on the specific difficulties currently surfacing on what the quality of citizenship in the unified society should be in more precise terms, and how this objective can be brought about by those involved in the immense challenge.

Whereas there is a general understanding prevailing between East and West Germany that the former's population should no longer be deprived of political rights, economic well-being and existing welfare benefits, there is widespread debate in both parts of the country regarding the time schedule and the means necessary to arrive at the realization of these targets. As Marshall (*ibid.*) noted, civil rights lay down the foundations to strive for certain goals, but by definition they do not guarantee their achievement. It is this dualism that the paper draws attention to when exploring the prospects and constraints of solidarity amidst rising unemployment and contextual uncertainty over numerous social, political and institutional problems in the former GDR.

Establishing Industrial Relations in East Germany

Contrary to the political revolutions and institutional transformations experienced by Poland, Hungary and Czechoslovakia in 1989/90, the sweeping changes in East Germany were in fact initiated by its own population. However, after the Honecker regime had been overthrown, the central actors and organizations in charge of unification came from outside. On that count, domestic change kicked-off by civil rights movements in East-Berlin, Dresden and Leipzig soon came under the influence and later dominance of political actors who had not been responsible for the initial ruptures, and who resided in Bonn, Frankfurt and Munich.

As a result, when one looks at the former GDR two years after the Berlin Wall crumbled, the search for East German organizations which were created during the sea of changes and managed to maintain autonomous structures yields an unambiguous finding: with the exception of civil rights associations, all other organizations either merged with their West German counterparts, or dissolved themselves after the respective organization of the West had assumed sole responsibility. While the former pattern chiefly applies to the political parties, with the exception of the Party of Democratic Socialism (the successor of the Communist Party), the latter predominantly concerns organizations in the emerging industrial relations system of East Germany. In short, the formation of associations, interest organizations and political parties in East Germany sooner or later only led to their incorporation into the existing West German counterparts.

For reasons of space, I shall limit the following comments to the trade unions. The establishment of the West German trade unions in the former GDR is described in order to provide the reader with an understanding of industrial citizenship under the conditions of system transformation.

As appealing as the slogan 'Unified unions in a unified country' initially sounded, the short history of independent labour organizations in the former GDR suggests that their capacity for self-transformation and the enhancement of organizational reforms were both deemed unattainable by their West German counterparts. This perception was best mirrored by the labour confederation in the West. The West German Trade Union Congress (DGB) renounced its formal co-operation with the East German Confederation (FDGB) on the grounds of the latter's undemocratic character and its reputation as a mouthpiece of the political goals of the communist regime.

The pattern emerging from this approach speaks for itself. West German unions did not opt for a direct merger with their respective sister organizations in the East. The members rather than the organizations themselves were the target of the West German unions. Hence, West German unions extended their services, and thereby gradually introduced the West German union system to the dissolving GDR. In other words, a formal and political 'take-over' through *Anschluß* became the order of the day. In the wording of West German trade unionists, the strategy was labelled *FÜ-Phase* (enemy take-over). This procedure implied that those seeking admission into the respective unions did not have any say in their regulatory framework and organizational provisions.

West Germany's largest union, the engineering federation (IG-Metall), illustrated this approach most tellingly. In the autumn of 1990, the statutes of IG-Metall were changed so that the West German union could expand its field of operation and responsibilities to the former GDR. Consequently, IG-Metall in the East had to dissolve itself and recommended its 1.8 million members (a union density of almost 100 per cent) to join ranks with the Western organization henceforth in charge. With 2.7 million members in West Germany, engineering union membership is now likely to exceed 3.5 million!

Single Union Status amid Socio-economic Cleavages

So far, my aim has been to outline the establishment of union structures in the former GDR. My primary focus was the *modus operandi* of imposing the West German union model on to the five new states. My special interest in this section will be possible repercussions deriving from the introduction of the Western industrial relations system into East Germany.

Ever since West German labour federations managed to establish single status in the eastern states, the predominant question on their agenda has been which services unions can offer to their new members. Because this aspect of union policy overshadowed all other considerations of industrial citizenship, West German unions have presented themselves in the former GDR as insurance organizations providing services for members who are trying to make their way amidst widespread uncertainty.

In that respect, the daily needs and fears of East German citizens are essentially centred around crumbling enterprises, rising unemployment, mounting prices for daily life requirements and increasing uncertainty with regard to services such as housing, education, public transport and insurance premiums. Given the mosaic of problems and challenges they face, employees in East Germany have every reason to seek responses to classical issues of union interest representation: fear of unemployment, wage levels and better living standards.

The economic and employment structure of the five new states largely corresponds to the West German standards prevailing around 1965: overproportional employment representation in both agriculture and manufacturing, while the service sectors are rather underrepresented. (*Die Zeit* 16 March 1990) If the structural transformations in East Germany follow the post-war West German pattern, and nobody seriously doubts such a trajectory, then large numbers of redundancies will be forthcoming: in agriculture and manufacturing over 500 000, in the energy sector predictions are for more than 100 000 lost jobs. By and large, estimators expect the economic changes to affect over 1.7 million jobs labelled as dispensable. With regard to such dramatic lay-off prospects, it is not unrealistic to contend that unemployment rates may reach over 35 per cent in the former GDR.

The tensions emerging from income disparities between two workforces suddenly having to confront each other and the expectations about overcoming such imbalances as fast as possible are considerable in the new states. Accordingly, the conflict potential residing in this juxtaposition has to be addressed by unions which now have to establish their profile as credible representatives and organizers of the interests and insecurities of the workforce in the former GDR. West German unions are assuming responsibility for this challenge, and are presenting tacit blueprints in East Germany which are at odds with the development of the industrial relations agenda in West Germany during the 1980s.

Formerly, the classical demands mentioned above were increasingly linked to qualitative considerations such as environmental objectives, gender dimensions of the labour market and new approaches in working time policies. The intra-union modernization debate which was spearheaded by the engineering and public service unions interferes with the present requirements to establish civil, political and social citizenship in the eastern part of Germany.

The organization of the social interests of the population in the former GDR has now became the order of the day. The possibility that this organizational drive may encounter considerable roadblocks stemming from divergent aspirations and experiences in the East and West German labour force is reflected in the following example. In 1991 the West German engineering union staged a national conference on alternative traffic policies. The congress was to elaborate environmental concepts outside private transport options. It quickly emerged that East German trade unionists, many of whom had only recently been able to realize their long-standing ambition to acquire a car from the West, voiced considerable reservations as regards the ecological implications of such a congress.

What took West German trade unionists many years to gradually popularize within their ranks – namely to introduce innovative strategies that incorporated changing value orientations within the labour force and reflected a new approach towards life quality, social rights and gender aspects – currently meets with serious constraints in the five new states. In the light of the fact that the eastern part of the country faces the reality of an underdeveloped region with high unemployment and limited resources for short-term change, the anxieties this produces inside the East German workforce calls for a union organization which many in the West consider outdated and one-dimensional.

This argument impels us to recall the profile of the successful trade unionist during the 'economic miracle' of West German reconstruction in the fifties and sixties. Such an interest representative of the rank and file focused his policy priorities on the increase of material well–being of the male blue-collar worker in manufacturing; he scarcely questioned the preconditions and consequences of production arrangements nor the products deriving from these, and expressed considerable reservations towards demands that introduced qualitative bargaining issues. The emerging diversity of union priorities between the West and the East is reflected in the following statement by Steinkühler, president of the union of metalworkers:

> With our 'Congresses about the Future' we have made a big step forward in the old Federal Republic, for instance regarding the discussion about environmental safety. This problem has not yet reached the state of political awareness in the former GDR... Hence, it is quite well possible that in ideological terms we are facing a splitting situation, and therefore have to proceed with a smaller step forward because we cannot leave the colleagues from the GDR behind. (Steinkühler 1991 p. 31, my translation)

Collective Bargaining in East Germany: the Trade-off between Equality and Efficiency

Industrial citizenship advanced by collective bargaining organizations currently follows very different trajectories in the eastern and western parts of Germany. Given the former's immense transition problems and the latter's mixture of an economy faring well amidst high unemployment and rising budget deficits, collective bargaining strategies are confronted with the challenge of bridging two elements which pose huge constraints of realization. Okun (1975) characterizes such a challenge as the trade-off between equality and efficiency.

Taking the East German situation into consideration, the two parameters imply finding the starting line for a fair race towards living standards and working conditions as they exist in West Germany. Precisely because of the double nature of the reform process, transition in East Germany is fraught with difficulties, and after its initial support is now facing increasing scepticism and even open rejection by a growing part of the population.

The debate over which trajectory the social unification process should take, mirrors the essential challenge and core dilemma of politics, not only in East Germany but also in Eastern and Central European countries: do equality and efficiency conflict irreconcilably under the conditions of a system's transformation? Here I am referring to the normative implications, actor constellations and procedural arrangements that are capable of channelling these two essential components of a transition process into an acceptable compromise.

My position is that the two parameters may currently and for some time in the future be incompatible, although all the actors involved are practically obliged to act as if the opposite were the case. In short, in order to establish the foundations for long-term investment, short-term distributional interests may have to be put on ice, thereby cementing social cleavages in the unification process.

Ever since its foundation, West Germany was a uniform country concerning the standardization of collective bargaining provisions. To a considerable extent, this uniformity guaranteed what has been labelled 'social peace' in the West German context. After unification however, two different pay standards have been evolving, causing growing discontent in both parts of the country. First and foremost, this dissatisfaction expresses itself by the constant movement of East Germans embarking on a westward trek in search of jobs, higher wages and a brighter future. The character of the exodus signals a domestic migration of predominantly young male workers, and recalls similar population movements in underdeveloped regions of Europe, like the Italian south or eastern Turkey.

What is needed, but apparently in short supply, is political patience, flexible adjustment to and tolerance for unequal trajectories. The central question in this context is how can the relevant actors in German politics contribute to the advancement of such an approach? Through repeated public claims, future promises, the rational implementation of political and economic instruments, the generation of institutional reforms? All this is necessary and currently also taking place, but on a scale that may prove inadequate in a situation which can be likened to a train running full steam ahead into a budget deficit disaster, sustained labour market problems and growing frustration over the price tags attached to German unification.

Under considerations such as these, collective bargaining is engaged in a tightrope walk. Employees in the five new states are seeking a perspective and a time schedule as to how long it will take until basic wage rates and income differentials have been harmonized in both parts of Germany. By contrast, employers and managers desire an investment perspective based on clear property rights and sustainable wage increase margins. Accordingly, they call for differences in income levels and working conditions (for example working hours provisions) to persist over a number of years. Employers repeatedly underline that during the transition phase industrial relations actors should refrain from generalizing and from overly ambitious collective bargaining agreements in the eastern part of Germany. Instead, they favour extended flexibility provisions which pay tribute to the respective situation of the sector and the individual enterprise being privatized.

The various collective bargaining agreements established in East Germany during 1990/1991 provide for income increases and reductions of working hours which aim at gradually harmonizing differentials with the West. But the time period foreseen for this objective extends to 1994 for wages in the engineering industry, and to 1998 (!) for standards of working hours.

In that respect, collective bargaining agreements may suggest a normality in pay standards and provisions concerning working conditions amidst a very abnormal situation at the macro-level. Collective bargaining in East Germany is currently taking place in a context where the old has not fully disappeared and the new continues to encounter numerous roadblocks.[3] A prime example of such a dilemma concerns the question of who was, and often continues to be, in charge. While the politico-economic changes have affected the workforce most seriously, the institutional power distribution in many firms remains largely unaltered. In other words, besides the structural difficulties of establishing a functioning collective bargaining system there is the problem that, in firm-level negotiations, democratically legitimized union representatives often meet employers who were in charge of firms under the Honecker regime.

Furthermore, since many companies still lack reliable calculations for investment decisions and the composition of their workforce, the collective bargaining agreements can only further a limited degree of economic and social predictability. Above all, what these settlements cannot furnish are perspectives regarding the scope and depth of structural transformations in each firm. In short, setting the terms for wage bargaining in the former GDR resembles Don Quixote's struggle against windmills. Unions, employers' associations, shop stewards and managers cannot assess precisely the consequences of their agreements.

What is clear and may reach catastrophic dimensions in the foreseeable future is the worrisome fact that with the present wage levels numerous companies will not be able to meet competition standards. Additionally, the prospects are that they will lose out even more if and when wages are substantially increased in order to approximate the West German standards. More broadly speaking, current wage bargaining in

East Germany is a political and social blind flight. While unions face the choice between higher wages and prospects of rising unemployment, employers are confronted with the alternative of reducing income differentials between East and West Germany or seeing large numbers of East Germans continuing to move westwards.

Finally, collective bargaining in Germany is currently confronted with the parameter of inter-class solidarity. Namely, trade unionists in the West are urged by employers and political decision-makers to engage in a commitment for East German reconstruction. In practical terms, such a demand calls on the responsibility of individual labour market organizations, and seeks voluntary wage restraint in the West in favour of the creation of employment in the East.

During the engineering Congress in November 1990, IG-Metall President Steinkühler called on the solidarity of West German workers. His proposition suggested a smaller part of income harmonization for the West while the colleagues in the East were to receive the larger share. In the context of this commitment, Steinkühler recalled the strategy of IG-Metall during the West German work-sharing debate in the 1980s: in order to gradually reach the 35-hour week, the engineering union accepted lower wage increases than might otherwise have been attainable.

In the face of the challenges deriving from the social unification process, a similar approach could now become the order of the day. As a means of preventing the prolongation of a society of two nations, wage increases should be shared according to specific requirements in the East. But as it turned out, Steinkühler's proposal received a stern rejection from the engineering union's rank and file. (Steinkühler 1991 p. 31) Having seen their own taxes and social security contributions increase due to the costs of German unification, West German trade unionists felt that they were already contributing enough solidarity and therefore declined to take part in a further foreign aid package for their colleagues in the East. Rather, employees in the so-called old states wanted to profit from the prosperous economic development in the West German engineering industry, and felt entitled to a growth dividend after years of voluntary wage restraint.

Conclusions

It has been my aim to elaborate some options and constraints when social citizenship combines with economic imperatives in a unique socio-political context: the unification process in Germany. The contribution of collective bargaining organizations towards that end has been given priority in this paper. In light of the immense economic and social problems emerging in a country which officially had not known unemployment, and whose labour force has no experience with a free market economy, the solution of letting 'market forces' do the work seems unbearable.

It is precisely the controversy over the trade-off between equality and efficiency which currently puts collective bargaining actors in a dilemma: it has not been agreed upon by the relevant labour market organizations if social and economic objectives should be realized simultaneously. Furthermore, controversies abound over who should pay the price attached to these targets. Finally, it remains unclear if the temporal suspension of one policy target at one point in time will generate cleavages and disparities over time.

But as illustrated in the course of this analysis, the wide range of problem areas in East Germany can hardly be resolved between employers and unions alone. Rather, the dramatic labour market developments and the general uncertainty over the future state of affairs in social, financial and economic areas of East German society highlight not only the uniqueness of the endeavour, but simultaneously the political legitimacy on which it is based.

Putting the problem this way suggests that those implementing policies cannot ignore the fact that the transition process in East Germany is consistently characterized by a combination of drastic economic transformation and democratic reform. Both in its procedural elements and normative objectives this concurrent undertaking is essentially 'political capitalism'. (Offe 1991 p. 877) In that respect, the arduous project of social unification implies putting a specific element of democratic citizenship, namely political participation, on the agenda of economic policy-making.

In practical terms, the order of the day would demand re-introducing a procedure of participation and direct democracy which had become so central during the crumbling of the Eastern European regimes in 1989: the establishment of 'round tables'. This short-lived institution accomplished what party democracy, transplanted with express delivery from West to East, can hardly achieve, given the complex demands it presently faces: that conflicts are dealt with and existing differences are not blurred, that those involved in decision-making are not dominated by tactical considerations, and that policy-making in the former GDR entails that the actors are not imported from or monopolized by the West.

Calling for such round tables does not carry with it the nostalgia of those November days in 1989, nor does it aim at establishing extraparliamentary institutions next to the existing five new state parliaments elected in October 1990. Instead, round tables could be set up with the objective of simultaneously encouraging the participation of citizens and acting as intermediary institutions in selected fields of crisis management. In both cases this endeavour could involve pressing problems like the creation of industrial holdings, the recasting of infrastructure in East Germany and working out blueprints for an environmental policy.

Regarding the location of such round tables, the regional and local levels are most suitable given the multi-dimensionality of problems to be confronted. All the more central to their establishment are the specific actor constellations and their linkages to the respective local authorities and state governments. In order for such round tables to have some say in current German politics, it is first and foremost essential that the latter two institutions establish an autonomy of revenue generation and budget dispersion. As long as monthly pay cheques from the Bonn Government constitute the single most important source of revenue, thus reinforcing the ill-advised notion of persistent subsidies being transferred to a dying patient, neither state governments nor round tables of any configuration in the East will be able to by-pass the dilemma of a limited and constrained capacity to act.

Thus, the specific actor constellation is a cornerstone of such round tables. They would have to incorporate state representatives and members of the Treuhandanstalt,[4] local authorities, firms present in the respective regions, unions as well as academic experts, environmental initiatives and the church. Adding to this enumeration, representatives from West German banks and enterprises, as well as EC-coordinators for regional policies would have a seat in such a 'social parliament'.

In establishing a forum with a feasible agenda and a clearly defined share of participation, those involved would be asked to pay up in political and moral terms. Still, their voluntary commitment would not consist in doing away with social inequalities or bringing about prosperity in due time. The benefits resulting from regional round tables are essentially by-products and they will only be forthcoming if participation, consultation and decision-making are valued for non-instrumental reasons. In that respect, the participants could very well establish some leeway to focus on policies oriented towards structural innovations and the aversion of normative deficits in the course of German unification.

Notes

1. I am particularly grateful to Prof. Dr. Werner Abelshauser and Mary Daly for helpful comments and to Michael Eggert for his unique insight as well as invaluable collaboration in understanding the dynamics of German unification.
2. Ever since this administrative procedure was implemented, confusion and controversy arose concerning the specific classifications henceforth to be used. The 'five new states', often also referred to as the 'former GDR' or 'East Germany' include: Sachsen, Sachsen-Anhalt, Brandenburg, Mecklenburg-Vorpommern and Thüringen. Often ignored or forgotten within this enumeration is East-Berlin which was unified with the western part of the city.
3. The West German 'Regulations governing establishment-level industrial relations' came into effect in the GDR on 1 July 1990. Until all the works councils elections had been carried out and the committees had been established, many firms faced a situation of non-existing formalized co-determination, so that employers were free to act on their own will.
4. Federal agency in charge of the privatization of state-owned firms in East Germany.

Part III

The Transformation of Work and Industrial Citizenship

9. With Every Pair of Hands You Get a Free Brain

Stephen Heycock

Introduction

Let me begin by explaining the title. Its origins lie in a remark made by a senior manager in a large international company which manufactures aerosol cans. This company was suffering from the recession and the problem of maintaining its position within a multinational company in which production could be shifted to its parent company's factories abroad. After a period during which cut-backs in the labour force had lead to strikes and conflict generally, management attempted another solution. They decided to seek the help and co-operation of the workforce to reorganize production in order to make savings in production times and costs.

This need not necessarily be seen as a conscious attempt to change significantly the relationship between management and labour. It may simply be an attempt to solve a particular problem during a period of recession. Although management did express their motives as being to increase the autonomy and participation of their workers in the production process, and although the word citizenship was used in this context, we do not need to take such statements at face value, but must look behind the rhetoric at the historical reality of what those words have meant up to now in industry.

What this particular management were saying was that they realized that they were not tapping the full potential of their workers, many of whom held responsible positions in the community but who were not expected to use those abilities and skills at work, and to take a meaningful part in the organization and running of the production process of which they were a part. The company only utilized their hands not their brains. We realized, he said, that with every pair of hands you get a free brain. With this phrase he summed up neatly the persistent problem which the labour process poses for capital.

Labour purchased in the labour market can be dissociated from the labourer, but when put to work this poses problems. It necessitates imposing discipline upon the labourer in order that his/her labour once bought is used as capital wants and not as the labourer wants. In the extreme conditions of recession this inherent conflict is increased as capital attempts to extract maximum value from the labour purchased. But this can be counter-productive, and then attempts are sometimes made to engage the whole labourer. Of course mental as well as manual skills are purchased in the labour market, but these are usually in the form of conceptual skills linked closely to the operation of manual skills.

What this particular manager meant was willing worker co-operation towards managerial goals. The implied confirmation in the phrase he used was that up to now this co-operation which would necessitate worker autonomy, participation, and most significantly citizenship at work has been very weak or non-existent to any significant extent in Britain.This industry, together with the clothing industry and coal-mining, forms part of a wider study now being carried out of these factors, with regard to teamwork and cell work.

My starting point is the reason why autonomy, participation, and citizenship at work have historically been so weak in Britain. Paradoxically, Britain, the oldest industrial society, with one of the oldest and strongest trade union and labour movements in Europe is nevertheless the one with the least well-developed forms of worker participation and autonomy, or industrial citizenship. These terms are used in Britain, but the meanings attached to them, and the examples we have of them are indicators that they are known more by their absence than their presence. Their weakness informs us only of their potential existence.

Citizenship through autonomy at work and citizenship through political power in the community are two identifiable forms of citizenship which the labour movement have seen as being mutually reinforcing. Employers also understand how in their own interests the two combine, and have sought to exploit their ownership and control of industry by controlling political bodies such as local councils.

In many working class communities the labour movement has sought a similar dual basis of power, most easily identified in coalmining communities under both private and public ownership.

Why does the concept of industrial citizenship in particular sound so hollow in Britain? To answer these questions fully would require an historical analysis of the peculiar path towards industrialization which Britain took as the first industrial society, and in particular of the way in which new class formations developed.

For example the newly forming bourgeoisie of industrial employers adopted many of the cultural forms of the pre-industrial aristocracy and landowning class, who were not overthrown and who married into and invested alongside this bourgeoisie in the new industrialization. The working class as it developed did not have a single polar opposite in whose mirror they could regard their own negative image and, according to Marx at least, see a possible positive future through its negation. 'Deference' to the old order remained amongst both bourgeoisie and working class. (Weiner 1981; Hobsbawm 1968)

After the end of a relatively brief revolutionary period in the 1840s trade unionism in Britain developed as a strong, confident, but basically moderate movement. First skilled and later unskilled workers developed and maintained their own position as an independent force based upon an implicit if not always explicit assumption of opposed economic interests. Once their legal right to exist and take effective action had been won and safeguarded by the law in the late nineteenth century, they neither sought nor wanted any real participation, legal, formal, or informal, in the production process, at the national, local or workplace level.

Britain developed what came to be called a voluntaristic system of industrial relations and collective bargaining in which agreements were voluntarily reached outside the law between organized employers and employees. (Clegg 1980; Donovan 1968)

Trade unions saw any form of participation as hampering them in their task of extracting the best wages and conditions they could from an employer. It was seen as co-optation not participation (Coates and Topham 1990). As late as the 1970s the Bullock Commission's recommendations and the attempts to introduce industrial democracy failed not just due to the opposition of organized employers but no less to that of organized labour too.

Within the labour movement most saw participation as meaningful only within a nationalized industrial economy, and they rejected along with the employers a European conception of industrial democracy.

So far I have referred only to participation – what of autonomy? Responsible Autonomy is a term which has been used by social scientists with quite different perspectives. (Trist *et al.* 1963; Friedman 1977) Generally it was used to describe or denote that form of autonomy gained by usually skilled workers over that part of the production process which they performed. It was therefore piecemeal, informal and unstable and under constant attack from Tayloristic forms of work organization.

A large part of the labour process debate has centred around an analysis of how and how far this form of autonomy has been eroded during the nineteenth century and twentieth century. (Braverman 1974; Burawoy 1979; Clawson 1980; Edwards 1979) In Britain this debate is especially important since this is almost the only form of autonomy workers have attempted.

Up until the advent of 'Thatcherism' the trade union and labour movement had developed very little legal or formal forms of participation and autonomy. After Thatcherism they have no choice, since whatever bodies had been created, have now been choked. Bodies like the National Economic Development Council, various Trades Union Congress committees, set up in the post-war era which engaged in some formal participation with Government and employers in the creation and running of industrial policy have been quietly strangled in the 1980s.

The message of the last twelve years has in contrast been loud and clear, Thatcherism is opposed to all forms of participation and autonomy by labour and its representative organizations.

However, the historical truth tells us that Thatcherism is not wholly to blame. Labour has not actively and enthusiastically sought such forms of participation and autonomy, and so cannot now complain that it is prevented from doing so. But this is not an entirely accurate picture either. The truth, as usual, is more complicated than that. Trade unionism sought autonomy and participation more indirectly through the creation of the Labour Party. But these then depended upon a programme of massive nationalization brought about by a Labour Government committed to this.

Neither has happened and the example of the coal industry is a good example of why not.

Autonomy, Participation and Citizenship in Coalmining

Coal was the first industry to be nationalized in 1947 by a Labour Government and was seen as the vanguard for the rest. The miners' union had campaigned long and hard for generations to gain what this, their Labour Government, had now achieved. The newly formed National Union of Mineworkers (NUM) therefore co-operated wholeheartedly with the National Coal Board (NCB) in making it a success. This was first seen in their ready concern to meet the post-war energy shortage during the first 10 years of their existence. The Union's hopes and plans for participation in the running of the industry were put on hold. For example schemes like the 'ladder plan' whereby miners could graduate into and up the management structure of the NCB.

When decline of the coal industry began suddenly in 1957 in response to amongst other factors a decrease in the price of oil, the NUM used to co-operation not consultation (another scheme put on hold) or participation was unable to control let alone prevent the rate of decline or its social consequences for its members and its communities.

They therefore slowly reverted to the sort of relationship they had with the former private coal companies – that of defensive, reactive attempts to mitigate the worst social effects of a rapid decline. Even this took a long time to develop and no overt industrial action to attempt to halt decline occurred for almost 30 years, until 1984/5. (Allen 1981)

What of autonomy? The coal industry provides us with a good example of what this meant for most workers in Britain. Coalminers have traditionally been taken as prime examples of workers, the nature of whose work gave them responsible autonomy. (Trist *et al.* 1963; Dennis *et al.* 1969) Their work was described as multi-skilled, carried out within a workplace which they were also responsible for controlling, and in a process of production in which they were almost the whole part. Supervisory control was very small or almost non-existent. However, this traditional picture is overdrawn. (Heycock 1986) Miners' work was usually effectively controlled by a price list which determined not only how work was to be paid but how it was to be done too. The actual degree of autonomy outside this was relatively small, being largely confined to claims for allowances due to adverse working conditions and which were made usually in on-the-spot workplace bargaining. (Heycock 1987) Such 'traditional' mining began to disappear in the late 1950s with increasing mechanization of coal production, with powerloading in the 1960s and even more dramatically in the 1970s and 1980s with the introduction of information and communication technology to control the operation and maintenance of this machinery, and the whole flow of the production process. Very little autonomy is now left to coalminers.

What then of citizenship? Coalmining produced strong, closely knit communities often with strong local community control reflected institutionally in local councils, trades councils, political party constituency parties, school boards, clubs, etcetera. At the national level this was reflected in TUC committees, sponsored Labour MPs, etcetera. Historically, coalminers were among the best examples of such citizenship amongst the working class. But after 30 years of decline, this is no longer the case in coalmining and is also no longer the case in the working class generally due to similar processes of decline as well as changes in the structure of industry and occupations in Britain.

However, even when they were at their strongest the link between work and citizenship was never a strong one in Britain. For example, miners would vote unhesitatingly for a known communist miner to be a trade union official, but they would not vote for the same man if he stood as a prospective communist councillor. (Heycock 1979) Trade unions were not seen as political institutions; economism and politicism were separated. In one case you acted as a miner with economic interests, in another as a citizen with political interests. If this was the case in mining communities it was even more the case amongst the working class generally. In addition, one of the most significant features of post-war Britain has been the decline of working-class communities as cultural and political entities and goes some way to explaining the lack of a coordinated political reaction to recession and very high levels of unemployment during the 1970s and 1980s. During the slump of the inter-war years the unemployed were still part of their communities and still had institutionalized means of expressing their opposition to unemployment through them. Today this is not the case. What link there was between citizenship and work has largely disappeared.

Autonomy, Participation, Citizenship and New Technology

Coalmining is not a special case, in fact its experience of the destruction of autonomy and participation are typical of managerial strategies in industries in Britain, particularly during the 1970s and 1980s. (Wood 1982; Thompson and McHugh 1990)

Although coalmining is a declining industry in terms of employment and output, its productivity has increased tremendously during the 1970s and 1980s as new advanced mining machinery and techniques have been introduced into new 'super pits' and older mines.

However, obstacles to increasing productivity have been seen since the 1950s as being social as much as technical by management in the coal industry. The study done for the NCB by Trist *et al.* in the 1950s suggested a socio-technical systems approach to recreating the autonomy and participation in work lost by miners through mechanization. When a second major technological change, powerloading, ended this method of production and destroyed the organization of work built upon it by Trist *et al.* the NCB decided upon a reversal of their social solution and in the 1970s began to organize work in order to reduce what remained of autonomy and participation.

This was achieved through the development of information and communication technology built into already existing mining machinery in order to control the work of miners who operated and maintained them, and through a central computerized control system for all mining operations. (Burns *et al.* 1985) This allowed management to develop new working practices in the 1980s which might be termed 'flexible working' but which were in fact more restrictive for miners so that flexibility in fact only existed for management. (Heycock 1989)

For example skilled craftsmen like maintenance men could now be informed by management when a machine needed maintaining or repairing through information relayed to them directly from microprocessors in the machinery about its performance via the mine operating system computer network. The maintenance men therefore no longer controlled the diagnostic procedure through which their work was organized, so that their whole pattern of work was now controlled by management. In a similar fashion other grades of miner lost autonomy over shift patterns, payment systems, and methods of work as management were able to monitor the production process better. To this extent the union found its participation in bargaining and negotiating over those issues greatly reduced.

A most significant change which indicates how autonomy and participation were lost was the increasing use of external contract labour for carrying out skilled maintenance work for example. This was a predictable progression from management's new practice of holding a reduced pool of maintenance men on standby as the machines' self-diagnostic capability now informed management in advance when a fault was likely to occur. The next logical step was for management to eliminate the maintenance men entirely or drastically to reduce them further, and only have to pay for maintenance or repair work done by contractors when it was needed, thus allowing them to reduce their labour force (numerical flexibility) and their labour costs (financial flexibility). But equally they could also monitor the work intensity of machines and therefore of miners too and as a result develop strategies to increase it. This aspect of information and communication technology is common to many forms of work in industry generally, for example in office work. (Webster 1990)

However, I am not suggesting a technologically determinist view of the labour process in which autonomy and participation are constantly eroded by the Bravermanesque march of Taylorism. Social and political factors are crucial. For example the 1984/5 miners' strike was a last desperate defence against a rapidly accelerating period of closures by the NUM, and a desire to defeat the power of the union by British Coal (BC), who felt that its economic strategy and its ability to increase productivity and work intensity necessitated breaking the power of the union to determine work rates, work methods, and pay. It was a political strategy to reduce the social significance of autonomy and participation. (MacGregor 1986) For this to happen the traditional centres of power in the coalmining communities had also to be broken – a very clear example of an attempt to break or critically reduce the link between citizenship and work.

For example the new pits of the 1980s like Selby in Yorkshire were not to be allowed to develop strong mining communities. British Coal did not build large estates for the miners as in the past, but dispersed the workforce throughout the small rural villages in the area. (Tomaney and Winterton 1990) There were historical precedents for this in the Kent Coalfield during the inter-war period when miners from Wales and elsewhere were brought into this new coalfield and settled into the rural villages of Kent, and the union struggled with the divisive effects of this. (Pitt 1979)

In the case of Selby it is suggested that the much lower than average support for the strike of 1984/5 can be attributed in part to this absence of a strong community. (Winterton and Winterton 1989) The same factors have been found to be important in explaining why some pits resisted closure more than others. (Heycock 1979) In particular newer or more 'cosmopolitan' pits in which miners were drawn from a number of older mining communities whose pits had already closed exhibited higher levels of resistance and industrial conflict than older or single community pits. At the same time this conflict was often more anarchic and less directed. There is a paradox here, in that stability, moderation, even co-operation and co-optation are found as aspects of industrial relations and even of industrial conflict, alongside high levels of autonomy, participation, and citizenship in traditional mining communities where conformity and even parochiality are enforced. However, this is not to suggest that technological change is not an important factor in itself. In the 1970s coalminers' work began to be reorganized significantly as powerloading machinery and methods were introduced. In order to be able to calculate and control labour costs more easily, miners were removed from piecework payment and paid a daywage. With the internalized control of piecework removed, management, in order to control the running time of these new machines, changed the role of the Deputies, formerly responsible for health and safety and local collective bargaining at the workplace into front-line supervisors more akin to a foreman in a factory. This reflected a move away from greater degrees of autonomy and participation in the production process and collective bargaining towards a more supervised and management-directed form of factory-type production. However, social and political factors once again impinged upon the technical, when after the first national coal strike since 1926, in 1974, the NCB engineered a return to a different form of piecework in 1978 – the pit level bonus scheme – in an attempt to prevent national daywage rates producing national pay strikes.This return to a more flexible system of payment was linked to an attempt to make the organization of work more flexible now that information and communication technology allowed management to increase the intensity of work. But 'it does not allow the workforce to use the information or make any decisions about more flexible patterns of work organization'. (Burns *et al.* 1983 p. 104)

As I have already commented, flexibility of this kind means flexibility for management not miners, and is part of a much wider managerial strategy to reduce autonomy and participation. According to the NUM it includes the new commercial orientation of BC with a view to possible privatization.

All of these changes significantly reduce the autonomy and participation of miners and their union in the production process, and the NUM believe that such a notion of flexibility is against the interests of their members. (NUM 1987)

This issue of flexible work organization has in fact caused splits in the NUM and helped further to reduce their effective participation in the running of the coal industry. It has been linked closely to the new technology 'super pits' and BC have made it clear that they will only be sunk if the union accepts it. This split areas which might gain from having new pits, like South Wales from the NUM leadership who were opposed to such flexible work schemes in principle on the grounds of health and safety and who put forward an alternative policy to reduce shift times and hours worked per week. (Heycock 1989) Such splits have tended to further weaken the union and reduce its ability to bargain collectively at the national level. In fact since the 1984/5 strike and the formation of the United Democratic Mineworkers (UDM) with whom the NUM refuses to bargain, the NUM no longer participates in such national collective bargaining with BC.

The major technical change in coalmining during the 1980s and into the 1990s has been the development of a computerized system for centralizing the monitoring and control of production, which reduced the autonomy and participation of miners and their union at all levels from workplace to national level.

The full impact of technological change could be modified as long as miners had sufficient control at the point of production to resist changes in work organization. However, there is evidence to show that BC formulated a management strategy to reduce the miners' autonomy over and participation in the labour process.

The balance of power between miners and management thus altered steadily in favour of management, and was demonstrated visibly in the 1984/5 strike. Since the strike management have consolidated their gains by victimizing union activists and restricting the role of the NUM at branch level, re-asserted managerial prerogative in a new disciplinary Code of Conduct, and institutionalized the divisions highlighted by the formation of the breakaway UDM in the new arrangements for consultation and conciliation. (Heycock and Winterton 1989)

So far the NUM has resisted these changes but it is uncertain how long the union can resist, given the additional pressure from the privatization of electricity and the possibility of privatization of the coal industry itself. The context of all these changes means that the link between citizenship and work has been constantly eroded for over 30 years in this industry, and I suggest that this has also been the case within industry in Britain generally during this period.

Conclusion

I have taken coalmining as an example in order to compare it with the more general limited nature of industrial autonomy, participation and citizenship in Britain, under the premise that if these were not developed more fully in this industry it helps to explain why they did not develop elsewhere either. Coalminers have always been regarded as having a high degree of autonomy at work, and to have developed a strong, confident union at the local and national level with strong roots in the community. This union was also well placed to develop autonomy, participation, and citizenship at work through its political position within the labour movement and the Labour Party, and as the first industry to be nationalized by a Labour Government in 1947. This was then clearly seen as a legitimate and obtainable goal, and a preferred route towards them by the labour movement.

However, those plans did not even last ten years, so that when decline of the industry began in 1957 they were scrapped. Decline has been typical of the environment workers in such basic industries as coalmining have had to exist in ever since.

The attempted socio-technical systems solution to autonomy and participation in coalmining formally approved of and introduced during the 1950s (Trist *et al.* 1963) did not survive the NCB's preoccupation with decline and indeed fostered an opposite solution in the re-assertion of direct control by management, although their ability to do this to any great extent had to wait until the new technologies of the 1970s and 1980s. In particular the NCB took the 1974 national coal strike as a warning to increase managerial control and reduce autonomy and participation through increased technological innovation and reorganization of work.

It is argued that after the 1984 national strike BC went further and attempted to break the NUM as well as autonomy and participation at the workplace level and citizenship at the community level. There is some evidence that individual pits, communities, and even coalfields were targeted on the basis that they were the strongest repositories of those very things.

If this has happened in coalmining where autonomy, participation, and citizenship have historically been stronger than in most industries, even if limited and incomplete, it shows what has been happening less clearly and in a more piecemeal fashion in British industry in general. The rapidity of decline and its scale may be greater in coalmining than in industry generally, but the fact of decline, and of the decline of autonomy, participation and citizenship is significant.

To return to the original more general questions then. First, why has autonomy and participation at work been so weak historically in Britain? Second, why has the concept of citizenship at work been a non-issue? Third, what is the link between technological change, economic restructuring, and fragmentation of the working class in Britain? Fourth, why has the labour movement seemingly become so marginalized?

Autonomy at work has usually been seen in terms of the ability of the (usually skilled) workers to control part of the production process they are directly engaged with, and not the whole process. Participation has been self-limited to collective bargaining within a voluntary, informal and non-legalistic system. Therefore the concept of citizenship at work has not been seen by trade unions as a goal since it would involve a formal, legal association with employers. Furthermore, individual trade unions did not want the Trades Union Congress (TUC) to act in this capacity on their behalf.

During the last Depression of the 1930s trade unions amalgamated into larger general unions for protection, but still they preferred to deal with employers directly at local level, only entering into very broad general agreements at national level which merely provided the frame-work for collective bargaining at local and shop-floor level.

During the present Depression these same factors have contributed to the impossibility of the trade unions securing greater autonomy and participation at work. The various Employment Acts passed during the 1980s have brought trade unions into the formalized, legal world of labour law, but without their consent and co-operation let alone their participation. They have been framed specifically to reduce the forms of autonomy trade unions have secured historically in Britain whether within or without the legal framework. Trade unions were powerless, it seemed, to prevent this. First, because they had always relied upon their individual powers within collective bargaining to oppose employers economically, and were ill-suited to opposing government politically. Those areas together with the law were areas they had kept away from, and therefore had developed no knowledge of, or experience, or exper-tise in.

Second, because the fractionalized collective bargaining at shop-floor level was seen as the cause of Britain's so-called strike problem during the post-war area, particularly during the 1960s and 1970s. The Employ-ment Acts of the 1980s were framed to destroy this form of autonomy and prevent this form of participation and not to create new forms. Philosophically, so-called 'Thatcherism' believed in the individual not the citizen. Technological change and industrial and economic restruc-turing during the 1970s and 1980s has produced the decline of traditional basic industries like coalmining with their strong trade unions and communities – even though their notion of citizenship was of community rather than industry. Existing industries which have been restructured and new ones which have grown within the new economic structure of Britain have tended to seek a company level relationship with their workers, utilizing the new control opportunities of new technology. In this they have been aided by the growth of smaller companies and the breaking down of larger companies, and the increase in part-time, temporary, or contract labour. Linked changes in the age and gender composition of labour and immigrant labour have further disrupted many trade unions' positions of power. Working class communities have also reflected those changes, declining in size and becoming more fractionalized. The recession has of course also reduced the power of trade unions and can be simply quantified by quoting the decline in trade union members from a high of 12 million members in the 1980s to a new low of less than eight million in 1992.

As during the Depression of the 1930s trade unions have amalgamated into even bigger unions, now called 'superunions', which seek agreements directly with employers, reducing the influence of the TUC, and within a legal framework which does not encourage autonomy and participation at work.

The link between autonomy or empowerment at work and political citizenship in the community has declined in Britain to a historically low level, and to such an extent that the causes of this decline cannot be vigorously opposed, by a fractionalised and weakened labour movement, with the same chances of success as in the past.

10. Participation and Autonomy at Work: a Segmented Privilege

Peter Leisink and Leni Beukema

Industrial Citizenship

Although economic citizenship rights did not receive much attention in Marshall's theory of citizenship, they were not completely absent. Marshall regarded the right of collective bargaining and the right to form trade unions as an 'extension of civil rights in the economic sphere". (Marshall 1973 p. 93) Participation at work is absent from Marshall's writings, at least as an economic civil right, but he does pay some attention to information, consultation, delegation and joint control as 'four degrees of co-operation' between management and employees. (Marshall 1973 pp. 221–222) Yet the way in which workers' participation at company level has been institutionalized in some West European countries may be compared to the institutionalization of political participation through town councils. In much the same way as local citizens elect their representatives to the town council, employees in Belgium, Denmark, France, Germany, the Netherlands and Spain elect their representatives to the works council. (Koene and Slomp 1991) We will use the term 'industrial citizenship' to indicate the opportunities for workers' participation at work.

In this chapter we will explore the extent to which industrial citizenship exists. As political citizenship rights have given rise to a longstanding debate about the model of political democracy (Held 1987), industrial citizenship raises the question of the requirements of industrial democracy. To tackle a subject like this one needs criteria that establish whether a system of decision-making may be called democratic. Following Held we will adopt the criteria that have been elaborated by Dahl (1985). These criteria may be adapted to industrial democracy as follows:

1. Votes must be allocated equally among employees.
2. Each employee must have an adequate and equal opportunity for expressing a preference as to the final outcome.

3. Each employee must have adequate and equal opportunities for discovering and validating his or her preferences on the matter to be decided.
4. The company's constituency must have the opportunity to decide what matters are and are not to be decided according to these criteria.
5. The company's constituency must include all employees except transients.

We will use these criteria to assess the actual state of industrial citizenship. Most criteria are rather self-evident the third criterion demands some further clarification at this point, however. It will be obvious that one needs information which is relevant to a particular matter in order to form one's opinion on that matter. It will be obvious as well that this information must be available at a timely moment so that one will have the opportunity to explore alternative approaches. With respect to industrial democracy one other condition pertaining to the third criterion comes to mind which has to do with the organization of work.

For many decades the Taylorist organization of work has been dominant. (Littler and Salaman 1984 pp. 73–74) The important point with respect to our analysis of industrial democracy is that the Taylorist organization of work takes the competence and resources from the worker which form the basis of participation, notably in terms of the third criterion specified above. The separation of mental and manual labour, the transference of planning and maintenance tasks from the workshop to auxiliary departments, and the stripping of work tasks have taken away the opportunity for many workers to gain insight into the economic and organizational framework of the labour process and their working life. In sum, the Taylorist organization of work erodes the autonomy of employees, which involves 'the ability to deliberate, judge, choose and act upon different possible courses of action'. (Held 1987 p. 270)

Throughout the 1980s there have been reports of forms of work redesign in some core sectors of industry that cross the Taylorist border. These provide workers with an integration of planning, executive and control tasks. (Kern and Schumann 1984) It may be assumed that the conditions for gaining access to decision-making processes in the company are enlarged considerably by this type of work redesign. It seems that until now only a minor group of employees have benefited from these reforms. Nonetheless, the importance of the organization of work and the concomitant worker autonomy as a condition of industrial citizenship requires that they are dealt with in a separate section.

We will go about our exploration of the extent of industrial citizenship as follows. We will start with an explanatory note on the sense in which we use the terms participation and autonomy. Secondly, we will examine the legal regulations concerning industrial democracy. We will focus on the Works Councils Act in the Netherlands and we will touch on workers' participation in the European Community. Thirdly, we will go into the extent to which formal rights are actually being used by employees. We will then enter into the question of autonomy and the organization of work as a condition that contributes to a fuller use of participation opportunities. Finally we will make some remarks on the way in which the exercise of industrial citizenship rights might be directed at goals of non-sectarian social solidarity.

Definitions of Participation and Autonomy

The variety of ways in which the term 'participation' is used is a welcome invitation to start by clarifying the sense in which we will use the term.

We want to define workers' participation as the access of workers to the decision-making processes in their company. (Leisink 1989 p. 15) Our concern is with the rights and opportunities workers have to influence company policy from their point of view. Terms like 'co-determination' or 'workers' control' are also used in this context. (*cf.* Poole 1986 p. 18) They draw attention to the scope of actual influence, ranging from influence by workers on decisions for which the management holds sole authority to decisions over which workers have actual control. The conceptual advantage of using these terms instead of 'workers' participation' is that the term 'participation' can be reserved to designate management initiatives like quality circles. These management initiatives may have a positive effect on worker satisfaction and productivity. However, they do not structurally enlarge the workers' access to decision-making because quality circles usually have no discretionary powers of their own and it remains up to management to decide whether proposals are accepted. By and large these management initiatives contribute to the humanization of work but they do not alter the structure of power in the company. (de Nijs 1983 pp. 82–83; Poole 1986 p. 19; Rueschemeyer 1986 p. 96) Therefore we will not deal with them here.

In the Dutch system of industrial relations, works councils are the main institution of workers' influence in company decision-making. Therefore we will concentrate on them. Although we would rather not use the term 'participation' in this context we will stick to the term here because of its analytical relationship with citizenship as essentially concerned with participation.

Depending on the changes in the division of labour it entails, work redesign may enlarge the workers' autonomy. We take autonomy at work to mean the degree in which workers are able and free to organize the job they have to do and the speed of their work. (Beukema 1987 p. 69) Autonomy in this sense is concerned with the influence workers have, individually or as a group, in performing their job.

Participation and autonomy at work complement each other. Together they come close to Held's general principle of autonomy which states that:

> individuals should be free and equal in the determination of the conditions of their own lives; that is, they should enjoy equal rights (and, accordingly, equal obligations) in the specification of the framework which generates and limits the opportunities available to them, so long as they do not deploy this framework to negate the rights of others. (Held 1987 p. 271)

Regulations of Workers' Participation in the Netherlands

The works council can be compared appropriately to the town council. The company's employees elect their representatives in the works council like local citizens elect their representatives in the town council. The Works Councils Act has indeed been presented as an invitation to industrial citizenship. (van den Heuvel 1983 p. 54) Some students of industrial relations even consider the Dutch Works Councils Act as the juridical completion of citizenship. (de Gier 1988 p. 15). We do not support this view. The legal regulations of workers' participation can be shown to entail substantial limitations to full industrial citizenship. In terms of the actual realization of participation rights the limitations appear even greater as we will show in the next paragraph.

The Works Councils Act prescribes the creation of works councils by companies employing at least a hundred employees or at least 35 employees working more than one-third of the normal working hours. (*cf.* Ministerie van Sociale Zaken en Werkgelegenheid 1987; Sociaal-Economische Raad 1991) It is the works council's function to represent the company's employees *vis-à-vis* the employer and to consult with the employer on company policy.

In companies with 35 to a hundred employees, only employees who have been employed for at least a year and for more than one-third of the normal working hours have the right to elect and to be elected.

In companies with a hundred or more employees all employees who have been employed for at least six months have the right to elect works council representatives. All employees who have been employed for at least a year may be elected as a works council member.

In companies employing more than 10 and less than 35 employees another regulation of workers' participation holds. In these companies the employer is expected to consult with all employees on company policy at least twice a year.

These statutory regulations show one major restriction to industrial citizenship. Not all employees are treated as industrial citizens equally. In very small companies employing less than 10 employees there is no legal regulation of worker participation at all. In companies employing 35 or more employees the citizenship rights depend on the labour contract and on the term which one has served. It might be argued that conditions concerning the term which employees must have served in their company may be compared to conditions concerning the age of citizens before they enjoy their political rights. But clearly the exclusion of all employees working less than one-third of the normal working hours has no parallel in the sphere of political citizenship and is an infringement on the fifth criterion of industrial democracy. Public awareness of this situation has led the Minister of Social Affairs and Employment to propose eliminating this exclusionist condition but, as late as May 1992, the employers' organizations are opposed to this idea.

The statutory regulations contain a second major restriction to citizenship rights. The scope of works council rights varies with the domain of company policy. With respect to personnel and social policy the council has a right to veto management proposals. It compels the company management to reach an agreement with the works council in cases of personnel management policy, working hours regulations and so on. With respect to financial and technical-organizational company policy the works council has advisory powers only. In the case of works councils in firms employing less than a hundred employees this advisory right is conditional, that is to say a management plan has to be submitted to the works council only if at least a quarter of all employees are affected by this plan. The company management is, therefore, not required to reach an agreement with the works council for instance in the case of decisions to invest in new machinery. If both parties disagree and the works council advises negatively, management may proceed as it intended if it observes certain procedural requirements.

Referring to the fourth criterion we have mentioned above, it is not the company's constituency which may decide what matters are to be decided. The law stipulates that in some matters the employees' representatives have the right to veto and in other matters have the right only to advise. This brings up the first criterion as well. Whereas the works council's right to veto comes close to co-determination and may be regarded as a more or less equal distribution of voting power between management and employees, the right to advise does not reflect an equal allocation of votes.

The differential distribution of rights to the works council reflects the basic asymmetrical distribution of power between capital and labour in a market economy. (Poole 1986 p. 29) The traditional management prerogative is not affected fundamentally by the rights assigned to the works council. The management is still the boss when it comes to investment decisions and the organization of work. The efforts of the labour movement have induced the state to intervene, resulting in the Works Councils Act. The rights of the industrial citizen have progressively been extended since the first act of 1950. However, the scope of these rights is still inversely correlated with the centrality of the various domains of company policy.

Trade unions have tried themselves to intervene in the distribution of power between labour and capital. The results they have achieved as far as the rights of works councils are concerned are limited. In some branches of industry, unions have succeeded in specifying the works councils' rights with respect to the implementation of shorter working hours and technological innovations. On the whole worker participation regulations in collective agreements are scarce, and if they do exist they are only a rather marginal extension of statutory regulations. (*cf.* Looise 1985)

These critical observations with respect to statutory regulations of industrial democracy in the Netherlands should, however, be qualified against the background of European industrial relations. Six European countries – Belgium, Denmark, France, Germany, the Netherlands and Spain – have institutionalized workers' participation along the lines of works councils. On the basis of statutory regulations concerning the rights of works councils, Germany and the Netherlands appear to have the more powerful forms of industrial democracy. (Koene and Slomp 1991 pp. 245–251)

This is not to say that other European countries do not have workers' participation. Where works councils do not exist, workers' participation usually takes place by shop stewards, as in the United Kingdom. The absence of statutory regulations, however, makes workers' participation more vulnerable to the vicissitudes of the economy and in particular to the resources which trade unions can mobilize to back up workers' participation. In this respect the United Kingdom illustrates that the crisis of trade unions goes hand in hand with the decline of workers' participation at shop floor and company levels. (Crouch 1991)

Although the systems of industrial relations and workers' participation will no doubt take years to converge, if they will ultimately do so at all, the works council appears to be attractive to European trade unions as a form of workers' participation. The European Trades Union Council (ETUC) promotes the idea of a 'Euro works council'. It supported the proposal by the European Community Commissioners which made it obligatory for enterprises with at least a thousand employees and with at least a hundred employees in two EC member states to have a works council. If this proposal had been accepted, the Euro works council would have met at least once a year to be informed by the central management on overall enterprise policy and would have had the right to be consulted on policy plans which may seriously affect employees. However, Unice, the European organization of employers, was flatly opposed to these proposals. The British government was unwilling to accept any 'social paragraph' and a Euro works council in particular. Therefore, the proposal was dropped and was not on the agenda of the European Community conference at Maastricht, December 1991. It may be that the other European Community member states will adopt the proposal but no firm regulation of transnational industrial democracy must be expected for the near future.

Obstacles to Workers' Participation in Practice

In the previous paragraph we analysed major restrictions to industrial citizenship that are inherent in statutory regulations as such. We will now discuss the state of workers' participation in practice, that is the extent to which statutory participation rights are exercised. Our focus, again, is on the Netherlands.

The first point to be noted is that the institutionalization of industrial citizenship is less extensive than statutorily demanded.

To be fair, 83 per cent of all companies employing at least a hundred employees which have to establish a works council have done so. However, of all companies employing at least 35 but less than a hundred employees only 41 per cent had a works council in 1987. This situation implies that 87 per cent of all employees in companies employing at least a hundred employees are represented via a works council versus only 45 per cent of all employees working in companies employing at least 35 and less than a hundred employees. (Ministerie van Sociale Zaken en Werkgelegenheid 1988 pp. 7–15)

Of companies employing at least ten and less than 35 employees 40 per cent do not hold a consultation meeting of employer and employees, about 30 per cent hold one meeting a year and only 30 per cent hold two meetings a year as legally prescribed. (Verstegen and Andriessen 1987 pp. 54–55)

A preliminary conclusion on the basis of these findings may be that the opportunities for employees to exercise their statutory citizenship rights at work increase with the size of their company. It has been supposed that detailed legislation does not fit in with the situation in small firms since actual informal consultation practices would be bureaucratized unnecessarily. (Verstegen and Andriessen 1987 pp. 3–4) However, the supposition that smaller companies organize worker participation of their own accord, albeit in a more informal way, is not confirmed by the findings concerning companies employing ten to 35 employees.

A second observation we would like to bring up concerns the gender bias in the formal regulations with respect to the company's constituency.

As mentioned before, only employees who have been employed for at least a year and for more than one-third of the normal working hours have the right to elect and to be elected in companies employing 35 to 100 employees. In companies with a hundred or more employees all employees who have been employed for at least six months have the right to elect works council representatives and all those who have been employed for at least a year may be elected themselves.

The consequence of these regulations is that a considerable number of employees are excluded from participation rights, particularly those with atypical employment contracts, such as part-time, temporary and trainee contracts. In practice this means that especially female workers are excluded. For instance, women make up 85 per cent of all part-time workers in the Netherlands, where the proportion of part-time work is relatively high when compared to other OECD-countries (24.9 per cent against an average 15.5 per cent; only Sweden and Norway score higher). (WRR 1990 p. 67) Again, among workers who do not have a labour contract, like some flexible workers and outworkers, women are by far the largest group. Together with the fact that it is still mainly women who are responsible for the organization of the household and childrearing, these conditions explain why 83 per cent of all works council members are male and only 17 per cent are female. (Looise and Heijink 1986 p. 106)

A third point we would like to raise has to do with the fact that the works council is a type of representative democracy. The works council can only be said to contribute to real participation opportunities for all employees in so far as the elected works council members act in close communication with their rank and file. However, the lack of interaction between works council members and their rank and file has been one of the deficiencies of the works councils from their very start in the 1950s. (Hövels and Nas 1976) Only 15 per cent of the works councils hold office hours. Again only 17 per cent of the works councils hold a consultation meeting with their rank and file twice a year. (Looise and Heijink 1986 p. 113) As far as there are contacts between works council members and ordinary rank and file they take place mostly on an individual and informal basis.

In some branches of industry, such as the metal and the food industry, trade unions have made an effort to organize trade union committees at shop-floor level. These committees may be found in 40 per cent of the manufacturing industry. Yet even if there is a trade union committee, only half of the works councils have contacts with the committee. (Looise and Heijink 1986 p. 114) The extent to which these networks exist, appears to depend on the trade union's policy itself. Works council members and shop stewards who are assisted by their unions with these kinds of contacts, have networks which are two to three times as extensive as those whose unions do not promote mutual contacts. (Leisink 1989 pp. 354–371)

The three empirical observations show that the idea of a community of industrial citizens participating through workers' representatives must be qualified in several ways. In addition to legal restrictions on the notion of industrial citizen it appears that many employees are excluded from the exercise of economic civil rights. This holds true for female workers especially. Immigrant workers are another category of employees that is largely underrepresented. It may be concluded that there is a segmentation between those who can exercise their economic civil rights and those who are formally or practically excluded. This segmentation in terms of industrial citizenship coincides to a large extent with a segmentation in terms of the quality of work (*cf.* Atkinson 1985), which, however, should not be conceived of in terms of neat divisions. (Wood 1989 p. 5) With respect to the latter segmentation the primary segment consists of secure, well-paid and highly-skilled jobs which offer a considerable degree of autonomy and promotion prospects. The secondary segment consists of low-paid and low-skilled jobs. Here job security varies, but the more peripheral a job the less secure it is due to flexible contracts and subcontracting.

Our analysis shows that those workers who occupy marginal jobs which offer little opportunity to develop qualifications on the job have no access to participatory institutions either.

The extent to which works councils can exercise their rights in practice qualifies the concept of industrial citizenship in yet another way. It appears that nearly 40 per cent of all cases of company policy that should have been submitted to the works council according to statutory regulations were in fact not put before it. (Looise and de Lange 1987 pp. 24–28) This finding concerns those cases of which works council members themselves are actually aware. It may, therefore, be assumed that the percentage is in fact higher. By far the most important reason for this infringement on industrial democracy appears to be the management's unilateral decision-making without asking the council's opinion or without paying respect to the council's opinion. The same finding was reported in another study of the involvement of the works council in decision-making with respect to technological innovations. (Warmerdam et al. 1987)

Apart from the actual request for the council's opinion, the moment at which the council is informed by the company management is an important factor which determines the extent to which the council can exercise its rights. The sooner the council is informed on some management intention that may (or may not) result in a decision at a later stage, the greater the opportunity for the council to influence the decision-making process effectively. It appears that in half of the cases of company policy in which the council can bring to bear its advisory rights, the council is informed as soon as management has preliminary plans and in the other half after management has reached a basic decision. With respect to cases of social company policy in which the council has veto rights, it is informed sooner. In three-quarters of all cases the council is informed after management has preliminary plans and in one-quarter after management has taken its basic decision. (Looise and de Lange 1987 p. 53) These findings reveal that the moment at which the works council is informed by the management is related significantly to the power that the council holds. Indeed, the veto right enables the council to block the continuation of management's work. (*cf.* Teulings 1989) This makes it much more important for the management to win the co-operation of the works council by informing the council at an early stage. By contrast the advisory rights of the works council in cases of financial and technical-organizational company policy are much weaker and enable the management to hold on to its management's prerogative.

Industrial citizenship is far from complete. In terms of statutory regulations workers' participation is to be improved both as regards the inclusion of peripheral workers into the company's constituency and as regards the distribution of voting rights between management and workers in different areas of company policy. It is to be strengthened, moreover, by the way both works council members and management deal with workers' participation. It is largely dependent on the works council members whether all employees will have an adequate and equal opportunity for expressing a preference as to the final outcome (our second criterion). It is dependent on management's attitude whether employees have real access to company decision-making, as far as the legal framework allows. This refers, among other things, to the supply of adequate information at a timely moment. It also refers to the organization of work, since 'the transformation of the rigid and technical division of labour is essential if people are to develop their capacities and involve themselves fully in the democratic regulation of political as well as economic and social life'. (Held 1987 p. 276) We will now turn to this topic.

Work Organization and Autonomy

At the end of the 1960s the dominant Taylorist forms of work organization were confronted with increasing problems. Among them can be mentioned: organizational inflexibility, negative consequences for work attitudes and underutilization of worker competence. These problems, in combination with increasing global competition, have led to the emergence of initiatives aiming at job redesign. There are various trends in job redesign but all types share one or more of the principles as summarized by Littler and Salaman:

1. The scope of the job should include all the tasks necessary to complete a product or process.
2. Incorporation of control and monitoring of tasks.
3. Task variety: workers should understand the general principles of a range of tasks so that job rotation is possible.
4. Self-regulation of the speed of work and some choice over work methods and work sequence.
5. A job structure that permits some social interaction and co-operation among workers. (Littler and Salaman 1984 pp. 80–81)

It will be evident that changes in the organization of work along these lines would significantly enlarge the autonomy of those workers whose job consists of performing low-skilled repetitive tasks. The greater range of individual tasks, the expansion of the worker's survey of the production process by including the planning and control of the work of his workteam or department, the extension of networks of social interaction and co-operation and so on generate opportunities to gain knowledge and develop capacities which underpin the competence to participate in decision-making processes.

However, questions concerning the real extent of job redesign programmes and the scope of workers which might benefit from them have been at the centre of heated debate. Indeed, the opposite position has been argued strongly. Orthodox labour process theory maintains that there is an uninterrupted trend of deskilling, resulting from management's compulsion to assert direct control over workers. It claims that new technologies are designed to arrest any remaining autonomy and control skilled workers may have had. (*cf.* Wood 1989) We will not enter this debate arguing for one overall trend or the other. It seems realistic to assume that a more differentiated pattern of work organization arrangements has emerged and will continue to develop. (Wood 1989 pp. 42–43; Rueschemeyer 1986 pp. 93–99)

Since we are concerned here with the relation between autonomy at work and workers' participation, it is interesting to examine the experiments at job redesign which have been reported from such a point of view. Our interests may be specified by a number of questions. First, which workers will benefit from these new production concepts? Second, will workers who see their autonomy increase participate more actively in company decision-making? Third, will work redesign result in a further loss of autonomy and a further marginalization of those workers who do not belong to the core work-force? We will try to answer these questions in so far as the knowledge we have of these experiments allows us to do so.

Various experiments at job redesign have taken place, notably in the automobile industry. Empirical studies report that in some core sectors of the industry new production concepts seem to be succesful, resulting in the upgrading and integration of different types of tasks. Still, the initial idea that all workers, at least those who have a job in these core sectors (Kern and Schumann 1984 pp. 300–315), might benefit from these new production concepts leading to more highly-skilled integrated jobs has later been qualified by Schumann. On the basis of new research in the automobile industry he estimated that only five per cent of the jobs could be classified as highly-skilled and all-round jobs. (Schumann et al. 1988) It appeared, moreover, that the segmentation between core and peripheral workers was not undone by these new developments. A tentative conclusion may be, therefore, that those workers, particularly those belonging to the periphery, who have the greatest interest in increasing their autonomy, have benefited from these new production concepts so far.

Theoretically one may assume that work redesign programmes will provide those workers who are involved in them with a larger degree of autonomy and an increase of power resources that can be mobilized in gaining access to decision-making processes. Alternatively, it is also conceivable that work redesign results in granting circumscribed spaces of autonomy and maximizing the generation of consent without the authority system being changed.

There are indications from the automobile industry that workers who saw their autonomy expanded did gain greater access to the decision-making process. Worker representatives did not restrict themselves to matters that were brought up for participation by the management but also raised topics of personnel policy, the allocation of rewards and the process of modernizing the organization of work. (Kern and Schumann 1984 pp. 120–121) Edwards, quoting a General Motors Director of Employee Research and Training, suggests that 'management's present monopoly of control can in itself easily become a source of contentior.' (Edwards 1979 p. 156) On the basis of Kern and Schumann's research in the automobile industry, however, it seems more likely that new technologies and new production concepts make for increasing inter-dependence of management and employees. As a result a pragmatic coalition emerges. Employees get a greater say in company policy-making and the agreements they reach contribute simultaneously to management's interest in stability and consensus as a basis of industrial modernization. (Kern and Schumann 1984 pp. 118–119)

There is only some evidence as to what happens to those workers who, in spite of earlier expectations, do not benefit from work redesign programmes. Those workers whose traditional craftsmanship used to grant them a privileged position but whose qualifications are no longer needed due to the new technologies usually continue to be employed with their former income being guaranteed. (Kern and Schumann 1984 p. 123) Because of the ongoing strategy of flexibility through atypical contracts, one may assume that peripheral workers have not seen any improvement of their position. Moreover, when access to core employment is reserved first of all for traditional workers with firm contracts, peripheral workers have little opportunity for mobility.

In the German automobile industry the persistence of segmentation seems to have been helped by the works councils. Works council representatives being recruited from the traditional workforce are more alert in looking after the interests of their colleagues whose job is being threatened than in offering opportunities for peripheral workers. This raises the question whether institutions which are a medium of workers' participation may not be used as an instrument to secure the rights of some and negate the rights of others. We will take up this question in our final section.

Workers' Participation and Solidarity

We noted that workers who occupy marginal jobs, among whom women and immigrants are overrepresented, have hardly any access to participatory institutions. In addition to this we observed that most works council members do not interact frequently with the rank and file whom they are supposed to represent. We think, moreover, that it is not very likely that peripheral workers will benefit from an introduction of work redesign by the management. Combining these considerations we may assume that there is a real danger of those workers who are relatively best off, using the participation opportunities which they have to promote their own interests. Such a kind of workers' participation would clearly not be a full realization of the principle of autonomy (Held 1987 p. 271) which we quoted above, in the sense that the access of some to the specification of the framework of work would negate the rights of others.

If one wishes participation to serve the interests of all employees including those who tend to be excluded, specific arrangements are called for. In our view collective organization is needed, not only for the effective pursuit of given interests but also to guide the definition of these very interests. (Rueschemeyer 1986 p. 102) What is needed, to begin with, is the collective organization of employees at shop-floor level. This should enable all workers to give voice to their respective complaints and wishes. The articulation of specific interests is a condition of finding common ground, though not a sufficient condition.

A trade union policy which aims at solidarity is another condition which assists the development of a kind of inclusive participation. The abstract idea of a non-sectarian solidarity should of course be operationalized in order to provide the collective discussion at shop-floor level with concrete reference points. Against the background of the preceding analysis we suggest that participation and autonomy at work may be a common reference point for all employees, without implying that this would ultimately mean offering every employee the same job.

Both collective organization at shop-floor level and a non-sectional trade union policy are no self-evident conditions in the history of Dutch industrial relations. Dutch trade unions are divided along religious-ideological and occupational lines. Women and immigrant workers are underrepresented among trade union members. (Visser 1991) The two main trade union confederations, however, explicitly have a non-sectionalist programme.

By and large all trade unions in the Netherlands have neglected collective organization at shop-floor level. Traditionally Dutch trade union policy has mainly been directed at national and branch level. (Windmuller 1969 pp. 435–438) During the 1960s and 1970s some unions promoted union organization at shop-floor level but most of them discontinued this policy. Since the mid-1980s it has been resumed in some branches of industry. Research we conducted in the dairy industry (Beukema 1987) and the printing industry and regional transport (Leisink 1989) shows that shop-floor organization and trade union policy may contribute significantly to a powerful and non-sectional promotion of interests by works council members and shop stewards.

In conclusion we must note that the prospects of workers' participation aiming at overcoming segmentation are highly uncertain. It may be that market changes which limit the potential for standardized mass production and open opportunities for less routinized and fragmented work, may offer new opportunities for autonomy and workers' participation. To avail themselves of these opportunities without simultaneously widening the divide between core and peripheral workers, employees need to be backed up by a trade union policy that is not directed at defending vested interests only. A clear choice to overcome segmentation, a creative view on alternative work designs and a constant effort to develop worker competence are essential ingredients of a trade union reply to the dominant trends of decentralization and flexibility. In this way industrial citizenship may come to mean more than a privilege of the core of employees.

11. The Concept of Work in the Trade Unions. Towards a Debate on Economic Rights

Harry Coenen

Introduction

The aim of this article is to make a contribution to the public debate on the concept of work as this is employed by the trade unions. I will emphasize the need of debate about the notion of a basic income scheme joined to the right not to work.

Within the context of this part of the book *Work and Citizenship in the New Europe* it is important to indicate the relevance of the debate on the concept of work for citizenship in general, exactly in an organization such as the trade union.

For various reasons it is important to discuss the trade union's concept of work in the context of the relation between work and citizenship, a fundamental social relation whose potential change will have far-reaching social consequences. As has meanwhile become clear in several countries, it cannot at all be taken for granted that the majority of the population which so far has been – relatively – well-off is prepared to support fundamental changes which may undermine their own position. Social solidarity does not extend that far any more at present. Moreover, the proletariat has made its exit as a revolutionary subject from Eastern Europe too, whereas the new social movements prove not to have the social appeal which many expected or hoped they would have. In such circumstances a lot is to be said for turning our attention to the trade unions, at least if we are not inclined to wait with resignation for various minorities to stir themselves, co-operate, and take the fate of the 'sub-classes' or 'the modern poor' to heart.

The trade union is an organization which has played an important part and gained a lot of experience in acquiring the political and social rights of the welfare state, which have now come under such pressure. Better than any other organization, the trade union knows the tensions which arise in social relationships when efforts are made to humanize labour.

It is pre-eminently aware of the tensed relation between adhering to the existing labour system and the transformation of that system. It has made a great contribution to the acquisition of social rights of citizens, and just such a role will be in store for it, or for a similar organization, in the future acquisition of both social and economic rights of citizens.

Turning our attention to the trade union, however, does not in the least imply that a new relation between work and citizenship can be defined unambiguously in this way. Such certainty is lacking exactly because it is the trade union's commitment to social change which raises some questions. The question, for example, whether an old social movement like the trade union will be capable of renewal without losing its clear identity. I would certainly not venture to answer this question in the affirmative, because at present the realization of the trade union's traditional objectives clashes with the reconsideration and reformulation of these objectives, and the trade union seems to me to be little disposed as yet to overcome this deadlock.

Another question is whether the trade union turns the everyday experience of its citizen members merely into an object of its central policy, or whether it is developing into an organization which takes citizens seriously and makes use of their competence. In the present context, this question has not only a general significance because liberty is a constituent element of citizenship, but it also has a particular significance because so far the trade union has given a virtually democratic-centralist account of solidarity: solidarity means unity, with little or no choice for the individual. This situation has not changed much: suggestions are merely being put forward in the trade union to interpret solidarity not as unity, but as a link between divergent positions, allowing room for mutual differences. (Hoffmann *et al.* 1990)

After these arguments for paying attention to the trade union's concept of work, I would like to make some remarks about the grounds for a debate on the basic income scheme in this context.

Such a debate has an exemplary value: it comprises fundamental as well as controversial issues, while the debate itself has been an important stimulator in questioning the nature of the concept of work and the functioning of the labour system. More pertinent to the context of industrial citizenship and economic rights is the point that a basic income scheme might correct the imbalance existing between employer and employee. Having a basic income linked to a right not to work, citizens would not be compelled to enter into an employment relationship. A basic income would provide all citizens with the resource on the basis of which they are free to choose whether they want a job to supplement basic income and what kind of work they would like to do (referring not only to wages but to the quality of work as well). From the Dutch perspective, it may be added that debates on the concept of work in general and on the basic income scheme in particular have also taken place in trade union circles. There are two reasons why this was possible:

a. The existence of an independent Women's Federation, recognized by the Federation of Dutch Trade Unions (FNV), which has been conducive to the debate on unpaid domestic work.

b. The fact that the Food Workers Union, a medium–sized federation affiliated to the FNV, has for years made the basic income scheme the main issue of its policy.

As I have mentioned above, I intend to contribute to the debate particularly by bringing up subject matter for discussion. I wish to draw attention to some major points which ought to be discussed publicly by paid and unpaid executive staff members in the trade union. However, I will begin by making some remarks about the rise and the future of the modern trade union movement and about the way the concept of work has been dealt with historically by the trade union and the labour movement in general. Subsequently I will enter into the subject of citizenship and the right and the obligation to work.

Rise and Future of the Trade Unions

In the course of the nineteenth century the industrial proletariat came into being as a consequence of the slow but sure disappearance of the old trades with their professional qualifications. The rise of the trade union as a mass organization at the end of the previous and the beginning of this century may be regarded as the collective answer of the industrial proletariat to the new way of mass production in large factories, set up according to the guidelines of Taylor and Ford. The massiveness and uniformity of the way of production is reflected in the collectivization of the workers' individual concerns by the trade union. Since then the trade union has aimed at protecting wage labourers in a uniform way (solidarity is strength) against the ceaseless infringements on their employment, income and social security. Equal pay for equal labour was and is its point of departure: wage labour is still central to trade union policy.

In the last decades of the twentieth century, new technologies, on the basis of microelectronics, have greatly influenced ways of production.

Some call this the third industrial revolution and believe that the end of the system of mass production is at hand. (Piore and Sabel 1984) In its wake, Müller-Jentsch (1988 p. 11) sketches how this will affect the mass trade union movement: membership is becoming much less uniform due to the changes in the production process, and as a consequence it can no longer be taken for granted that a homogenous trade union can satisfy all these various groups. All this is reinforced by the process of state withdrawal, while the social-democrat and denominationally oriented trade union is still incapable of repressing its wish to rely on that (strong) state.

Against this backdrop, questions concerning the trade union's future may have more than one meaning and may be asked with various accentuations. A first possibility is the question whether the trade union has not outlived its usefulness due to the sweeping social changes that have occurred or that are still in the process of occurring. What will be the trade union's future potential to attract groups of employees from those new booming economic sectors?

The question of the trade union's future acquires a different meaning when it is taken to refer to its future as an emancipation movement. This doubt is phrased as follows: is not the crisis of the trade union that it has become or is becoming an elite organization, a stronghold for the relatively strong: those who (still) have paid work? Is the trade union able and prepared now to protect more vulnerable groups such as claimants, women, foreigners and young people, as it protected the wage labourers in the previous century?

Both questions concern the trade union's organizational skills and the groups to whom it attunes – or ought to attune – its policy. The problem which then becomes the centrepiece is whether paid work nowadays can play the same unifying role for the trade union in organizing interests as it played in the past. Within and between the Dutch trade unions that is also a matter of doubt or, respectively, dispute.

Furthermore, there is the question to what extent labour is still a central social issue: is not the environmental issue more dominant? (*cf.* Beck 1986; Touraine, Wieviorka, Dubet 1984) Will the trade union remain focused on labour or will it develop into a social movement co-operating with other social movements and linking up its labour policy with demands that are made by the women's movement and the environmentalists?

Paid work still assumes pride of place in Dutch trade union policies. Issues of unpaid work only play a subordinate role in these policies and are virtually absent from policy considerations. All this despite actions of the Women's Federation and the Food Workers Union, which are often experienced as annoying by other unions. There has been no sign yet of general, publicly-held debates with respect to the central position of paid labour in policy, let alone policy changes. Due to this omission, the possibilities to formulate and implement (new) policies are severely restricted, which does not make the trade union's future look any the brighter, on the contrary. Hence the objective of this contribution: to supply subjects for debate on and within an organization such as the trade union of all organizations, because it is still so very much involved in the way society deals with labour and the way the concept of labour is determined.

First of all, however, I would like to make some remarks on the way the concept of work has historically been treated by the trade union and the labour movement in general. I do so to clarify the relevance of this debate on the concept of work. As will become clear, conceptions of work within socialism have been ambivalent. Without any debate worth mentioning, efforts have been made to put an end to this ambivalence by turning one particular conception of labour into the point of departure for reflection and policy of the left-wing movement. This debate which never took place has presented itself once more in recent years with renewed vigour, due to public interest in the issues of basic income schemes, domestic work, etcetera.

Opportunities for holding the debate have increased, not only because of the higher educational level of the population, but also because the trade union's concept of labour has run up against its limits: a structural lack of opportunities for obtaining wage labour in the current labour system. The debate on work is also being spurred on by various social movements such as the women's movement and the environmentalists.

The Concept of Work within the Labour Movement

Reflection on labour within the labour movement derives its most important impetus from Marx. Referring to Marx does not in the least remove the problems surrounding the concept of labour. On the contrary. According to some interpreters of Marx, such as Kolakowski (1978), Marx himself is a source of confusion surrounding the concept of labour. Conflicting motives are evident in Marx's thought about labour (see Achterhuis 1984 p. 92 *ff.*), several roads lead to the realm of liberty where labour is no longer a burden but a joy. According to these interpretations

Marx employs the concept of labour in two different ways. On the one hand labour belongs to the realm of necessity. From this perspective he looks upon labour as imposed coercion. Reducing or abolishing labour would then have to terminate this coercion too. On the other hand Marx looks upon labour as man's highest value. In the future, he expects, man will find complete self-fulfilment in labour. After the revolution the obligation to work would be perfectly suited to labour as man's prime need.

The principal idea in Marx's thought about labour is the reduction of imposed coercion. Marx was predominantly concerned with the liberation of wage labour. Abolishing wage labour signifies the end of capitalism, in which man works to live, and heralds the beginning of socialism, in which man lives to work. Marx shares his bourgeois-opponents' appreciation of capitalism, for that matter, as regards the great progress it brought about in the productivity of labour.

Besides thoughts on the liberation of wage labour, we encounter to a lesser extent ideas in Marx tending in another direction: the liberation from labour. Arguing from this perspective, Marx advocates pushing back labour as much as possible. Then he postulates that the realm of liberty starts only where labour stops.

Paul Lafargue, Marx's son-in-law, is diametrically opposed to his father-in-law in his conceptions about labour, at least where the latter describes labour as the highest human value. Lafargue (1974) proclaims the right to laziness and counters the right to work. His ideas go well with fantasies of Cockaigne. He remarks for instance:

> A strange insanity keeps the workers of the capitalist civilized countries captive ... That insanity is the love of labour, going so far as to exhaust the vigour of the individual and his off-spring. The medieval craftsman still had ninety compulsory rest days (52 Sundays and 38 holidays), but the protestantism of the tradesmen and industrialists dethroned the saints in heaven so as to abolish their holidays on earth. (van Strien 1978 p. 167)

For Lafargue labour is a terrible nuisance. Nor is he the only one in the socialist movement, or on its periphery, with such a view. Lafargue is a figure of importance and *The Right to Laziness* is an important book. He emphatically makes use of Marx's analyses. There is, however, one major difference between Marx and Lafargue: according to the latter not only the capitalists but also the workers have themselves to blame for their exploitation. They are incriminated because their religious attachment to labour prevents them from rising against bourgeois society.

As early as the previous century Lafargue's ideas were banished from the labour movement. Bernstein made a start by removing the subtitle of *The Right to Laziness* – 'Refutation of the right to work'. Within really existing socialism Lafargue was indeed granted a prominent place in the historical surveys, but *The Right to Laziness* was never mentioned, which makes sense with a view to the enormous emphasis which was put on the obligation to work by the state and the party. This emphasis is considered justified because the state ensures that the right to work is substantiated: there is work for everyone, there is no unemployment according to official sources. Those selfsame sources fail to add that the right to work only existed in a formal sense, and that there were far-reaching material limitations as regards one's liberty to choose a profession and a place of residence according to one's own judgement and preference.

Citizenship and the Right and the Obligation to Work

The above-mentioned will suffice to indicate the ambivalence in thought about work. It indicates to a lesser extent (only in the last few remarks) how a one-sided stand was taken without any debate with respect to this ambivalence. A procedure which has continued to determine thought about work to the present day, within the trade union too, and which clearly finds expression in thought about the obligation to work and the right to work.

The right to work was first formulated by Louis Blanc in 1848. Blanc was well aware of the relativity of such a right. For what use is this right to someone who possesses no power? What use is the right to a cure to a terminal patient? (*cf.* Köbben 1988)

The right to work is included in the Universal Declaration of Human Rights. In the Netherlands the right to work is not laid down in the constitution. In 1983, however, the following cautious provision was included in the constitution: 'The promotion of sufficient employment is an object of care of the state'. This provision only indicates that exactly at a time of economic recession – such as the beginning of the eighties – the government, even a withdrawing government, cannot escape its duties with respect to employment. This does not in any way mean that the government will create job opportunities, though, formally speaking at least, it would have been obliged to do so – just as in the countries behind the former Iron Curtain – had the right to work been constitutionally laid down.

The remarks above are made from the viewpoint of a positive appreciation of the right to work. The reference to really existing socialism, with its right and obligation to work, which has given rise to a situation in which an unemployed person is regarded as a state enemy, shows the reverse side of the right to work. Against this backdrop, a simple positive appreciation of the right to work falls short. The issue is more complicated than that, and the concept of citizenship may be useful in putting the right to work into perspective and in determining the balance between the right and the obligation to work.

In the Netherlands everybody has the right to vote (in so far as one has Dutch nationality) but there is no compulsory voting. This is optimal liberty: one may but need not vote. Compulsory voting would imply a restriction of the liberty of one's right to vote. The vote offers citizens opportunities which they can seize or not as they see fit.

With the right to work and the obligation to work, matters are exactly the other way round. Nobody has the formal right to work, but in social security regulations and in public opinion there is such a notion as the obligation to work and derivations from that notion, such as the obligation to apply for jobs. There can be no optimum liberty here when one has to sell one's labour force without anyone else having to buy it. Large sections of the left-wing in general, and the trade unions in particular, play a considerable role in public opinion. They fear that the government will cease to concern itself about employment if they do not keep insisting on the obligation to work.

Nevertheless it is a moot question if the trade union is doing itself and its members a good turn by taking up a line of 'one good deed deserves another' with respect to citizens' social rights. This is more or less a tough variety of the position which was imported from the United States and which reads that poverty is not the problem, but the non-participation of the poor in society is, because they have more rights than duties. (Mead 1986)

The trade unions in the Netherlands are not appreciably rewarded by the government for this 'tough' attitude which, moreover, might well imply an impairment of citizenship. For Dahrendorf (1988a) at least the emphasis on discharging one's duties in order to acquire or preserve one's rights is a reprehensible matter. Pursuing such a policy and thinking in that way impair the core of citizenship. For him equality and liberty go hand in hand with the notion of citizenship: equal opportunities, not as an actually existing situation in society, but as rights with accompanying facilities open to everyone; liberty to make citizenship as accessible as possible to as many citizens as possible, and liberty to avail oneself at will of the rights and facilities intended for all citizens. 'In principle the rights of citizenship are not conditional. What citizenship offers does not depend on the readiness of people to pay a price in the private domain'. (Dahrendorf 1988a p. 34) That way the citizen remains free and the state is prevented from predominating.

If the trade union wishes to maintain the attainments of citizenship, in whose development it has played a major role, if it does not wish to revert to a lower level of rights, it will have to keep advocating equal rights and equal duties for all, and it will have to advocate those rights for citizens which are attainable as civil rights.

The impossibility of determining a right to work for all citizens in the current social constellation is based on the fact that labour is realized in private contracts between persons in unequal power relations, which are only equalized to a very limited extent by the present civil rights. These unequal relations between private persons do not play a role in realizing the right to vote, which is a right in which only the relation between the state and the citizen matters. That is why this right may serve as a model for other civil rights. In an attempt to rule out unequal relations in the economic domain, really existing socialism opted for public ownership but meanwhile it has become clear that there are too many disadvantages to this 'solution'.

What to think and what to do? Abandoning the pursuit of the right to work entirely seems premature. It concerns an extremely important right, whose realization has been aimed at for quite some time by many a social movement. Perhaps the thought process may be helped on by referring to the historical development which citizenship has undergone up to the present day and which, supposedly, has not finished as yet. In his renowned study of citizenship, Marshall (1973) distinguishes between three stages in the historical development of citizenship in the United Kingdom: in the eighteenth century civil rights came into being, in the nineteenth century political rights and in the twentieth century social rights. Against this backcloth, the inclusion of the right to work (meaning paid work) in the Universal Declaration of Human Rights may be considered the herald of the twenty-first century development in which the economic rights of citizens are about to be realized.

In order to be able to realize economic citizenship, sweeping changes will have to occur, not only in trade union policy and in the way citizens think and act, but also in the general conventions, norms and rules bearing on labour. The concept of work will be central to the debate which is to be held. Dichotomies such as labour versus non-labour, labour versus leisure, paid versus unpaid work will have to be discarded. In this differentiation of the concept of labour, Gorz's work (1989a; 1989b) may play an inspiring role.

I hasten to add that the above merely sketches the outline of a possible development. There can be no such thing as an irreversible evolutionary process in which the political rights grew to full stature in the previous century and will turn out to have been maintained of their own accord in the next century. (*cf.* Held 1987) So although this sketch may appear somewhat too evolutionistic, putting it this way has the advantage of offering a way of grasping the tension in the development of citizenship. The current tension is caused by the fact that economic citizenship is already presenting itself on the one hand, whereas profound controversies concerning the possibilities and impossibilities of realizing social citizenship are rampant on the other hand. In this situation a right has meanwhile been formulated which is characteristic of the above-mentioned tension. That right has been designated in negative terms as the right not to work by Dahrendorf among others. In order to be able to realize this right, he advocates the introduction of a basic income scheme, which in his view will encourage citizens to look after themselves as they will no longer be dependent on the market value of their labour force. In this way Dahrendorf believes that the paradoxical development of a growing economy on the one hand and growing poverty on the other may be arrested and replaced by a growth of citizenship, which has not occurred during the past decade. The right not to work, linked to the introduction of a basic income scheme, implies a reinforcement of the possibilities to realize both social and economic citizenship. If this right is realized, it will strongly support citizens in their search for paid work in the present circumstances, both because they will be less obliged to accept paid work of any quality whatever and because the choice between paid and unpaid work becomes a valid one. Put that way, it is a first concretization of economic citizenship.

The right not to work goes well with the concept of citizenship because it promotes the equality and liberty of all citizens and because it can be applied unconditionally: it does not impose duties in order to acquire or safeguard rights.

There is, however, also a problem involved in the right not to work. What work will we have the right to refuse? A moot question, even if it seems self-evident that we are talking about the right to obtain paid work, because there is no trace of social consensus on the question what work ought to be paid (*cf.* the debate on domestic labour).

Finally a remark provoked by the ideas of Marx, which were presented as ambivalent. Have I not taken up a comparable position in the above by advocating both the right to work and the right not to work? I can only answer this question in the affirmative. Nevertheless I do not wish to drop the right to work, while I also stick to my view that formulating the right not to work is necessary, not only in order to be able to debate the matter with clarity, but also to make new developments possible. Perhaps the above-mentioned ambivalence will be solved in the future. It is conceivable at least: the right not to look for a job in its current sense of wage labour, but instead to perform socially meaningful work which is unpaid work as yet, with a basic income plus a possible extra allowance as remuneration.

The Debate on Work in the Trade Unions

The proposed right not to work linked to a basic income scheme, plus the concomitant debate on the concept of work, put the trade union-movement in a very uncomfortable position because it has made itself part of the majority in the labour movement without much debate as regards content and has only concerned itself with problems regarding the liberation of wage labour, rather than with problems regarding liberation from wage labour. It is precisely this distinction as such which has now come under attack in proposals for a basic income scheme and in the debate on the concept of work.

Avoidance of this debate or its being conducted too inadequately to have any consequences for policy will lead to a situation in which the trade union changes into an elite organization which only has eyes for the concerns of the strong who still have paid work, and which is no longer able or willing to contribute to the reinforcement of citizenship in general and the emancipation of more vulnerable groups in particular. In that case, Dahrendorf (1988b) has rightly announced the end of the trade union and Gorz (1980) would be right after all in dismissing the trade unions as an emancipatory movement.

The gravity of the situation is reflected in the items which need to be entered on the agenda for the debate within the trade unions. Amendments to the proposal will obviously remain possible. The choice of subjects is predicated by the desire to prevent the trade union movement from not debating an important issue at a time when historic choices have to be made, as has happened before in the past.

After the preceding, the following subjects for debate will not be a cause for great surprise:

a. trends which lie at the root of the fundamental social and political reorientation which are expressed in the debate on the concept of work in general and the basic income scheme in particular;

b. the concept of work;

c. the basic income scheme.

The first two subjects provide a framework for the debate on the basic income scheme. They follow naturally from the train of thought which has been developed in the preceding, so that my position in the debate on the basic income scheme is clear, where I sketch a relationship between the main points which have been put forward by supporters and opponents of the basic income scheme.

For the debate on trends (a) I would like to refer, for brevity's sake, to a concise summary by Mückenburger, Offe and Ostner (1989 pp. 175–176):

> There are unmistakable signs of a crisis of the labour market and the welfare state which can no longer be solved by the means which have been employed so far.
> With the failure of a model of social progress which is based on full employment, economic growth and social security, the drawbacks of the system also come to light. Some of these are: the centrality of the industrial view of society in which the normal course of life of the individual is based on paid work; the exclusion of women from this view; the destruction of traditional forms of labour and living which are not organized via the labour market or the state; the overloading of the environment.
> A traditional strategy aimed at full employment by means of more growth, either by means of 'more growth', or by means of 'more market', or by means of 'more state' seems an illusion. Such a return to the model which is considered 'normal' is economically not feasible, ecologically not justifiable, and socially irresponsible.

For the debate on the concept of work (b) I would like to draw attention to the creative work of André Gorz (1989), who has concerned himself systematically with a redefinition of the concept of work.

In his treatment of the concept of work, Gorz does not opt for the common distinction between paid and unpaid work.

> This we consider the strength of the concept of work developed by Gorz. He attempts to reveal what the consequences are of paying particular activities and organizing these activities in the shape of jobs. That way he tries to develop criteria for a choice between shaping such activities into paid jobs or not. (van Berkel and Hindriks 1991 pp. 85–86)

Gorz wants to have done with what he calls the 'ideology of jobs for the sake of jobs', that is the tendency to ward off the crisis of paid work by organizing a growing number of activities in the shape of paid jobs. Only one kind of work qualifies for payment as a matter of course. That is economically rational labour: labour which creates practical value, that is labour yielding more or better products than the buyer himself can make; which is carried out not in a relationship of personal dependency but in the public domain; and which makes maximum productivity possible, that is labour which is measurable in time so that time can be saved.

It is participation in economically rational labour exclusively which, according to Gorz, contributes to full citizenship, rather than participation in paid work generally. As examples of paid work which does not contribute to emancipation he mentions not only domestic service, social work and service industries, but also surveillance and control activities.

Besides income-generating activities, Gorz also distinguishes work-for-oneself (production of consumer commodities, the producer of which is at the same time the consumer) and autonomous activities (which are a goal in themselves, not subjected to an external goal).

Finally the debate on the basic income scheme (c). Let me first of all mention a number of subjects for debate which are raised by opponents of the basic income scheme.
- Labour and labour conflicts have not lost any of their political importance and ought to remain a priority in the shaping of society.
- Labour is easy to politicize: problems in the area of labour relating to the autonomy of employees in their jobs and the remuneration for their work are clearly familiar to many.
- Introduction of the basic income scheme erodes the right to work and does not contribute to a distribution of power.
- The solidarity between the employed and claimants is at issue. Opponents of the basic income scheme fear that the basic income scheme will do away with this solidarity. Also because the solidarity of the employed with claimants has a drawback: the distance between wages and unemployment benefits ought not to become too small.
- A further democratization of the welfare state, decentralization, and a great influence of clients ought to remain the main issues of the political debate.

What subjects for debate, finally, are brought up by those who hold that labour and income ought to be unlinked further, the supporters of the basic income scheme?

- The proposition that it is time rather than work which is central to the shaping of one's personal life and of society. Labour ought not to be the most important political controversy any longer.
- The second point concerns the relation between labour and leisure. The commonest form of this relation is based on the situation of the full-time employed, and the question is to what extent full-time work is still desirable and to what extent it is still attainable by the many.
- The basic income scheme is an effective means of meeting the demands of an ongoing individualization and of taking measures against an increasing state control.
- A concept such as the basic income scheme makes it possible to search for a combination of social self-determination and minimal governmental tasks. This does not render government redundant: the point of departure being that the government supplies a set of things which people do not control (such as a minimum wage and minimal basic facilities). In this view the loyalty of citizens is based on a government taking a modest position and acting fairly.
- The basic income scheme is economically founded on the fact that labour will get cheaper. Net wages are going down, since earnings will be supplementary. Both for the government and for business, therefore, a saving in expenses occurs. On top of that, the basic income scheme encourages a further redistribution of paid labour.

At present the concept of citizenship is prevalent both in social–scientific and in political debates. It offers good prospects to keep debating important concepts such as liberty and equality at a time when familiar ideologies such as liberalism and socialism are liable to wear, and the distrust of 'grand narratives' is considerable.

Yet the concept of citizenship means different things to various parties to the debate on labour participation by citizens. Some will have the present social order and its economic system function as well as possible by letting as many citizens as possible participate in paid work (WRR 1990). Others have little or no faith in its future prospects and try to develop new concepts. (Beck 1986; Coenen 1992; among others)

Both strategies are represented in the trade union. Its policy programme reflects the actual social development with respect to (paid) work. Its actions demonstrate the feasibility of innovation proposals with respect to the labour system in the foreseeable future. As regards that I see no reason for great optimism, but at any rate the trade union is one card in the pack which must be played.

Part IV

Work, Rights and Obligations

12. Labour Force Participation, Citizenship and a Sustainable Welfare State in the Netherlands

Hans Adriaansens and Willem Dercksen

Unemployment Versus Labour Force Participation

Socio-economic problems in the Netherlands have always been analysed in terms of employment and, particularly, unemployment. The problem with this line of reasoning is that it starts from an only seemingly unproblematic notion of what the labour force consists of. As far as unemployment statistics are concerned, they do not usually account for the socio-cultural peculiarities which make for an extended or a restricted labour force. The decision as to who do and who do not form part of the labour force is usually taken for granted. If it is considered normal for women not to work, they are not seen as belonging to the labour force. The labour force will then be small and unemployment figures will relate only to a seriously limited part of the population. If by contrast female employment is socially and culturally accepted in the formal labour circuit, the labour force will be large and unemployment figures relate to a substantially larger proportion of the population. International comparison of unemployment statistics tends to ignore such socio-cultural differences and therefore provides us with an unreliable picture of the employment situation in a specific country.

With respect to socio-economic policy, analysis in terms of unemployment also has its disadvantages. For as long as unemployment figures in the Netherlands are at approximately the same level as those in other Western countries, it remains tempting to think that unemployment is a consequence of rather autonomous macro-economic developments and has nothing to do with national policies. If, by contrast, one realizes that under these comparable unemployment figures major differences in labour force participation rates are hidden (in some cases by more than 20 percentage points!), national socio-economic policies suddenly become important once again. In yet another respect the focus on unemployment has made for policy-lines which, from the point of view of

191

labour force participation, seem at least paradoxical if not ridiculous now: measures to combat unemployment, such as redistribution of work, as a matter of fact reduced the size of the labour force! The net result of many people making use of pre-retirement or disability schemes is, of course, that unemployment decreases. This may flatter the overall picture (for they simply disappear from official statistics), but it does not alter the often dramatic reality of employment and labour force participation.

Labour force participation is therefore a better concept to start from than unemployment. It is defined as the ratio of the number of people in paid employment and the population aged between 15 and 65 years (excluding students). In doing so it becomes clear that unemployment is just one of the factors which keeps down the participation rate. Other forms, whether they be 'hidden' or 'desired', are disability, sickness, pre-retirement and various forms of non-paid labour. By placing labour force participation at the centre of attention these other factors come more clearly into view. Disability, for example, has now become a much larger problem in the Netherlands than officially registered unemployment. Out of every hundred people in the labour force, 14 receive a disability benefit. This ratio is two to three times as high as in neighbouring countries. (Prins 1990; Aarts and de Jong 1990) International comparison of participation rates shows differences which cannot easily be explained by macro-economic developments alone. Institutional and socio-cultural explanations are needed to get a clear picture of what these differences are about.

Low Participation: the Weak Spot of the Dutch Welfare State

International comparison shows that labour force participation in the Netherlands is relatively low. Since the mid-1950s – when the welfare state came into being – the participation rate has gradually declined. This trend was not finally reversed until the second half of the 1980s, thanks primarily to the growth of part-time employment. The present level, however, is still several percentage points below the 1960 rate. By international standards the Netherlands have a low participation rate, particularly when measured in man-years (full-time jobs). In comparison with the United States, Japan and the Scandinavian countries, most EC-countries have low rates of labour force participation. The participation rate is 71 in Japan, 72 in the USA, and 78 in the Scandinavian countries. The weighted average for the EC member states is 59. (1987 figures) Within the EC, participation rates differ considerably between member states. In Spain, the Netherlands, Ireland, Italy, France, Greece and Belgium the participation rate is under average. When the amount of part-time labour is accounted for, Spain and the Netherlands have an extremely low labour force participation. The Dutch rate is six percentage points below the EC-average, that is six full-time jobs per hundred adults.

Table 12.1
Labour Participation Rates in European Community Countries in Persons and Man-Years, 1987

Countries	total		men		women	
	(1)	(2)	(1)	(2)	(1)	(2)
Portugal	63	63	81	83	53	50
Luxembourg	65	62	87	86	46	40
Denmark	78	62	84	74	72	49
FR of Germany	63	60	77	78	50	41
United Kingdom	68	56	77	74	58	37
Belgium	56	53	69	70	44	36
Greece	54	53	72	73	37	33
France	59	53	70	68	48	38
Italy	54	50	73	71	35	30
Ireland	51	49	68	70	33	27
Netherlands	58	47	73	65	42	26
Spain	46	44	65	63	27	24
EC-average	59.0	53.3	73.0	71.5	44.9	35.0

(1) Labour force participation in persons
(2) Labour force participation in man-years

Based on: OECD, *Historical Statistics 1960–1987* Paris, 1989

The question can be asked whether such a low participation rate constitutes a real problem. For in terms of the 1970s' 'leisure society' it might even be regarded as an accomplishment. Similarly in terms of the family-centred philosophy of the 1950s and 1960s, a low level of labour force participation generally did not pose a problem, as long as there was sufficient employment for breadwinners. In those days a country was regarded as 'affluent' and 'rich' if it could permit its women, children and elderly people to remain outside the industrial labour system. Seen in this light it also becomes understandable that 'full employment' was achieved in that period at a relatively low participation rate.

Instead of unemployment, the low level of labour force participation is the key problem of the Dutch welfare state in general, and its social security system in particular. The ratio between economically active and inactive people has much to do with the volume of social security spending. The affordability of the increasing claims on social security facilities and schemes was one of the main reasons for the Dutch government to review expenditure programmes in the 1980s. The past 30 years have seen a substantial rise in the number of benefit claimants. Whereas the figure was just 1.2 million in 1960, by 1985 it had risen to 3.77 million and in 1990 it exceeded the 4 million mark. The ratio between employed people and benefit claimants (that is, between the economically active and inactive people) therefore changed substantially during that period: from 3.4:1 in 1960 to 1.3:1 in 1984. Since that time no further changes have taken place in the ratio up to 1990, and no further changes are anticipated in the next few years. If old-age pensioners are left out of account, the distortion in the ratio becomes even more dramatic: whereas each benefit claimant in 1960 was matched by nearly 13 employed people, the figure since 1985 has dropped below three. Looking further to the future, the ratio including old-age pensioners will once again come under pressure with the ageing of the population. Naturally these developments have boosted the volume of spending considerably. Until 1960 income transfers amounted to no more than 10 per cent of net national income, whereas in 1991 it had risen to 29 per cent.

In the remainder of this contribution we will first go into the main institutional and socio-cultural factors which can be held responsible for the predicament of the (Dutch) welfare state. Then we will discuss the main reasons why a higher labour force participation level is necessary. In the next section, labour force participation will be related to the concept of citizenship. The last section will deal with concrete participation policies which should be pursued if a higher level of labour force participation, and consequently a serious implementation of social citizenship, are to be realized.

The Rise and Fall of the Dutch Welfare State

After the Second World War there was a general conviction that the unemployment of the 1930s could be avoided. Full employment could be attained by Keynesian methods. It became one of the principle objectives of socio-economic policy and it even became codified as such in the 1950s. Several decades later, in 1983 to be precise, at the very point where the axiomatic nature of full employment was once again swept aside by the wave of mass redundancies, the objective of full employment was even enshrined in the Dutch Constitution. The formulation, however, reflected the hard times and was in fact rather cautious.

The original foundations of the welfare state go back far into Dutch history. For our purposes, however, it is sufficient to look back at the 1950s and 1960s. Two basic principles formed the foundation of the construction which we now know as the welfare state: a dominant industrial economy, underpinned by a religiously inspired work ethic, and a dominant family philosophy, in which the (male) breadwinner was responsible for the economic independence of the family household and his (female) partner for the family's well-being. As it developed, the welfare state (that is, the system of welfare arrangements) was moulded by these uncontested starting points. During the 1950s and 1960s this system of foundations and arrangements developed into a successful discourse. The marriage between the traditional economy and family philosophy resulted in an ever more advanced system of social security and welfare.

Since the 1970s the situation has changed. What happened was that the two pillars of the welfare state edifice have been shaken over the past two decades. Both the traditional family philosophy and the religiously inspired work ethic have changed radically. The industrial economy of the twentieth century underwent a development towards an economy of a 'post-industrial' type. As part of this process, science, technology and (international) economic competition have radically changed the face of work. This amounts to a shift in work based, broadly speaking, on human muscle power to work based on mental capacity. Computerization has not just reduced industrial labour demand but has also changed the quality of work. Old industries have died out and totally new ones have arisen. Tertiary and non-profit sectors have evolved. Since 1970 the latter categories account for over half of total employment (measured in man-years) in the Netherlands, and for 67 per cent in 1987. Employment in the industrial or manufacturing sector now accounts for only 27 per cent of total employment, and agriculture for just 6 per cent. Besides, the increasing industrialization in both the Third World countries and the East Newly Industrializing Countries (NICs) has led to a further decline in industrial employment in the West, thereby accelerating the emergence of the post-industrial society. Industrial activity itself has also become more knowledge-intensive, thereby placing new demands on training and education levels. The result has been an erosion of the relative share of unskilled professions in employment.

Apart from these shifts in nature and scale of employment, radical changes have also taken place in the are(n)a of household formation. These have had major consequences for both the production and the consumption side of the economy. The trend towards individualization has meant that families in recent years have generally become smaller; that a shift towards a more equal sharing of tasks has begun to take place within families; that new forms of primary relationships have evolved; and that the number of one-person households has grown strikingly. This has placed the traditional breadwinner structure of the labour economy under a lot of pressure: consequently, a movement towards a more individualized employment and wage structure can be observed. Various categories of people, such as women, who previously entered the labour market on a very limited scale and, given that prospect, had no great interest in education or training, are now anxious to apply their educational qualifications in the formal labour system.

Thanks to such major developments as the restructuring of the economy and the individualization process, the pillars of the traditional welfare state began to erode. The economy got its post-industrial flavour and the traditional focus of family dependence was – at least to some extent – replaced by new and more individualistic structures. The building itself, that is, this complex bundle of institutions and arrangements which we used to call 'welfare state' proved to be such a stable construction in itself that at first it did not give in: no visible cracks in the ceilings, not even in the wallpaper. It was not until the late 1970s that these cracks indeed became visible. The welfare state building was shaken to its very foundations. From that moment on the welfare state became a politically and economically contested issue.

Starting in 1979 unemployment grew at a very fast rate until it reached its peak in 1984. For a lot of people unemployment became long-term unemployment, and many turned their backs on the labour market and found alternative ways of life. The absence of sufficient labour market provisions such as training, places to obtain new work-experience or additional (temporary) jobs enabled them to do so. Moreover, in the 1980s the number of people receiving disability benefits continued to grow at a fast rate, as disability regulations were – and still are – misused as a so-called 'social' route of premature exit. Finally, starting with the 1982 Central Agreement between federations of employers and unions on wages and redistribution of work, the number of pre-retired also grew enormously. In 1990 one out of every three men aged 60–65 was on a pre–retirement scheme. To a certain degree these three routes of premature exit are communicating vessels, pre-retirement being financially the most, and unemployment the least attractive for those concerned. In the 1990s these three regulations of premature exit together have become a main cause of the low participation rate in the Netherlands.

It was not before the second half of the 1980s that the Swedish active labour market policy attracted Dutch attention. Sweden had succeeded in maintaining a very low level of unemployment. Starting from the premise that the Swedish model (as it existed until 1991) is indissolubly bound up with an active labour market policy, but that such a policy is not indissolubly bound up with the Swedish model (*cf.* Meidner 1990), an active labour market policy is now gradually being implemented in the Netherlands. This implementation is difficult and time-consuming.

The absence of sufficient active labour market measures in the 1980s has disturbed the balance between rights and duties. Unemployed and recipients of disability benefits were offered, as a matter of fact, a free choice between withdrawing from the labour market and an (in many cases desperate) effort to (re-)enter. Now that the labour market situation has changed, neither all long-term unemployed, nor all recipients of disability benefits who have a capacity to work, are eager to re-enter the labour process or to participate in training and work-experience places, especially when they regard low qualified jobs or job prospects. Moreover, very often financial incentives are absent or meagre. It now gradually dawns upon the boards and administrations of the social security system that the choice between full benefits or paid employment should not be left entirely free any more, as became practice in the 1980s due to the lack of jobs.

Regulations allowing or providing premature exit are one cause of the low employment rate. Breadwinner provisions enabling partners (in practice women) to withdraw from the labour market without causing undue effects on the household's income are a second cause. Examples of breadwinner provisions are to be found in the transferable personal tax allowance on income tax, the non-contributory status of dependent partners in the national old-age pension scheme and national health insurance, and in the statutory minimum wage.

The third cause is what may be called a 'negative cycle'. The crisis of the early 1980s triggered a downward spiral in which the high costs of labour are preventing many low-skilled people from getting jobs, as a result of which they cannot but claim welfare benefits, which in themselves raise labour costs once again. This downward spiral has contributed to a situation in which the Dutch welfare state does not seem to be able any more to provide those who need it with what they can rightfully claim, as too many people have become victims of a typically Dutch and therefore idiosyncratic socio-economic policy.

Arguments to Raise the Level of Labour Force Participation

There are many reasons why participation policies should be pursued. To a certain degree these reasons also apply to other EC-countries, especially those with a lower than average participation rate.

The first argument is of a sociological nature. Employment is an important form of social participation. By means of (paid) employment individuals contribute significantly to the maintenance and further development of the system of social relations that makes up society. The lower the proportion of the population participating in society through employment, the heavier the burden on other institutions to generate the necessary social cohesion. Precisely at the present time, in which traditional integrative links such as the church, family and neighbourhood are subject to erosion, and insufficient new institutions are emerging to take over these functions of social integration, participation in the labour system is a significant factor for social cohesion. A higher level of labour force participation is also consonant with a society in which individualization and other demographic trends mean that only a minority of the population will live in single-income households consisting of a husband, wife and children.

Secondly, demographic developments will put an extra burden on European welfare states in terms of social security, health care and social services. Other things remaining equal, demographic pressures will raise the number of benefit claimants even further and diminish the number of workers in paid employment. In the Netherlands, as well as in all other

EC-countries, this is due to a decreasing number of young people and the ageing of the working-age population; consequently the number of unemployed, disabled and pre-retired people will grow. In most EC-countries the percentage of people older than 65 will also grow. (ILO 1989) A demographic projection for the Netherlands provides an impression of the influence of demographic trends on social security (including old-age pensions). Instead of the present 65 benefit claimants for every hundred persons in paid employment (1990), the corresponding number of benefit claimants will rise to 70 in 2000, 80 in 2010 and 93 in 2020. (WRR 1990) If expressed in man-years (full-time jobs) and 'full' benefits, the 1990 ratio is considerably higher: 86. The future trend of this ratio is comparable to that of the ratio in terms of persons.

The maintenance of living standards in both absolute and relative terms poses a fundamental economic argument for a higher level of labour force participation. The achievement of a broader base for social security can provide a significant impulse for economic growth. That impulse may derive from both an increase in the number of persons in paid employment and a reduction in the number of benefit claimants. The improved utilization of the 'human capital' formed by education – especially among women – is another significant economic argument for a higher level of labour force participation.

Unemployment, including hidden unemployment among females and disability benefit claimants, is expensive in an economic sense, particularly if the unemployment is protracted, and it is socially unacceptable. The desire of a large and increasing number of women for paid employment is one argument for pursuing a higher level of labour force participation. In addition a large number of unemployed experience unemployment as something decidedly negative, without being able to find a job, whereas others turn their backs on the labour market and drop out of the labour system. Many disability benefit claimants aspire to a paid job; even if this were not so, there are good reasons for helping those physically and mentally capable of doing so to return to work fitting their capacities.

The last argument is of an international political nature. Because of the process of European integration, member countries will increasingly be exposed to policy competition from abroad. For countries with a low rate of labour force participation (in man-years), an effort to attain a level not too different from that in competitor countries is opportune. Although countries do not compete in terms of the actual rate of participation, the effects of such participation, including the level of taxation and social security contributions, in turn affect the competitiveness of private industry and the government's financial room for manoeuvre. The latter in turn affects a country's ability to compete in terms of education and the physical and scientific infrastructure.

Labour Force Participation and Citizenship

The massive unemployment following the second oil-crisis led to renewed attention to what T.H. Marshall as early as 1950 referred to as the social dimension of citizenship: a 'decent' standard of living, education and health care. The project of citizenship proved to be vulnerable in the 1980s. Rights of citizens had to be curtailed because of the economic crisis. In the Netherlands this vulnerability was aggravated by the low participation rate.

The number of adults not participating in paid employment, has grown during the past decades. As a result of intended and unintended consequences of welfare state arrangements, many categories that are hard to define have settled on the continuum of a hundred per cent employment disability on the one hand and full-time labour force participation on the other. From a macro-perspective, for most groups on this continuum, the standard of a 'decent' living is related to the combination of the participation rate (in man-years), and the degree of social solidarity that can be generated.

Broadly speaking, two opposing future policy options have been put on the agenda. One may be referred to as activating social policies, the other as the basic income option. Their common denominator is to go along on the path of social citizenship.

Therborn referred to the Netherlands as a 'soft' welfare state. (Therborn 1986) Insufficient provisions are institutionalized to prevent and combat unemployment, disability and pre-retirement. 29 per cent of Netherlands Gross Domestic Product (GDP) regard income transfers, of which one-third is for unemployment, sickness and disability benefits. In the OECD the proportion of transfer expenditure in GDP is ten percentage points less. (OECD 1991) One remedy is to be found in the concept of an activating welfare state. The primary objective of such a welfare state is in providing people with opportunities to participate in paid employment: directly, or indirectly, by way of training, counselling, work-experience places, sheltered jobs, temporary jobs, child care, parental leave, and so on. Income support is considered as a second-best option in an activating welfare state. This concept not only applies to social security, but to other social services as well. A main objective of social services might be to activate people to help themselves as much as possible, instead of treating them as mere objects of professional care.

The opposite policy option is to take the number of adults not in touch with the labour process for granted. One version is the basic income option, for instance by way of a negative income tax. The advantages of this policy option are clear (as far as a basic income may allow for a decent standard of living). It implies freedom for citizens not to opt for a job and it releases those citizens who are unable to find a job from the duty to be available for work at short notice. Moreover, a basic income is said to be a solution to poverty traps. Finally, it fits what Dahrendorf refers to as a 'free society', a society 'which offers chances and does not impose ways of using them'. (Dahrendorf 1988a)

A material objection is the affordability of a 'decent' basic income. A replacement of the actual income support provisions by a(n) (individualized) basic income would be too expensive, because non-working adults who do not yet receive social security (mainly housewives) would also be entitled ot it. Another objection is that a basic income implies cutting the link between labour and income. This is not without serious risks. Young people might be encouraged to opt for a basic income and to drop out of school prematurely and uncertificated. This might cause unbridgeable time-lags if they should desire alternative options later on in adult life. In a certain way this argument also applies to adults turning their backs to the labour system, and consequently losing skills and work-experience. A basic income also enlarges the risk for society of not being able to afford 'decent' minimum standards of living. This applies especially to the Netherlands because of its low participation rate. Finally, the basic income option is principally contestable in so far as it discharges citizens from the duty to take part in the social division of labour. At the same time a basic income may function as a legitimation not to provide job-seekers sufficient opportunities for (re-)entering the labour system.

Policies Towards Labour Force Participation

There are a large number of policy options for increasing the employment rate. Effective policies should be in line with major developments like the restructuring of the economy and the individualization process.

A central objective of all the policy options will be to create a 'positive cycle'. This should be understood as follows. In the Netherlands the low participation rate is related to substantial costs of social security. The resulting taxes and social premiums lead to high wage costs which in turn depress the level of employment. By an increase in the participation rate the burden of transfer incomes will fall, with a consequent decline in wage costs. As a result, on the basis of the laws of supply and demand, the demand for labour (that is employment) will increase. A reduction in the burden of taxation and social insurance contributions will also significantly boost purchasing power, which will in turn have a positive effect on employment. In this way an increase in the labour force participation rate can have a flywheel effect.

The flywheel effect can be set in motion by a coherent package of policy measures. Important policy options in this respect lie in the fields of income policy, fiscal policy, labour market policy, recurrent education and vocational training, child care, maternity leave and in the prevention of early exit. More specifically, such policies relate especially to the participation of women, ethnic minorities, the elderly, the unemployed and the disabled – overlapping categories not participating in paid employment or with a (very) low participation rate.

The most significant measures to improve participation in paid employment are:

- (Further) implementation of a labour market policy activating the long-term unemployed and women who have withdrawn from the labour market. In the Netherlands the essence of such a labour market policy consists in making it possible for the unemployed and people who want to (re-)enter to obtain qualifications on demand in the labour market. In this respect, training and work-experience placements are indispensable. Also exceptionally important is an adequate manpower service, study and careers counselling, training in job application and counselling of the unemployed and returners;
- (further) flexibility of the labour market. As the male breadwinner is no longer the standard, the full-time employment relation for unlimited duration as a corresponding standard is also in need of revision. Part-time employment, temporary employment and agency employment do not deserve to be put aside with the label secondary labour market (or worse). Moreover, flexibility of working hours, operating hours and opening hours of shops can contribute to an increase of participation in paid employment;

- institutionalization of a system of 'permanent education'. This is also in line with technical, market-economic and demographic developments. These will necessitate the (further) development of a competitive training infrastructure for those in, as well as those seeking paid employment;
- integration of ethnic minorities by way of education (pre-school activities, Dutch as a second language, basic education for adults, and so on), vocational training and access to paid employment; (WRR 1989)
- encouragement of women to participate in paid employment, particularly via incentives (for example gradual abolishment of the system of tax transfers for non-working partners), as well as via provisions to facilitate the combination of parenthood and paid employment (child care, parental leave);
- continuing wage restraints. While Dutch net wages are relatively low, total labour costs are high in comparison with competing countries;
- increased differentiation in labour costs. Wages in the Netherlands are built on high foundations, due to the level of the statutory minimum wage. Minimum wages in collective agreements are on average another 10 per cent higher;
- prevention of early exit of older employees;
- prevention of incapacity to work and the reintegration of the long–term ill and disabled in so far as they are capable of performing work.

These measures may affect labour force participation via the supply and the demand side of the labour market. The main goal would be a sustainable welfare state and consequently a serious implementation of social citizenship in a prosperous, and hence competitive nation. The main road would not primarily be a matter of enlarged social solidarity between those in, and those out of paid employment, but – in line with the trend in society towards greater individualization – a larger average number of incomes per household. In a neo-corporatistic country like the Netherlands support from employers' associations and unions is inevitable. Consequently a sustainable welfare state and social citizenship can only be the result of a joint, and therefore coordinated effort of politics and social partners.

13. Basic Income, Citizenship and Solidarity: Towards a Dynamic for Social Renewal

Jacques Vilrokx

Regardless of the 'classic' discussion on basic income (which is, for a large part, an ideological one) it can hardly be denied that the current labour market situation has fundamentally altered reflection on the relation between work and income. The hypothesis we shall put forward is that it is socio-economically inefficient to maintain the existing link between work and income because such a connection limits the potential for economic and social innovation that meta-industrial (or post-modern?) society badly needs in order to overcome the inertness and lack of societal renewal which so many writers today are commenting on. I shall point to a certain number of trends in the evolution of social interaction processes that can enable our societies to develop new possibilities for social integration.

Contrary to what is generally argued, that citizenship can only be arrived at through participation in the labour market, I shall adopt the opposite position that full citizenship is only possible when the link with the labour market is not a condition. Basic income will be discussed in this context.

Citizenship Through Basic Income

In this chapter I shall introduce some arguments to support the case against the link between work and income and, as a corollary, between work and a more complete citizenship. A preliminary remark has to be made, however, concerning an overly idealistic approach with regard to the possibilities of a more or less immediate introduction of a Basic Income System (BIS). Basic income, rather, has to be seen as a dynamic process towards a gradual establishment of a fully-fledged BIS. At this point it is necessary to state clearly what we understand by basic income: a generalized citizen's right attributed to every natural person throughout his or her complete life and which consists of a guaranteed income established along decent subsistence criteria regardless of any possible participation in the labour market and/or quaternary sector.

A BIS also serves as an alternative to the current social security system, replacing a number of functions and services such as family allowances, study grants, health insurance, etcetera. Solutions can be worked out with regard to capitalizing schemes, heavy impact events (handicapped children, serious health problems, major accidents, etcetera). It is also conceivable that a move towards a BIS be initiated on a rather limited scale, for example on a national level without requiring one country to go in the same direction at the same speed and at the same time as other countries. In many fields such differentiated tendencies can already be observed: European collective agreements concerning labour conditions are signed without necessarily having the same conditions of application in each country. In this sense Attali is right in saying that great achievements (he is talking about the European unification process) mostly move necessarily at many speeds. (*Financial Times*, 14 October 1992)

The voluntaristic tendency towards a BIS has to be seen as a process of change. If we consider a basic income, indeed, within the context of more complete citizenship, basic income is not a state but a dynamic evolution towards an ever increasing global emancipation and a relative autonomy of minority groups and individuals.

The separation of income from work is the next step in the achievement of a fuller citizenship after the recognition in the nineteenth century of people as social beings (when their rights to defend their interests in an organized way were established) and as political beings (when the principle of universal suffrage was adopted) in the first quarter of the twentieth century. The third phase, economic emancipation, is material independence from work as a source of subsistence. The discussion on the shift from men as producers to men as consumers within the postmodern theoretical framework is very relevant here.

Jobloss Economic Growth in a Differently Organized Capitalism

Economic emancipation through the establishment of basic income is a recognition of the growing impossibility for society to create conditions of full employment. Or, rather, this impossibility triggered off the renewed interest in the question of basic income because the social and economic significance of work has gradually come under increasing pressure. The circumstances of this evolution are well known, although some of its most fundamental aspects are taken into account only seldom or not at all. One of them is the historical uniqueness of the full employment situation we knew from the 1950s until the early 1970s. This 20 to 25 year period was an exception to economic functioning since the start of the industrial revolution, and even before that. Probably very few people, if any, will today maintain the viewpoint that, even if the economy recovers periodically, the present unfavourable employment situation is likely to change structurally in a positive way.

How fragile the labour market situation is, can easily be demonstrated. If we look at the 'rise' in employment figures in the second half of the 1980s (after a decline of more then 10 years) we can observe that fundamental differences exist between the increased employment in this period and the increase during the 1950s and 1960s. This latter period was characterized by a global rise in employment, higher qualification levels, considerable internal and external labour market mobility, etcetera. In the period 1985–1990 a completely different picture emerges: for Belgium, as an example, increased employment resulted mostly from a higher participation by women (+169 000 against +34 100 men). More than half of these female entrances took part-time jobs (+91 000 against only +2 000 men). Also, the whole of this rise is in the private service sector, the public and industrial sectors remaining at their previous levels. Although industrial output increased in the same period, this was produced by the same number of industrial workers. This is what undoubtedly will happen in the service sector too, in the longer term, when comparable productivity gains will be made on a larger scale, as is already the case in the distribution and fast food sector.

This phenomenon of economic growth with ever fewer workers we call jobloss growth. It represents a break with the 1950s and the 1960s, when capital investments (notwithstanding the fears of the trade-unions) were coupled with ever higher employment levels, mostly because domestic and foreign markets continued to expand. The negative relation between economic growth and employment seems to be one of the most critical characteristics of the use of information technologies and organizational innovation in industrial and service production because traditional domestic growth sectors are saturated and because for new foreign markets production can be easily (and more cheaply) organized on the spot.

'The fine art of flexibility' (to quote the title of an article from the *Financial Times*) thus forces us to approach the labour market and the (un)employment situation from new angles. The starting point is the recognition that the three main instruments that have been used to combat unemployment (working-time reduction, measures directed at specific categories of unemployed, (re)training programmes) have been almost completely unsuccessful. Without a really drastic redistribution of working time (implying a working week of three and a half or four days) it has to be feared that the unemployment situation will be a permanent one. Current structural labour market trends in most industrialized countries seem to confirm this analysis. In the second half of the 1980s some five million (mostly atypical: other than full-time/full-year) jobs were created in the OECD countries. With the economic decline and with the slimming-down movements in some key sectors such as the car industry, micro-electronics and consumer electronics, all this job creation was cancelled out by the end of the 1980s or the beginning of the 1990s. Now more than 30 million people are unemployed in the OECD countries and this figure will undoubtedly increase.

In such an economic environment it would appear as quite idealistic to think that a drastic reduction of working time could represent a feasible solution for the unemployment crisis. Still it is the most favoured scenario for trade unions and some other collective actors. Very few reasons exist, however, to assume that a three- or four-day working week would generate a more equal distribution of work among citizens. Quite a number of people would take two jobs, as is the case already at this very moment in different professional situations. Furthermore, a reduction of working time is very difficult to organize for large sections of the working population: self-employed, people in creative professions in, for instance, the marketing and publicity sector, managers, and so on. And, since it is hardly conceivable that such a reduction of working time would be accompanied by an equivalent reduction of individual wages, labour costs would rise in an unacceptable way for firms.

In what follows we shall argue that the unemployment crisis is only part of the global socio-economic restructuring that Western societies are facing on all kinds of levels. A radical redistribution of working time in order to solve the unemployment problem, does not address these other issues. That is why, apart from the technical reasons just mentioned, the shortening of the working week is not enough. What is needed are measures that can influence some core aspects of a social fabric threatened with disintegration. Our socio-economic system (whether we call it industrial or capitalist or whatever) has entered a phase of different organization with the transitional period of the 1970s and the first half of the 1980s. Even in excellent recent accounts of citizenship (for example Roche 1992) the issue of basic income is hardly analysed in relation to these global transformations of work and society and the resulting value systems.

Differently organized (we prefer this term instead of Offe's term 'disorganized' (Offe 1985), although we generally agree with his analysis) means that the same mechanisms are no longer operating and, therefore, that the same intervention procedures as in the past can no longer be applied. We have the impression, to quote the French sociologist Chouraqui (*Le Monde*, 15 April 1992), that no person or institution at this moment is able to understand, and to control, the ongoing economic, social and technological evolutions. This is also apparent with regard to political developments, as recent elections in several countries make clear. It is, then, no exaggeration to speak of a crisis. The emphasis in post-modern analysis on the *ad hoc* functioning of individuals in society without much theoretical legitimation, on market orientation, on the shift from people being consumers instead of producers, etcetera, offers a number of inspiring starting points which concur extremely well with the conceptual and theoretical disorientation with regard to the solidarity mechanisms in present-day society. (see Bauman 1992; Avineri and de-Shalit (eds) 1992) We shall discuss the basic income issue within this framework.

Relative Autonomy and Citizenship

It is a sociological truism that work has been the most critical institution with regard to the integration of individuals and groups in society. In this section we will put forward some arguments that show that work has (and will have in the future) rather different functions, and that therefore, it is doubtful that via the institution of work the same integration mechanisms will operate as they have done in the past. We consider this shift as part of a much wider range of socio-economic transitions that have occurred since the mid-1970s.

A useful way to look at this matter is offered by Durkheim's treatment of social solidarity. We shall summarize quickly the basic insights of Durkheim's thinking and then try to take his model a stage further.

As is well known, Durkheim (1973) links the division of labour in society to social integration mechanisms. Distinguishing two types of society, he states that in the first type the division of labour is characterized by similarities or resemblances. These societies (mostly of an agricultural or hunter type of organization) are less advanced, often clan-based with few interdependencies. In such a society integration is obtained in a 'mechanical' way because there is almost no division of labour.

If the first type is clearly of a pre-industrial nature, the second one is industrial. Solidarity is not governed by the fact that there is little division of labour, as in the first type, but, on the contrary, because an elaborate system of division of labour exists. The growing mutual dependence of subsystems and units within the global societal structure gives way to what Durkheim calls an 'organic solidarity'.

Of course it would be quite easy to criticize the schematic character of Durkheim's model. (see Lukes 1973 p. 157; tr. p. 167 for an overview) We have to bear in mind, however, that we are confronted here with an ideal-type approach that summarizes Durkheim's (in some cases incorrect or incomplete) very detailed analysis. The overall heuristic theoretical usefulness is, however, not affected by this criticism. That is why it seems very fruitful to expand the proposed typology in order to define some of the fundamental trends underlying meta-industrial societal development.

This meta-industrial (or post-industrial, or information, or knowledge, or service) society that has been defined in order to point to the crucial difference with the industrial type of socio-economic functioning, is indeed marked by a different kind of integration pattern we can call 'selective solidarity'. No longer do the collective interdependencies between collective actors (trade-unions, employers' organizations, the state, etcetera) constitute the nature of social relations, through which 'organic solidarity' was organized in industrial society, but these relations are defined rather by the relative autonomy of individuals or specific small groups in meta-industrial (and post-modern) society.

The reason for this is that the industrial type of division of labour (Fordist/Taylorist) based on differentiation and specialization, has also undergone fundamental changes, which have been widely studied. (for example Wood (ed.) 1989) The most apt way to define these transformations in the division of labour is to emphasize the network character of present and forthcoming systems for the production of goods and services.

This analysis brings us to a typology (Vilrokx 1987) as pictured in Figure 13.1.

Figure 13.1
Typology of the Nature of Social Relations in Different Types of Societies

	Agricultural Society	Industrial Society	Meta-Industrial Society
Division of Labour	Similarity	Differentiation	Networks
Social Integration Mechanisms	Mechanical Solidarity	Organic Solidarity	Selective Solidarity
Nature of Social Relations	Individual Dependency	Collective Interdependency	Relative Autonomy

The concept of relative autonomy is of central importance in the analysis of socio-economic and cultural changes and it implies a new perspective on citizenship. Without going into too much detail, we can say that relative autonomy refers to the tendency towards an ever growing importance of smaller (lower-level) organizations or units, be it individuals (or groups of individuals) or subsystems within, respectively, global society or global organizations. This tendency pertains to the increased accountability accorded to smaller units. We call this relative autonomy because at the same time autonomy *and* dependency become the attraction poles of social organization and social relations and because on the one hand binding forces are operating (for example globalization) *and* on the other hand greater possibilities exist for the creation of smaller unit relation patterns. All this implies new power and control relations between the global organization and its organizational subsystems.

The concept of relative autonomy (in fact the trend towards an ever expanding relative autonomy) can be related to the socio-cultural evolution that Attali (1990) calls the proliferation of nomadic objects. He considers this as one of the basic trends in current Western culture.

Everything that can easily be transported or is portable and can be connected with other in time and space distant (possibly nomadic) objects or information carriers are thus nomadic. Portable PCs, credit cards, walkmans, recorders, teleshopping and telebanking are the obvious examples to which Attali refers. But other objects also become nomadic: pizzas, chicken (fried, of course!), all kinds of information that can be delivered in quasi real time when asked for. Similarly, more and more professional expertise from accountants, medical personnel, etcetera, is becoming nomadic via expert systems. Examples of this are plentiful.

The idea of an increasing nomadization of objects can be carried further to production processes and people. They also become less and less fixed to specific spaces, become more mobile, more flexible. Production processes, or parts of them, are indeed to an increasing degree less attached to their traditional locations and more and more externalized from their initial organizational environment. People too can be involved in production processes without being 'on the spot': teleworking comes immediately to mind, but on a non-technological level too people become nomadic: temporary workers and short-term contracts are booming in all kinds of production settings adding to the creation of the nomadic society. All this is made possible by the use of information technology and organizational innovation allowing people, organizations and processes to function in a relatively autonomous way.

Basic Income as an Egalitarian Strategy?

Throughout this book the relationship is emphasized between unemployment and phenomena such as poor health, the emergence of an underclass, diminished life chances, etcetera. The question can be legitimately asked if these social inequalities will wither away with a BIS-based citizenship. First, it has to be observed that our currently functioning social security system itself does not provide, not even potentially, the conditions necessary to move out of unemployment situations. It is for this reason that totally different actions from those taken in the past have to be considered. Secondly, an awareness of the fact that unemployment is a completely misleading term, which distorts social reality, has to be developed. People cannot, morally or technically, be termed unemployed when they cannot be employed.

Basic income, then, also serves the purpose of declaring 'by decree' that unemployment no longer exists. Two practical (related) arguments are in general advanced against the introduction of a basic income. On the one hand, it is said, all possibilities of sanctioning people because of their unwillingness to participate in the labour market will disappear and, at the same time, people will not be encouraged to enter the labour market at all because they will receive an income anyway. Neither argument is valid. The first one refers to the concept of social contract. According to this concept, people contribute to the general interest by offering their labour power in exchange for the welfare and social security coverage they receive. As has been demonstrated convincingly (Showler and Sinfield (eds) 1981), this conception is deeply rooted in the post-Second World War welfare-state situation. Again, this argument cannot be maintained in a jobloss growth economy.

As for the second argument, of course there will be, at specific moments in the lifecycle, pressure on people to take jobs in order to supplement their basic income. Other people will have such social, cultural or financial needs that they will wish to work full-time/full-year. The freedom to work or not to work will certainly create different power relations between the demand and supply sides of the labour market but it would be nonsensical to think that shortages on the labour market would automatically result. New equilibria will emerge, based on a better balance between economic-financial and social-cultural rationalities. Exactly because of the possibility that both rationalities can be more fully exploited, the basic income scenario is an innovative one. Economic-financially as well as social-culturally interesting projects can be initiated and pursued by people who now will have the room for manoeuvre, created by a BIS, to follow with less risks new trajectories. An optimalization of individual and collective social and economic potential is made possible: these synergies can only create conditions for both higher social participation and more economic growth.

To come back to the question asked at the beginning of this section, BIS an egalitarian scenario? It is not. A certain minimum equality of income is established and social power relations will, therefore, in some way be affected, but the basic existing control mechanisms in global society will not be 'undermined'. In this sense economic citizenship through basic income will not lead to an equality of individual economic outcome. A parallel can be drawn with the social and political citizenship mentioned earlier, which did not produce social and economic equality either. It will, however, put an end to socio-economic exclusion of the large categories of people now being marginalized. And that is much more than can be said of all social security and welfare schemes brought into practice until now.

14. A Non-Productivist Design for Social Policies

Claus Offe

The Political Semantics of Welfare and Social Security

The basic mission of the modern welfare state is to legally guarantee social security (or welfare) through monetary transfers, services, physical infrastructure, and regulatory policies in the areas of health, education, housing, social insurance, social assistance, labour protection, and assistance to families.

'Security' is an objective that is by no means limited to the welfare state. The quest for security dates back to the philosophical defence of the liberal state and its principle of limiting state action. What was to be made secure through the liberal principle of 'rule of law' ('Rechtsstaat') was the enjoyment of life and property. This security was to be safeguarded by the state's inaction or non-interference.

In contrast, social security and welfare can only be safeguarded through state action. The change is from prohibited state action to mandated state action. This action takes the form of establishing positive legal obligations and entitlements to categories of people pertaining to conditions, risks and contingencies which are recognized as requiring public regulation, transfers, or services. If a person belongs to category x and meets conditions $a,b,c...$, then he or she is entitled to services and transfers. The working of these three components (categories, conditions, entitlements) is then supposed to implement the values of security and welfare. An important logical difference between the principle of the liberal state and that of the welfare state is this: while the inaction or restraint principle is always operationally precise, the action or commitment principle tends to invite the question of 'how much' and 'what kind' of action on behalf of 'what categories of people' (and naturally, at the expense of whom) is required in order to actually achieve the objectives of welfare and security. None of these questions is easily settled. Hence the elusive nature of 'social security', the semantics of which seem to be essentially and eternally contested.

The fact that the state cannot simply eliminate the problem by ignoring it and by returning to a liberal agenda of inaction results from some basic features of economic, political, and cultural modernization. First, a large portion of the individuals who are affected by conditions of need and distress cannot justifiably be 'blamed' for this condition, as some part of the condition of need, however contested and hard to determine, must and can always be attributed to factors beyond the control of those affected. Second, there is no universally valid moral standard according to which individuals affected by the risks of social insecurity, unmet need, or poverty, could possibly be expected to 'accept' this condition fatalistically as a burden that is imposed upon them, for instance, by the will of God. Not only have the religious foundations for such acquiescence eroded; the economic wealth that modern societies have accumulated, as well as their evidently vast capacity for technical and administrative control, render the view highly contestable that things must be accepted as they are, as nothing can be done about them.[1] Third, this view does not only become indefensible in moral terms, but equally so in strategic terms. That is to say, individual conditions of unmet need are widely known to be not only caused by processes beyond the control of individuals, but also collectively consequential through a variety of negative externalities (ranging from the spread of contagious diseases to disruptive social conflict).

As a consequence of all three of these features, the typical material risks and insecurities of individuals (having to do with illness, inability to find or to keep a job, inability to work due to the lack of skills or employment opportunities, lack of adequately priced housing, inability to cope with the conditions of maternity and childbearing, death of the breadwinner of a family household, and the destruction of life and property following from wars) must be provided for through collective arrangements, and this means not through voluntary charity or mutualism, but through the only robust and inclusive form of collective action that is available in modern society, namely state action based upon formal law and purposive administrative and professional intervention. (de Swaan 1988)

The inescapable politics of demanding and granting entitlements proceeds along three evolutionary dimensions (Alber 1982): substantive growth as to categories of risk and need (that is, first income maintenance for those affected by industrial accidents, and only much later also for those affected by unemployment), successive inclusion of more and more groups (first civil servants, industrial workers, or war veterans, last housewives), and upward equalization of levels of benefits. As a consequence of the dynamics of democratic mass politics, party competition, and the strategies of corporatist actors, any standard of entitlement is subject to potential upward as well as downward revision and qualitative change.

A related and similarly persistent issue in the ongoing social and political conflict over the operational meaning of social security and welfare concerns the supply side, that is, the fiscal resources that are needed to cover recognized needs. Who is to bear the costs (through taxes, contributions, prices, or through in kind services), and how much of these costs can we afford without running the risk of inadvertently doing more harm than good to the economy as a whole or to the moral fabric of society? Is it really a 'public good' to the production of which 'we' are contributing, or is it undeserved private gain of the beneficiaries of social security and welfare programmes? Does in fact everyone pay a fair share, or are there opportunities for free-riding and moral hazards? Are existing programmes sufficiently effective and efficient, or are there better and less costly ways to meet the intended objectives? These and related questions must be continuously settled in a reasonable consensus and support for social policy programmes. Given the ambiguities and the contested nature of both the demand and supply sides, or of entitlements and burdens, the operational meaning of 'social security' and the adequate level of welfare provision is always a moving target.

Having reviewed some of the reasons why, and aspects in which, the politics of the welfare state does appear to be an essentially and eternally contested matter, affecting as it does many of the core social and economic interests of large and powerful groups in society, we may wonder why and in which ways this inherent potential for conflict and controversy is in fact contained for most of the time in most welfare states. At least at the surface, the particular social policy arrangements that characterize various national welfare states appear to be, in the light of the above observations, surprisingly stable over long periods of time. In some countries, such as Germany, Austria, and the Scandinavian countries, reforms that do actually occur are usually not highly controversial, and often supported by bipartisan coalitions. How is, at least in these countries, the semantic vagueness, and hence the potential political explosiveness, of the notion of social security being overcome? How is, in spite of these dynamic forces that operate on the demand and supply sides of the welfare state, a relative and temporarily valid political support established? These questions need to be answered, and the often relatively calm and conflict-free nature of the politics of social policy explained, with reference to a number of political, economic, institutional, and moral ingredients of consensus formation. Taken together, these ingredients appear to work quite effectively in producing relatively stable and widely shared views on issues concerning the distribution of welfare and its financial burdens.

Any welfare state must operate upon the basis of a socially and politically validated conception of 'how much is enough under given circumstances', a definition which in turn implies a notion of which levels of inequality, of social need and insecurity of which categories of people of risk must be accepted, at least for the time being, as tolerable and affordable contingencies that do not require intervention, be it because they are considered minor in their nature or because those affected by them are thought to be able to rely on their own social and monetary resources in order to cope with them. The practice of the welfare state is embedded in a widely shared set of background assumptions concerning some operationally appropriate notion of social justice which specifies the (social and substantive) limits up to which, but not beyond which, security-enhancing public arrangements are called for, and who is to carry the burden of such provision.

The consensus that emerges among the various collective actors that take an interest in social policies will be an agreement concerning a set of demarcation lines. They specify, within the space of potential programmes and action, a subset of 'adequate' (as opposed to an 'excessive') provision of social security. A parallel distinction is established between 'legitimate' and 'illegitimate' cases of need and corresponding claims to public provision. A line is drawn between the universe of persons and conditions that are the appropriate object of collective responsibilities assigned through public policies, on the one hand, and the remainder of those contingencies which are to be covered by private and individual responsibility through market, family, and other arrangements.[2] Only those policies are likely to become effective which make sense (that is, are widely accepted as plausible, tolerable or sufficiently meaningful) in the context and by the criteria established by these considerations, which thus would delimit the 'possibility space' of social policies.

Determinants and Ingredients of the Social Policy Consensus

How does the negative component of this implicit theory of justice come into being, that is the components defining 'undeserving' social categories and 'illegitimate' kinds of claims to public provision, or 'excessive' levels of it? To come closer to an answer to this complex question, I wish to single out four hypothetical factors which play a role as ingredients in the formation of the operating consensus of the welfare state and social policies.

The first of the factors determining the possibility space of social policies is of a purely normative sort. It consists in the scope of moral universalism. There are basically two thresholds which must be overcome if a high level of moral universalism is to be achieved. The first threshold is passed if we stop coding members of social categories, and the claims they can legitimately make, according to a logic of we and them; universalist morals require the further abstraction from patterns of conduct, that is from what we see people doing (for example, complying to some notion of 'the work ethic' or a 'normal conduct of life'). The roots of moral universalism (or the lack thereof, that is of the willingness to abstract from identities and patterns of conduct) are probably to be found within the political, historical and religious traditions which determine the degree of inclusiveness of which a society is capable.

The second factor is cognitive. If I deny the legitimacy of a category of claims or claimants, I refer them by implication to other ways of coping with their needs. This in turn implies that such other ways, such as finding a job, learning the required skills, depending on one's personal savings, relying on the help of family members, relatives or friends, leading a healthy life, are in fact affordable and available to them. Passing such judgements involves a lot of implicit everyday sociology, in which perceptions about the resources and life chances of ordinary people under normal circumstances play an important role. The greater these chances, resources, and opportunities are in my perception (or the more limited my cognitive access is to pieces of relevant counter-evidence), the less I am likely to grant the legitimacy of claims and claimants.

The third factor is interest-related and structural. My commitment to existing or new social policies will depend, among other things, on the subjective probability that I assign to the event that I will find myself among those whom the social policy in question is designed to serve. We may call this the 'potential self-inclusion' consideration. Suppose that I happen to be a middle-aged, middle-class, male, married, healthy, skilled, home-owning private sector employee. The implication is that being in this kind of position will increase the moral effort required to adopt a thick veil of ignorance concerning all those social policies that are aimed at unemployed youth, foreigners, tenants of public housing projects, public sector workers, single mothers, the chronically ill, unskilled workers, the poor, etcetera. Furthermore the more specialized social policies become in terms of social categories and categories of need, the more they tend to undermine that portion of public support that derives from this probabilistic calculation of one's own interest. The more social structures become individualized, the more life patterns differ, and the more collective actors are fragmented, the less reason exists for individuals to look upon themselves as belonging to an encompassing social category with a shared commonalty of social-economic fates and risks, and the more reasons will social policy-makers have to target programmes at ever narrower social categories and categories of need.

The fourth factor that plays a hypothetical role in the ongoing formation of social policy consensus follows a functional or consequentialist logic. Here, the concern is with second-order, indirect, and long-term collective consequences of social policies. The key question is how individual social policy programmes affect not only (potential) claimants and their current need situation, on the one hand, and the bearers of direct costs, on the other, but each of us as actors within an economic, political and social system. Such global systematic variables that are often thought to be affected, positively or negatively, by social policies include the labour market participation rate; demographic variables including migration; the rate of economic growth, inflation, public debt, or unemployment; the terms and outcomes of party competition; and the work ethic, the educational system, the role of the professions and of public bureaucracies, the viability of communal bonds as well as the strength of the family as an institution.

The growth and spread of social science information have probably contributed a great deal to sensitize the general public opinions concerning such long-term repercussions of individual social policies and the welfare state in general. The awareness of social and economic phenomena, cliches, and paradoxes such as unintended consequences, exploitative coalitions, the dynamics of relative deprivation, prisoners' dilemmas, *tertius gaudens*, moral hazards, rising expectations, adverse selection, self-serving professions, budget maximizing bureaucrats, and fiscal crises seems to be sufficiently common to have become part of the reality which is described and observed in these terms.

I have thus far described four types of considerations that contribute to the ongoing formation of the operative social policy consensus. Needless to say, this consensus and its robustness is not only a limiting parameter of what policy-makers can do, but also the object of the strategic action of political elites and collective actors who shape and change the consensus. Interpretation of reality is itself a political process in which not only individuals take part on the basis of their particular experience and value orientations, but also actors such as political parties, trade unions, associations, churches, and professions.

Structural Change and the Shifting Welfare State Consensus

The analysis has so far focused on questions having to do with how welfare state citizens see the world, interpret the relations and dynamics inherent in it, and arrive at reasonably coherent interpretations and perceptions; the latter are in turn shaped by the conflicts among collective actors and political elites which draw upon codified normative knowledge. This one-sided interpretive view which is rooted in an analysis of the social and political construction of reality (or a 'political sociology of knowledge' perspective) must be complemented by a more structural approach which focuses on the 'raw material' of the social and political interpretation and ongoing 'negotiation' of reality. The question then becomes: which features and tendencies of 'objective' social change will give rise to (support, favour, select, confirm, validate, and confer plausibility to) certain patterns and beliefs about society in general and social policies and their appropriateness in particular? The general theoretical notion from which this pair of perspectives, the interpretative and the structural, derives is the idea that social reality is both the determinant and the outcome of interpretation.

A set of factual, if not outright ontological assumptions, all of which are actually challenged by the experience of advanced industrial societies in the seventies and the eighties, belong to what one could term the 'productivist syndrome'. Let me just mention what I think are the five most important of these empirical assumptions which have been rendered questionable by recent trends of social and economic change. I refer to them as 'productivist' assumptions because they are centred around the notion that production and productivity are both individually and collectively desirable and hence the morally self-evident criterion of material reward.

Most people live in families and derive their means of subsistence from an income in which all members of the family share; family households thus provide, and can legitimately be required to provide, a precondition for (future) productive activities of its members as well as a micro social security network for the benefit of those belonging to the family household; at the same time, the family contributes to the viability of the macro social security system (in particular old-age pensions) and to the maintenance of a demographic balance through the procreation and primary socialization of children.

Most families, unless they belong to the small sector of self-employed, have at least one permanently employed breadwinner, which presupposes as the normal case both a prevailing (subjective) orientation towards employed labour as well as the (objective) availability of employment. The income that is generated through employment helps to accumulate, individually as well as collectively, the funds out of which the social wage and other welfare state expenditures are to be paid. At the same time, the fact that people are normally employed and derive a family wage out of this employment limits the extent to which claims against the funds for the social wage will be made. That is to say, most people can rely on their own income (rather than transfers) for most of their needs for most of the time.

A societal system of collective actors, representing labour, employers, self-employed people, agriculture, the professions, and the public sector employees, performs the function of aggregating, mediating, legitimating, and negotiating distributional conflicts, the continuous outcomes of which constitute a meso social security network for those broad social categories represented by them. They also serve to define and consolidate broad social categories within which socio-economic fates are relatively homogeneous.

The welfare state, both in its social security and its social assistance branches, is a supplementary macro social security mechanism which takes care of all those residual needs and deficiencies in social security that are not covered by either the micro or the meso system. It will be able to do so, via a growth dividend extracted by the welfare state, to an ever wider extent, the more the productive potential of a national economy increases.

One of the main modes of operation of the welfare state, namely its reliance upon mandatory contributory schemes covering (at least) old-age and health expenditures, is in fact supported by citizens largely out of considerations of economic prudence alone, and is hence morally undemanding, politically relatively uncontroversial, and hence supported by a broad and stable consensus. This consensus derives partly from interest-rational considerations of the broad majority of the population and partly from the certainty that cases of risk and need that the welfare state covers are not behaviour-contingent, that is, not attributable to deliberate (and morally objectionable) acts of those who are entitled to those benefits.

All of these five productivist assumptions have become much harder to accept as valid and reliable representations of the social and economic reality of advanced industrial societies. The family as an institution, the labour market, the intermediary system of negotiations between representative collective actors, the effectiveness of social security and social assistance in covering all social and substantive categories of need and risk, as well as, finally, the consensus supporting this set of institutional arrangements are undergoing symptoms of stress and widely perceived insecurity.

Political Responses to the Perceived Insecurity of Security-Generating Mechanisms

There are basically four strategic options that one can adopt in response to the uncertainties and insecurities concerning the premisses of the welfare state. I want to briefly specify them and then explore the case for one of them, the basic income proposal.

First, economic liberals propose that after the empirical premisses of the welfare state as stated above are partly and progressively fading away, what remains to be done is to bid farewell to overly generous standards and promises of security and let the market decide. This strategic option involves in part the outright abolition of transfers and services, in part a more narrow targeting and means-testing of the clientele of the welfare state. It also involves a lesser role for collective actors, particularly unions, in negotiating wage and other agreements. Less regulations and protection will in the long run, according to the liberal philosophy, be rewarded by increases of productivity, competitiveness, employment and eventually per capita income, which in turn will and should rightly be the main source of individuals to buy security in the market.

Second, the conservative strategy recommends the selective punishing and rewarding of people's attitudes towards work, education, health, the legal order, and the family. Instead of favouring a lesser role for organized labour as well as fiscal austerity, conservatives set out to strengthen society's 'moral fibre' and emphasize the line that demarcates 'deserving' from 'undeserving' and illegitimate categories of claims and claimants.

Third, the social democratic version of strategic responses, even to the extent it is prepared to reluctantly recognize the fragility of the assumptions underlying the welfare state, still denies the need for a basic reorientation and insists instead upon the need and feasibility of defending and even further expanding the welfare state and its productivist premises. All that is needed for such defence is political determination and its potential for activating solidaristic and universalistic moral and political commitments among employees and voters.

Finally, there is a poorly defined and clearly undertheorized bundle of strategic proposals that comes from what I would like to term the 'post-industrial left' and that can be described as left-libertarian in its ideological orientation. It emphasizes the values of security and autonomy, and it envisages the possibility of reconciling the alleged antagonism prevailing between the two in relying upon the idea of citizenship and the positive rights and entitlements, such as the entitlement to a basic income, associated with it.

The case for citizenship-based entitlements to a basic income differs from some or all of the preceding options in that:

a. not class, occupational status, earnings, or employment record, but citizenship is the basis for entitlement to transfers and services,

b. not paid labour, but 'useful activities', including activities performed outside employment and the labour market and hence escaping formal measurement and accounting, is the moral justification of the claim to benefits, to the receipt of which no behavioural preconditions are to be attached.

c. not the protection of (relative) status or the rewarding of desert, but coverage of basic needs is the criterion of justice, and

d. not (absolute) security, but a sustainable level of risk and the maintenance of autonomous options concerning the citizen's responsible conduct of his or her life is the key value.

In contrast to this set of moral intuitions, the social democratic project of defending (on the European Continent) a contributory and incomes-graduated system of transfers is based upon not citizens', but employees' rights and duties. Mandatory contributions to the systems of old-age pensions, health insurance, and unemployment insurance are (within upper and lower limits) tied to the legal status of being an employee, and benefits are allocated (with the limited exception of the case of health services) in accordance with the duration of employment and the income earned during that employment. What are the reasons to question the moral validity (as well as to the fiscal viability) of this employment-centred model of the welfare state that social democrats are so eager to defend in most West European countries?

(a) The maintenance of expensive universalist social security systems, even the mainly contributory ones, requires, due to labour market and demographic imbalances, an increasing amount of fiscal subsidies. These subsidies can only, under the premises of an open economy, be financed by a steady process of economic growth and the growth dividend it generates for the state budget in general and for social policy programmes in particular. Economic growth, in its turn, whether or (more likely) not it is accompanied by the attainment of full employment, has in all its presently visible varieties and paths an unequivocally disruptive impact upon the natural environment. The continued dependency of social security upon economic growth conditions the immediate interests of employees in ways which will favour growth even at the expense of environmentally and ecologically sound policies. The productivist link that ties social security to economic growth and budgetary growth dividends operates as an effective brake upon more stringent varieties of policies aiming at environmental protection, as the clients of this type of welfare state will be naturally inclined to prefer economic growth over the preservation of natural resources.

(b) The employment-centred arrangements of social security and social welfare reserve the rights and entitlements of full welfare state citizenship to those enjoying stable employment and their dependents. As the functional link between economic growth and employment has become more uncertain, and as the link between the gainfully employed earning a family wage and the family as an institution serving as a micro social security network has also become more tenuous, the dispersion of wealth through employment and family relations has become more restricted, for example to the majority of what is often referred to as the 'two-thirds society'. At the same time, the emphasis that the welfare state and the arrangements for social security place upon formal employment makes it counterintuitively attractive for many to enter the labour market in spite – or even because – of the relatively shrinking demand for labour. The influx of those who have no other claim to the means of subsistence (and no other hope for the recognition of their social worthiness) than through labour market participation, marginal and unstable employment in an increasingly deregulated labour market, and unemployment and other benefits that are contingent upon their 'preparedness to accept formal employment' moves the system ever further away from anything approaching a labour market equilibrium.

Moreover, wage- and payroll-related modes of financing social security have the obvious effect of burdening the market prospects of labour with the costs of its own 'security', thus generating a rational incentive for employers to restrict their demand for labour still further.

Taken together, these two effects of the employment-centred social security system, making the status of being employed relatively more attractive as compared to other life forms outside employment and making it more costly to employ labour, are likely to positively contribute to a permanent labour market imbalance.

(c) Fiscal, labour market, and demographic strains will give rise to a politics of welfare state retrenchment and consolidation which, while protecting the interests of those in stable employment, deprives everyone else of welfare rights, such as the unemployed, the poor, many women, adolescents, the disabled and chronically ill, survivors, and, to an extent, even pensioners. The alleged universalism of employment-centred social policies thus turns into its opposite under conditions of retrenchment, namely into a particularism favouring the productivist core of employed members of society.

(d) The historical roots of the post-war welfare state accord are to be found in the appreciation of the political forces representing the middle class (including the privileged sectors of the working class, that is, skilled male workers) that they stood to gain significantly from the arrangement. It is probably only a slight simplification to argue that social security universalism based upon employment status was a means to 'bribe' the middle class to support the welfare state, or to buy its political consent (or at least its political acquiescence, as suggested by the 'hush-money' metaphor that some commentators have employed).

Gains for the middle class became the necessary precondition for making social security for the 'underclass' (including the less privileged segments of the working class) politically feasible. Had such gains not been provided for, the predictable political response of the middle class would have been a very effective appeal for stringency and austerity in welfare spending. To the extent that this interpretation is valid, it highlights a noteworthy contradiction between the economic and the political rationalities of the welfare state. Seen from the point of view of economic efficiency, any non-selective or non-targeted social policy arrangement, and certainly a fully universalistic one, is vastly inefficient, in that it spreads limited resources to all where only some actually need it, thereby depriving the system of its capacity of providing the latter with even their minimum requirements. But seen from the point of view of politics, this blatantly inefficient use of resources makes perfect sense, as the practice of spreading entitlements to benefits to all is the inescapable political precondition that must first be met in order to make the arrangement sufficiently popular with the middle class. Thus the consent-buying portion of total expenditures can be looked upon as a political investment the yield of which is the benefit that is eventually channelled to the 'truly' needy target group which depend upon the welfare state's support.

Does that allow us to conclude that a return to strictly selective principles of social welfare, based on large-scale needs tests and means tests, is called for, such as is advocated by the proponents of the neo-liberal welfare backlash?

I do not think so. Instead, I believe that a universal and adequate basic income could be designed to become a synthesis of the more desirable features of universalism and selectivity. Such a synthesis would have to consist of several components. The most important one is an unconditional, subsistence level, tax-financed right to income based upon citizenship rather than labour market participation. The extreme universalism embodied in such a basic income would have to be complemented by a tax structure that makes sure that all who participate in gainful employment and thus do not really depend upon the basic income will contribute – through direct and indirect taxation and in distributively progressive ways – to its financing. As it will be not surprising to see a massive middle-class opposition mobilizing against such a scheme that does in fact involve considerable downward redistribution of income and income security, the arrangement would have to be based upon a legislation that provides for something like the following procedural rule: revisions of the scheme that would restrict access to the basic income and/or its (GNP-indexed) level will only be possible to pass with a majority that equals, say, 90 per cent of the net-contributors. For instance, if at a given point 20 per cent of the adult population actually claim the basic income, a downward revision of levels or eligibility criteria would become effective only if it were supported by a majority of at least 72 per cent of the legislative body. Such procedural protection of structural minorities would decline in strength as the minority increases: the more it approaches parity, the closer we would come to the standard simple majority rule. Extensive co-operative and other institutional forms of non-wage labour outside formal employment must be experimentally developed in order to expose the near-monopoly that the institutional arrangement of formal employment holds over the universe of useful human activities to the competition of alternative modes of 'getting things done'. While emancipating society from the dictatorial imperatives of economic growth (as conventionally measured), such a scheme would not only provide individuals with the option of 'opting out', temporarily or permanently, of formal employment (if on a probably very moderate level of state-provided subsistence), but it would also free them to develop their skills and their potential for useful activities, alone and in co-operation with others, that are normally underutilized in employment in general and in unemployment in particular. (*cf.* Offe and Heinze 1990)

The Politics of Basic Income Proposals

(1) The basic income can and should not be presented as a panacea to open the road to a 'good society'. First, because, should the proposal eventually turn out to be a strategy to that end (which I believe to be the case), it will just be an element in a policy package within which other elements are equally important. Second, because we cannot claim to know enough about the short-term and long-term effects of the proposal once it is implemented, unpleasant surprises cannot be excluded, or rather they must be excluded in practice through thoughtful experimentation and the cautious exploration of the many questions, problems, and potential side-effects about which we simply don't yet know enough. Third, rather than being a formula for the foundation of a new social order, it might be more realistic and honest to argue for basic income in terms of a defensive measure to preserve and expand notions of social justice against a welfare backlash that has partly been going on and more of which must be anticipated in view of the above structural changes.

(2) The political implementation of basic income schemes involves two steps. The first and by far the more uncertain one concerns the problem of how a sufficiently broad alliance of social and political forces can be built that will be required to win support for such a proposal of tying the right to sufficient (subsistence) income to citizenship rather than employment (or the preparedness to accept employment). This problem cannot fully be dealt with here. (*cf.* Mückenberger *et al.* 1988) The second problem concerns the question how, after the scheme has once been instituted, its proponents and direct beneficiaries might be able to withstand the foreseeable pressure to revise it in negative ways, be it outright abolition, be it gradual restrictions of eligibility or levels of transfers.

(3) The obvious question to which proponents and direct beneficiaries of the basic income will be most vulnerable is this: If 'you' are not engaged in gainful employment, and not even prepared to find and accept such employment once it is made available to you why should 'we' be forced to subsidize your voluntary unemployment? To resist the tempting consequences of this Victorian logic, which are by no means a specialty of conservative and economic liberal political authors (*cf.* Elster 1986), it will probably not be enough to point to the limited capacities of the labour market, the family, and the system of corporate actors to spread effectively an adequate portion of society's wealth to each and every citizen. In addition, it will be necessary to be able to demonstrate that (a) the voluntary unemployed are actually, at least in the typical and quantitatively relevant case, involved in useful activities, although the usefulness of these activities is not measured by the institutional procedures of the employment contract and paid work; and (b) that the labour invested in the self-development of human resources (such as health, training, and other components of human capital) deserves as much to be remunerated as the actual utilization of human capital in paid labour itself. If one wishes to be able to make this point as compellingly as it will be needed to be made, one would have to provide for institutional alternatives to employed work as well as for meaningful arrangements for manpower development, rehabilitation, and training.

(4) Even if the Victorian unwillingness to reward 'work-shyness' can be successfully overcome by this argument on social justice, the question remains why people should actually prefer the general idea of citizenship-based rights to income over the conventional full employment alternative. Even if the idea can be shown to be acceptable in terms of

social justice, why should it also be desirable in terms of individual and collective interests? Even if the majority grants the right, would the minority of those who directly benefit from it at any given point in time be willing to use it without feeling marginalized by it? What kind of consideration should make a life outside formal employment desirable for relevant portions of the citizenship? To answer this question, individual as well as collective gains may be cited, not only the definitive infeasibility of the supposedly most preferred alternative of full employment. Individual gains consist in the options that a basic income scheme would create. These options consist in the possibility to choose any combination between the amount of employed work and the income that goes with it, on the one hand, and other activities that a person wishes to pursue, on the other. This option, which amounts to the availability of a choice concerning the individually most appropriate free time/income-mix, is normally precluded in a society where full social and economic membership status is tied to full-time and life-long employment, and where any deviation from this (male) standard is considered deficient. (*cf.* Gorz 1989) My intuition is that the taste-forming impact of this choice, once it becomes available, will be strong enough to offset not only the losses in income from employment on the part of (potential) employees, but also to partly neutralize the obvious and opposite interest of employers to make the most extensive possible use of any individual employee and the human capital embodied in him/her. To the extent that this intuition turns out to be valid, the option of discontinuous participation in employment would cease to be considered the second best (due to the unavailability of 'full' employment), and would instead be seen as the most preferred alternative, even under conditions where full employment were thought to be feasible.

(5) As to the collective benefits of the optionality of labour market participation created by the basic income scheme, three points appear to be relevant. First, while the right to income as an unconditional citizen right would certainly not by itself alleviate the environmental and ecological risks and dangers involved in industrial growth and the full employment that is contingent upon such growth, it would probably contribute in indirect ways, for it removes some of the productivist pressures and anxieties and thus paves the political road toward targeted and selective environmental policies, some of which are bound to entail the very termination of certain lines of production and production processes. The basic income makes an ecological critique of industrialism politically more affordable. Second, a major impact is to be expected

upon the level of overall social integration: as people who are, temporarily or permanently, outside of employment lose their stigma of deficiency and failure, and are instead looked upon as legitimate citizens involved in respectable activities other than paid work, many of the symptoms and social pathologies of marginalization are likely to disappear. Third, the temporary escape from employed work that a basic income would make feasible and indeed attractive would contribute to an ongoing process of the creative regeneration of skills, health and training, thus helping to maintain and enhance the productivity of human capital.

(6) The basic income would also induce conditions which amount to an indirect strategy of work humanization. Employees would find it affordable to refuse many of the least attractive and poorly paid jobs, as the alternative of claiming a basic income without being employed on such jobs becomes an attractive alternative. As a consequence, the recruitment of labour for such jobs would become significantly more expensive to employers, which in turn would induce efforts on their part to eliminate such jobs through technical or organizational innovations.

(7) Finally, the extent to which people will actually claim the basic income, and for what portion of their life-time, is an open question. Much of the alarmed responses to basic income proposals seem to be based upon the implicit fear that a wholesale defection from employed work would be the inevitable consequence. This is by no means a plausible conjecture. First, under all realistic calculations the level of the basic income, while being (by definition) sufficient for subsistence, would remain so moderate as to maintain much of the relative preferability of employment, wherever it is in fact available at decent wages and working conditions. Thus the disincentive effect will remain limited. Second, the overall incentive effect of the basic income may well turn out to follow a logic of what might be called, in view of the mass exodus of East German refugees during the summer of 1989, the 'GDR-paradox'. The paradox is this: had the government of the GDR granted its citizens the right to leave, many of them would have stayed. The failure to grant this right has been one of the immediate causes of the decision of many to leave illegally. Applying this logic to the labour market and the effects of the basic income scheme, one might arrive at the anticipation that the right to leave will certainly (as intended) cause many persons to withdraw their labour power from formal employment, which they now can afford to do, given the unconditional safety net of the basic income and the consequent effective optionality of employment. In particular

use of this option will be made by those marginal employees who have stayed in the labour market mainly for fear that leaving would involve the definitive decision never to come back. But this right to leave will also, to an unknown but hardly negligible extent, be used for the purpose of the acquisition of new social and technical skills and the generation of energies and preferences that will eventually facilitate the return into voluntary gainful employment. Thus the net effect will be a more flexible and optional life pattern, on the one hand, and a requalification of the work-force, on the other, both of which may well add up to a new condition of full employment on the basis of a significantly reduced share of his or her life-time that the average person spends in employed work.

Notes

1. For an insightful sociological plea for 'neo-fatalism', however, see N. Glazer. (1990)

2. One rather ingenious and influential method to solve this boundary problem of social policy is proposed by the Roman Catholic doctrine of Quadragesimo Anno (1931) and the principle of 'subsidiarity' established therein. It basically claims that the smaller social unit (family, local community, church, etc.) should always be given priority in providing transfers and services, and that only after the limits of the potential of the 'small units' are reached collective and public forms of responsibility should step in. The operational problems of implementing this apparent solution are well known. First, it is by no means certain which kind of 'smaller community' is to be given priority in concrete cases. Second, the proposal suffers from a certain circularity in that the capacity of the 'small' unit to provide help and services often depends itself upon public policies that enable it to do so.

Bibliography

Aarts, L.J.M., Ph.R. de Jong (1990), *Economic Aspects of Disability Behaviour*, Dissertation, Rotterdam

Achterhuis, H. (1984), *Arbeid een eigenaardig medicijn*, Ambo, Baarn

Alber, J. (1982), *Vom Armenhaus zum Wohlfahrtsstaat. Analysen zur Entwicklung der Sozialversicherung in West-Europa*, Campus, Frankfurt am Main/New York

Allen, V.L. (1981), *The Militancy of British Miners*, Moor Press, Shipley

Andrews, G. (ed.) (1991), *Citizenship*, Lawrence & Wishart, London

Andrews, K., J. Jacobs (1990), *Punishing the Poor. Poverty under Thatcher*, London

Andrusz, G. (1992), 'The Causes and Consequences of Recent Legislative Changes in Soviet Housing Policy', W. Joyce (ed.), *Social Change and Social Issues in the Contemporary USSR*, Macmillan, London

Armstrong, C.W. (1929), *The Survival of the Unfittest*, C.W. Daniel, London

Atkinson, A.B., J. Micklewright (1988), 'Turning the Screw; Benefits for the Unemployed, 1979–1988', *ESRC Research Report*

Atkinson, J. (1985), 'Flexibility: Planning for an Uncertain Future', *Manpower Policy and Practice*, Vol. 1, Summer, pp. 26–29

Attali, J. (1990), *Lignes d'horizon*, Fayard, Paris

Auletta, K. (1981), *The Underclass*, Part I, 16 November 1981, Part II, 23 November 1981, Part III, 30 November 1981, *The New Yorker*

Avineri, S. and A. de-Shalit (eds) (1992), *Communitarianism and Individualism*, Oxford University Press, Oxford

Baglioni, G., C. Crouch (1990), *European Industrial Relations*, Sage Publications, London

Barbalet, J.M. (1988), *Citizenship*, Open University Press, Milton Keynes

Barclay, P. (1988), *The Guardian*, April 1988

Beck, U. (1986), *Risiskogesellschaft. Auf dem Weg in eine andere Moderne*, Suhrkamp Verlag, Frankfurt am Main

Becker, J.W., R. Vink (1984), *Werklozen, arbeidsongeschikten en werkenden vergeleken*, Sociaal en Cultureel Planbureau, Rijswijk

Bell, D. (1976), *The Cultural Contradictions of Capitalism*, Basic Books, New York

Berghman, J., H. Deleeck et al. (1985/2), *Sociale Indicatoren van de Vlaamse gemeenschap*, C.B.G.S., Brussels

Berghman, J., R. Muffels, A. de Vries (1988), 'Armoede en armoedeonderzoek in de EG', *Tijdschrift voor Arbeidsvraagstukken*, Jrg. 4, Nr. 2, pp. 15–26

Berkel, R. van, T. Hindriks (1991), *Uitkeringsgerechtigden en vakbeweging. Over de modernisering van het arbeidsbestel*, van Arkel, Utrecht

Beukema, L. (1987), *Kwaliteit van arbeidstijdverkorting*, Konstapel, Groningen

Bloomfield, J. (1991), 'Citizen Power in Prague', G. Andrews (ed.), *Citizenship*, Lawrence & Wishart, London

Braams, M.M., R.C. Kloosterman (1988), *De smalle beurs breed uitgemeten*, Regioplan Nr. 27, Amsterdam

Braverman, H. (1974) *Labor and Monopoly Capital: The Degradation of Work in the Twentieth Century*, Monthly Review Press, New York

Brent Community Health Council (1981), *Black People in the Health Service*

Brighton Distress Committee, *Annual Report 1906*, East Sussex Record Office, DB/49/1

Bromlei, Y. (1983), 'Ethnic processes', *Soviet Ethnographic Studies*, No. 3

Bullock Report (1970), *Report of the Committee of Inquiry on Industrial Democracy*, HMSO, Cmnd 6706, London

Bunich, P. (1990), 'New Law on Lease', *Moscow News*, 7 January 1990

Burakovsky, I. (1992), *Ukraine: Economic Transformation*. Paper presented at the Annual Conference of the Centre for Russian and East European Studies (University of Birmingham) Cumberland Lodge, Windsor

Burawoy, M. (1979), *Manufacturing Consent*, University of Chicago Press, Chicago

Burns, A., D. Feickert, M. Newby, J. Winterton (1983), 'The Miners and New Technology', *Industrial Relations Journal*, No. 14

Burns, A., M. Newby, J. Winterton (1985), 'The Restructuring of the British Coal Industry', *Cambridge Journal of Economics*, No. 9

Burtseva, I. (1992), 'Gde zhe mne zhit', *Argumenty i Fakty*, No. 25–26, p. 4

Byrne, D., J. Jacobs (1988), 'Disqualified from Benefit; the Operation of Benefit Penalties', *Low Pay Pamphlet*, No. 49, Low Pay Unit

Clawson, D. (1980), *Bureaucracy and the Labor Process. The Transformation of US Industry, 1860–1920*, Monthly Review Press, London/New York

Clegg, H. A. (1980), *The Changing System of Industrial Relations in Great Britain*, Blackwell, Oxford

Coates, K., T. Topham (1990), *Trade Unions in Great Britain*, Spokesman, Nottingham

Coenen, H. (1990), 'De vakbeweging tussen industriële en risicomaatschappij', *Tijdschrift voor Arbeid en Bewustzijn*, Jrg 14, Nr. 2, pp. 125–130

Coenen, H. (1992), *Erosie en modernisering in het arbeidsbestel*, ISOR, Utrecht

Conolly, M., G. Parsell, K. Roberts (1990), *Black Youth in the Liverpool Labour Market*, unpublished manuscript, Liverpool

Coser, L.A. (1965), 'The Sociology of Poverty', *Social Problems*, Vol. 13, No. 1, pp. 140–148

Crouch, C. (1991), 'United Kingdom: The Rejection of Compromise', G. Baglinoni, C. Crouch (eds), *European Industrial Relations*, Sage, London

Dahl, R.A. (1985), *A Preface to Economic Democracy*, University of California Press, Berkeley/Los Angeles

Dahlgren, P., C. Sparks (1991), *Communication and Citizenship*, Routledge, London

Dahrendorf, R. (1988a), *The Modern Social Conflict: an Essay on the Politics of Liberty*, Weidenfeld & Nicolson, New York

Dahrendorf, R. (1988b), 'Meer spelers in een spel met minder nieten', *De Volkskrant*, 5 November 1988

Dahrendorf, R. (1988c), *Burgerschap – het nieuwe vraagstuk*, Van der Leeuw-lezing, Groningen

Dahrendorf, R. (1991), *Some Remarks on the Quality of Citizenship*, Paper presented at the Conference on the Quality of Citizenship, Utrecht

Davydova, N. (1991), 'Unemployment is on the Rise, but Jobs exist', *Moscow News*, No. 24, 16–23 June

Deacon, A. (1976), *In Search of the Scrounger*, Occasional Papers on Social Administration, No. 60

Deleeck, H. (1977), *Ongelijkheden in de welvaartsstaat*, De Nederlandse Boekhandel, Antwerpen/Amsterdam

Deleeck, H. (1985), *De ongelijke verdeling der sociale overheidsuitgaven en de armoede*, Rede uitgesproken bij aanvaarding Cleveringa–leerstoel Rijksuniversiteit Leiden

Demographic and Socio–Economic Characteristics of the Population (1988), Vol. I, Central Statistical Office, Sofia

Dennis, N., F. Henriques, C. Slaughter (1969), *Coal is Our Life*, Tavistock, London

Department of Employment (1987), *Lo Code 7 Circ 26 (Rev.)* , December

Die Zeit, 16 March 1990, 'Erwerbstätigkeit in der Bundesrepublik und in der DDR'

Dimitrov, R. (1991), *The Nomencultura*, Publishing House of the University, Sofia

Disraeli, B. (1839), *Speech to Electors at Maidstone*, 3 July 1839

Donovan, L. (1968), *Royal Commission on Trade Unions and Employers' Associations*, HMSO, Cmnd 3623, London

Durkheim, E. (1973), *De la division du travail social*, Presses Universitaires de France, Paris (first edition 1893)

Durkheim, E. (1984), *The Division of Labour in Society*, Macmillan, London

Durlacher, G.L. (1973), 'Armoede: een poging tot analyse', *Mens en onderneming*, Vol. 27/1, pp. 45–65

Edwards, R.C. (1979), *Contested Terrain. The Transformation of the Workplace in the Twentieth Century*, Basic Books, New York

Elster, J. (1986), 'Comment on Van der Veen and Van Parijs', *Theory and Society*, Jrg. 15, pp. 709-721

Engbersen, G. (1990), *Publieke bijstandsgeheimen, het ontstaan van een onderklasse in Nederland*, Stenfert Kroese, Leiden/Antwerpen

Engbersen, G., R. van der Veen (1987), *Moderne armoede*, Stenfert Kroese, Leiden/Antwerpen

Engbersen, G., K. Schuyt, J. Timmer (1991), *Cultures of Unemployment*, typescript, Leiden

Esam, P., C. Oppenheime (1989), *A Charge of the Community*, CPAG, London

Esping-Andersen, G. (1990), *The Three Worlds of Welfare Capitalism*, Polity Press, Cambridge

Federov, S. (1992), 'Intellekt natsii spacet stranu', *Argumenty i Fakty*, No. 25–26

Field, F. (1989), *Losing Out: the Emergence of Britain's Underclass*, Blackwell, Oxford

Friedman, A.L. (1977), *Industry and Labour: Class Struggle at Work and Monopoly Capitalism*, Macmillan, London

Galbraith, J.K. (1992), *The Culture of Contentment*, Houghton Mifflin Company, Boston

Gans, H. (1973), *More Equality*, Vintage Books, New York

Gans, H. (1990), 'Deconstructing the Underclass', *Journal of the American Planning Association*, Summer 1990, pp. 271-277

Gellner, E. (1983), *Nations and Nationalism*, Blackwell, Oxford

Genchev, N. (1987), *Social-Psychological Types in Bulgarian History*, Septemvri Publishing House, Sofia

Genov, N. (1992), *Political Modelling of the Perception of Environmental Risks: The Bulgarian Experience*, paper presented at the International Conference on 'Nation-building: Yesterday, Today and Tomorrow', Blagoevgrad, Bulgaria

Giddens, A. (1982), *Profiles and Critiques in Social Theory*, Macmillan, London

Giddens, A. (1985), *The Nation-State and Violence*, Polity Press, Cambridge

Giddens, A. (1989), 'A Reply to my Critics', D. Held, J.B. Thompson (eds), *Social Theory of Modern Societies: Anthony Giddens and his Critics*, Cambridge University Press, Cambridge

Gier, H.G. de (1988), 'Arbeid en burgerschap', *Tijdschrift voor Arbeidsvraagstukken*, Jrg. 4, Nr. 4, pp. 15–22

Glazer, N. (1988), *The Limits of Social Policy*, Harvard University Press, Cambridge

Glazer, N. (1990), *Globalization and Systems of Welfare*, Turin, Unpub. Ms

Goodin, R. (1982), *Political Theory and Public Policy*, Chicago University Press, Chicago

Goodin, R. (1985), *Protecting the Vulnerable, a Re-Analysis of our Social Responsibilities*, Chicago University Press, Chicago

Goodin, R. (1988), *Reasons for Welfare*, Princeton University Press, Princeton

Gorz, A. (1980), *Adieux au prolétariat. Au delà du Socialisme*, éditions Galilée, Paris

Gorz, A. (1989a), *Critique of Economic Reason*, Verso, London/New York

Gorz, A. (1989b), 'Over het verschil tussen maatschappij en gemeenschap. Waarom invoering van een basisinkomen alleen geen volledig lidmaatschap van één van beide oplevert', *Tijdschrift voor Arbeid en Bewustzijn*, Jrg. 13, Nr. 4, pp. 459–468

Grancelli, B. (1988), *Soviet Management and Labour Relations*, Allen & Unwin, London

Grigoriev, L. (1990), 'Taking Stock of Our New Plan for Share Deals', *Moscow News*, 13, July 1990

Grint, K. (1991), *The Sociology of Work: an Introduction*, Polity Press, Cambridge

Hagenaars, A.J.M. (1985), *The Perception of Poverty*, Dissertation, North-Holland, Amsterdam

Handler, J., E. Hollingsworth (1971), *The Deserving Poor*, Chicago University Press, Chicago

Harrison, M.L. (1991), 'Citizenship, Consumption and Rights: A Comment on B.S. Turner's Theory of Citizenship', *Sociology*, 25/2, pp. 209–213

Hayek, F.A. (1990), 'The Road to Serfdom', *Voprosi Filosofii* 11, pp. 123–165

Heater, D. (1990), *Citizenship: The Civic Ideal in World History, Politics and Education*, Longman, London and New York

Held, D. (1987), *Models of Democracy*, Polity Press, Cambridge

Held, D. (1989), 'Citizenship and Autonomy', D. Held, J.B. Thompson (eds), *Social Theory of Modern Societies: Anthony Giddens and his Critics*, Cambridge University Press, Cambridge

Held, D. (1991), 'Between State and Civil Society: Citizenship', G. Andrews (ed.), *Citizenship*, Lawrence & Wishart, London

Heuvel, G. van den (1983), *Industrieel burgerschap als uitnodiging*, Kluwer, Deventer

Heycock, S. (1979), *The Effect of Legal Regulation upon the Nature of Industrial Conflict*, British Sociological Association Annual Conference, University of Warwick, March 1979

Heycock, S. (1981), *Trade Union Consciousness and Action in Declining Industries*, Sociologists in Polytechnics Annual Conference, Bulmershe College

Heycock, S. (1986), *Effects of Collective Bargaining Structures on the Nature of Industrial Conflict*, Dissertation, University of Leeds

Heycock, S. (1987), *The Effect of Changes in Technology and Techniques of Production upon the Organisation of Labour and Work in Coalmining*, British Sociological Association Annual Conference, University of Leeds

Heycock, S. (1989), 'New Technology in the Coal Industry and Its Effects upon Patterns of Work Organisation', J.B. Agassi, S. Heycock, *The Redesign of Working Time: Promise or Threat?*, Edition Sigma, Berlin

Heycock, S., J. Winterton (1989), *The Labour Process at the Coal Face: Evidence from One Hundred Years. Organisation and Control of the Labour Process*, 7th Annual Conference UMIST, March 1989

Himmelfarb, G. (1984), *The Idea of Poverty*, Knopf, New York

Hint, M. (1989), *Human Rights and the Minorities in the Soviet Union*. Paper presented at the Conference East meets West on Human Rights in a New Climate of International Cooperation, Sintra, Portugal

Hint, M. (1991), 'The Changing Language Situation: Russian Influences on Contemporary Estonian', *Journal of Multi-Lingual and Cultural Development*, Vol. 12, No. 1 and 2, p. 111

Hirschman, A.O. (1991), *The Rhetoric of Reaction; Perversity, Futility, Jeopardy*, Harvard University Press, Harvard

Hobsbawm, E. J. (1968), *Industry and Empire*, Weidenfeld & Nicholson, London

Hoffmann, J., R. Hoffmann, U. Mückenberger, D. Lange (Hrsg) (1990), *Jenseits der Beschlußlage. Gewerkschaft als Zukunftwerkstatt*, Bund, Köln

Hövels, B.W.M., P. Nas (1976), *Ondernemingsraden en medezeggenschap*, Samson, Alphen a/d Rijn

Howe, S. (1991), 'Citizenship in the New Europe: A Last Chance for the Enlightenment?', G. Andrews (ed.), *Citizenship*, Lawrence & Wishart, London

ILO (1989), *From Pyramid to Pillar*, Geneva

Jahoda, M. (1982), *Employment and Unemployment. A Social-Psychological Analysis*, Cambridge University Press, Cambridge

Jalland, P., J. Hooper (1986), *Women from Birth to Death*, Harvester Press, New York

Jonas, H. (1984), *The Imperative of Responsibility*, Chicago University Press, Chicago

Jong, M. de (1989), 'Toenemende apartheid in het Nederlandse onderwijs: oorzaken, gevolgen en een mogelijke remedie', *Pedagogische Studiën* (66), pp. 61–73

Kagan, R. (1978), *Regulatory Justice*, Russell Sage Foundation, New York

Katz, M.B. (1989), *The Undeserving Poor, from the War on Poverty to the War on Welfare*, Pantheon Books, New York

Kern, H., M. Schumann (1984), *Das Ende der Arbeitsteilung?*, Verlag C.H. Beck, Munchen

Kevles, D.J. (1986), *In the Name of Eugenics: Genetics and the Uses of Human Heredity*, Pelican, p. 116

Köbben, A.J.F. (1988), 'Recht op arbeid', *De Volkskrant*, 5 November 1988

Koene, A.M., H. Slomp (1991), *Medezeggenschap van werknemers op ondernemingsniveau*, VUGA, 's–Gravenhage

Kolakowski, L. (1978), *Main Currents of Marxism: its Rise, Growth and Dissolution*, Clarendon Press, Oxford

Kornai, J. (1990), *The Road to a Free Economy: Shifting from a Socialist System*, Norton, New York

Kroft, H., G. Engbersen, K. Schuyt, F. van Waarden (1989), *Een tijd zonder werk: een onderzoek naar de levenswereld van langdurig werklozen*, Stenfert Kroese, Leiden/Antwerpen

Labour Code (1951), Nauka i Iskustvo, Sofia

Labour Code (1986), Nauka i Iskustvo, Sofia

Lafargue, P. (1974), *Het recht op luiheid*, Arbeiderspers, Amsterdam

Leisink, P.L.M. (1989), *Structurering van arbeidsverhoudingen*, van Arkel, Utrecht

Lewis, O. (1968), *A Study of Slum Culture, Backgrounds for La Vida*, Random House, New York

Lipsky, M. (1980), *Street-level Bureaucracy; Dilemma's of the Individual in Public Services*, Basic Books, New York

Lister, R. (1990), *The Exclusive Society; Citizenship and the Poor*, CPAG, London

Littler, C.R., G. Salaman (1984), *Class at Work*, Batsford Academic, London

Local Government Board (1906), *Annual Report*, House of Commons Papers 1906 XXXV

Looise, J.C. (1985), 'Medezeggenschap via de CAO', *Tijdschrift voor Arbeidsvraagstukken*, Jrg. 1, Nr. 2, pp. 6–20

Looise, J.C., J.Z. Heijink (1986), *De OR en zijn bevoegdheden*, ITS, Nijmegen

Looise, J.C., F.G.M. de Lange (1987), *Ondernemingsraden, bestuurders en besluitvorming*, ITS, Nijmegen

Lukes, S. (1973), *Emile Durkheim: His Life and Work*, Allen Lane The Penguin Press, London

MacGregor, I. (1986), *The Enemy Within*, Collins, London

Macnicol, J. (1987), 'In Pursuit of the Underclass', *Journal of Social Policy*, 16, 3, pp. 293–318

Marshall, T. (1950), *Citizenship and Social Class*, Cambridge University Press, Cambridge

Marshall, T.H. (1973), *Class, Citizenship and Social Development*, Greenwood Press, Westport, Connecticut

Marshall, T.H. (1964/1977), *Class, Citizenship, and Social Development*, University of Chicago Press, Chicago

Marshall, T.H. (1977), *Class, Citizenship and Social Development*, Doubleday, Garden City New York

Marshall, T.H., T. Bottomore (1992), *Citizenship and Social Class*, Pluto Press, London

Mashaw, J.L. (1983), *Bureaucratic Justice, Managing Social Security Disability Claims*, Yale University Press, New Haven Connecticut

Mathiessen, T. (1965), *The Defences of the Weak*, Tavistock Publishers, London

Mead, L.M. (1986), *Beyond Entitlement, The Social Obligations of Citizenship*, Free Press, New York

Mead, L. (1989), 'The Logic of Workfare: The Underclass and Work Policy', W.J. Wilson (ed.), 'The Ghetto Underclass: Social Science Perspectives', *The Annals of The American Academy of Political and Social Science*, Vol. 501, January 1989

Meidner, R. (1990), 'The Swedish Model: Goals, Methods and Experiences', *The Future of Industrial Relations in Europe*, W.J. Dercksen (ed.), SDU-uitgeverij, 's-Gravenhage

Ministerie van Sociale Zaken en Werkgelegenheid (1987), *Inzicht: een toelichting bij de wet op de ondernemingsraden*, Staatsuitgeverij, 's-Gravenhage

Ministerie van Sociale Zaken en Werkgelegenheid (1988), *De instelling van ondernemingsraden 1987*, Staatsuitgeverij, 's-Gravenhage

Moore, R. (1977), 'Migrants and the Class Structure of Western Europe', R. Scase (ed.), *Industrial Society: Class, Cleavage and Control*, Allen & Unwin, London

Moynihan, D.P. (1965), *The Negro Family: the Case for National Action*, US Department of Labor

Mückenberger, U., C. Offe, I. Ostner (1988), 'Das staatlich garantierte Grundeinkommen – Ein sozialpolitisches Gebot der Stunde', H.L. Krämer, C. Leggewie (Hg.), *Wege ins Reich der Freiheit, Festschrift für Andre Gorz zum 65. Geburtstag*, pp. 247–278, Rotbuch Verlag, Berlin

Mulgan, G. (1991), 'Citizens and Responsibilities', G. Andrews (ed.), *Citizenship*, Lawrence & Wishart, London

Müller-Jentsch, W. (Hrsg) (1988), *Zukunft der Gewerkschaften. Ein internationaler Vergleich*, Campus, Frankfurt am Main/New York

Murray, C. (1984), *Losing Ground, American Social Policy 1950–1980*, Basic Books, New York

Murray, C. (1990), *The Emerging British Underclass*, IEA

Myrdal, G. (1964), *Challenge to Affluence*, Victor Gallancz, London

Nijs, W.F.M. de (1983), 'Medezeggenschap', W.H.J. Reynaerts (red.), *Arbeidsverhoudingen, theorie en praktijk*. Deel 2, Stenfert Kroese, Leiden/Antwerpen

Nove, A. (1979), *Political Economy and Soviet Socialism*, Allen & Unwin, London

NUM (1987), *Current Industrial Reorganisation and New Technology in the British Coalfields*, Industrial Relations Research Department

Oakley, A. (1974), *The Sociology of Housework*, Martin Robertson & Co. Ltd., London

OECD (1989), *Historical Statistics 1960-1987*, Paris

OECD (1991), *Economic Surveys; Netherlands*, Paris

Offe, C. (1985), *Disorganized Capitalism: Contemporary Transformations of Work and Politics*, Polity Press, Cambridge

Offe, C. (1991), 'Capitalism by Democratic Design? Democratic Theory Facing the Triple Transition in East Central Europe', *Social Research*, 58 (4), pp. 865–892

Offe, C., R.G. Heinze (1990), *Organisierte Eigenarbeit. Das Modell Kooperationsring*, Campus, Frankfurt am Main/New York

Okun, A.M. (1975), *Equality and Efficiency – The Big Trade-off*, The Brookings Institution, Washington D.C.

Oude Engberink, G. (1984), *Minima zonder marge*, GSD-Rotterdam, Rotterdam

Oude Engberink, G. (1987), *Minima zonder marge, de balans drie jaar later*, GSD-Rotterdam, Rotterdam

Pavlov, N. (1992), 'Ne kchochu lyudoedo usatogo', *Argumenty i Fakty*, No. 24, p. 2

Perushkin, V. (1992), 'B Estoniyu, za granitsu', *Argumenty i Fakty*, no. 25–26, p. 4

Piore, M., C. Sabel (1984), *The Second Industrial Divide: Possibilities for Prosperity*, Basic Books, New York

Pitt, M. (1979), *The World on Our Backs*, Lawrence & Wishart, London

Plant, R. (1991), 'Social Rights and the Reconstruction of Welfare', G. Andrews (ed.), *Citizenship*, Lawrence & Wishart, London

Poole, M. (1986), *Towards a New Industrial Democracy*, Routledge & Kegan Paul, London

Poor Law Commissioners (1936), *Second Annual Report*

Praag, B.M.S. van, A.J.M. Hagenaars, J. van Weeren (1982), 'Poverty in Europe', *The Review of Income and Wealth*, Vol. 28

Prins, R. (1990), *Sickness Absence in Belgium, Germany (FRG) and The Netherlands; A comparative Study*, Dissertation, Maastricht

Rayner, Sir D. (1981), *Payments of Benefits to Unemployed People*, DHSS and DE

Regulation of Economic Activity (1989), Council of Ministry, Sofia

Report of the Departmental Committee on Prisons (1895), C7702

Rex, J., R. Moore (1967), *Race, Community and Conflict*, Open University Press, Milton Keynes

Rex, J., S. Tomlinson (1979), *Colonial Immigrants in a British City*, Routledge Kegan Paul, London

Ringen, S. (1984/4), 'Toward a Third Stage in the Measurement of Poverty', *Social Compass*, Vol. XXXI

Ringen, S. (1987), 'Poverty in the Welfare State', R. Erikson, e.o. (ed.), 'The Scandinavian Model', *International Journal of Sociology*, Vol. XVI, No. 3–4

Roche, M. (1992), *Rethinking Citizenship: Welfare, Ideology and Change in Modern Society*, Polity Press, Cambridge

Royal Commission on the Poor Laws and Relief of Distress (1909), Cd. 4499, Separate (Minority) Report

Rueschemeyer, D. (1986), *Power and the Division of Labour*, Polity Press, Cambridge

Schumann, M., V. Baethge, U. Neumann, R. Springer (1988), *Trendreport on Industrial Rationalization*, Siswo, Amsterdam

Schuyt, C.J.M. (1983), *Tussen macht en moraal*, Samson, Alphen aan de Rijn

Schuyt, C.J.M, A. Tan (1988), *De maatschappelijke betekenis van armoede*, rapport voor Nationale Raad voor Maatschappelijk Welzijn

Seabrook, J. (1985), *Landscapes of Poverty*, Blackwell, Oxford

Sen, A. (1983), Poor, Relatively Speaking, *Oxford Economic Papers*, Vol. 35, pp. 153–170

Sheehy, A. (1991), 'The Ethnodemographic Dimension', A. Mc Auley (ed.), *Soviet Federalism Nationalism and Economic Decentralisation*, Leicester University Press, Leicester

Shmelev, N. (1992), *The Current Economic Situation in Russia*. Paper submitted to the Conference on the Change of the Economic System in Russia, 15–16 June 1992 at Stockholm. Institute of East European Economics

Showler, B., A. Sinfield (eds) (1981), *The Workless State*, Robertson, Oxford

Shumeiko, V. (1992), 'Ot pervogo litsa', *Birzhevye Bedomosti*, No. 11

Sociaal en Cultureel Planbureau (1988), *Sociaal en Cultureel Rapport 1988*, Staatsuitgeverij, 's-Gravenhage

Sociaal en Cultureel Planbureau (1991), *Sociaal en Cultureel Rapport 1990, The Netherlands*, Staatsuitgeverij, 's-Gravenhage

Sociaal-Economische Raad (1991), *Voorbeeldreglement Ondernemingsraden*, Sociaal-Economische Raad, 's-Gravenhage

Statement by Prison Commissioners (1898), C 8790

Statistical Yearbook of the Peoples Republic of Bulgaria (1988), Central Statistical Office Sofia

Steinkühler, F. (1991), 'Verzicht schadet nur', *Die Zeit*, 1 February 1991

Stone, D. (1984), *The Disabled State*, Temple University Press, Philadelphia

Strien, P.J. van (1978), *Om de kwaliteit van het bestaan*, Boom, Meppel/Amsterdam

Swaan, A. de (1988), *In Care of the State. Health Care, Education and Welfare in Europe and the USA in the Modern Era*, Oxford University Press, New York

Taylor-Gooby, P. (1991), *Social Change, Social Welfare and Social Science*, Harvester Wheatsheaf, New York/London

Tazhin, M., M. Tazhimbetov (1991), *Sotsial'naya spravedlivost' i Politika. Territorial'nyi aspect*, Alma-Ata

Teulings, A.W.M. (1989), 'A Political Bargaining Theory of Co-determination', G. Szèll, P. Blyton, C. Cornforth (eds), *The State, Trade Unions and Self-Management*, Walter de Gruyter, Berlin/New York

Therborn, G. (1986), *Why Some Peoples are more Unemployed than Others*, Verso, London

Thompson, P., D. McHugh (1990), *Work Organisations*, Macmillan, London

Tomaney, J., J. Winterton (1990), *The Transformation of Work? Technological Change and Work Relations in the British Coal Mining Industry*, 12th World Congress of Sociology, Madrid

Touraine, A., M. Wieviorka, F. Dubet (1984), *Le mouvement ouvrier*, Fayard, Paris

Trades Union Congress (1929), *Genuinely Seeking Work*, evidence submitted to the Morris Committee on Unemployment Insurance

Trist, E.L., J.W. Higgin, H. Murray, A.B. Pollack (1963), *Organizational Choice*, Tavistock, London

Trombley, S. (1988), *The Right to Reproduce, a History of Coercive Sterilisation*, Weidenfeld & Nicholson, New York

Turner, B.S. (1986), *Citizenship and Capitalism*, Allen & Unwin, London

Turner, B.S. (1990), 'Outline of a Theory of Citizenship', *Sociology*, 24/2, pp. 189–217

Turner, B.S. (1991), 'Further Specification of the Citizenship Concept: A Reply to M.L. Harrison', *Sociology*, 25/2, pp. 215–218

Ustinov, A. (1992), 'The Perspective of 10 Million Jobless in Russia by 1993', *Moscow News*, No. 23, 7–14 June 1992, p. 11

Veen, R.J. van der (1990), *De sociale grenzen van beleid*, Stenfert Kroese, Leiden/Antwerpen

Verstegen, R., J.H.T.H. Andriessen (1987), *Medezeggenschap in kleine ondernemingen*, IVA, Tilburg

Vilrokx, J. (1987), *Self Employment in Europe as a Form of Relative Autonomy: Significance and Prospects*, FAST-Commission of the European Communities, Brussels

Visser, J. (1991), 'Continuity and Change in Dutch Industrial Relations', G. Baglioni, C. Crouch (eds), *European Industrial Relations*, Sage, London

Vroom, B. de, M. Blomsma (1988), *Vervroegd uittreden uit betaalde arbeid*, HRWB, Den Haag

Wachter, M. de, Y. Somers (1989), 'Job Creation Programmes in an International Comparison', J. Muysken, C. de Neuborg (eds), *Unemployment in Europe*, Macmillan, London

Warmerdam, J., G. Kraaykamp, J. van den Berg, J. Heijink (1987), 'Flexibele organisatie: krijgt de OR er vat op?', M. Akkermans, H. Doorewaard, F. Huijgen (red.), *Autonomie als arbeidssociologisch vraagstuk*, Kerckebosch, Zeist

Watts, A.G. (1983), *Education, Unemployment and the Future of Work*, Open University Press, Milton Keynes

Webb, S., B. Webb (1910), *English Poor Law Policy*, Longman's Green and Co.

Webster, J. (1990), *Office Automation. The Labour Process and Women's Work in Britain*, Harvester Wheatsheaf, New York/London

Weiner, M. (1981), *English Culture and the Decline of the Industrial Spirit*, Cambridge University Press, Cambridge

Wilson, W.J. (1987), *The Truly Disadvantaged, The Inner City, The Underclass, and Public Policy*, The University of Chicago Press, Chicago/London

Wilson, W.J. (ed.) (1989), 'The Ghetto Underclass: Social Science Perspectives', *The Annals of The American Academy of Political and Social Science*, Vol. 501

Wilson, W.J. (1990), 'Social Theory and Public Agenda Research: The Challenge of Studying Inner-City Social Dislocation', Presidential Address, Annual Meeting of the American Sociological Association

Windmuller, J.P. (1969), *Labor relations in the Netherlands*, Cornell University Press, Ithaca, New York

Winterton, J., R. Winterton (1989), *Coal, Crisis and Conflict*, Manchester University Press, Manchester

Wolf-Phillips, L. (1968), *Constitutions of Nation States: Selected Texts*, Pall Mall Press, London

Wood, S. (1982), *The Degradation of Work*, Hutchinson, London

Wood, S. (ed.) (1989), *The Transformation of Work?: Skill, Flexibility and the Labour Process*, Unwin Hyman, London

WRR (1987), *Activerend arbeidsmarktbeleid* , Leiden/Antwerpen

WRR (1989), *Immigrant Policy*; Summary of the 36th Report, The Hague

WRR (1990), *Een werkend perspectief*, SDU-uitgeverij, 's-Gravenhage

WRR (1990), *Work in Perspective; Labour Participation in the Netherlands*; Summary of the 38th Report, The Hague

Yakovlev, A. (1992), 'Reliving the Past', *Moscow News*, No. 28, 12–19 July, p. 2

Young, J. (1992), *What's to be Done about Law and Order*, Pluto Press, London

Index

European Community (EC),
99–100
citizenship rights in, 2, 23–4
Eastern Europe and, 22–3, 24
immigration and, 53
industrial democracy and, 163

family relations, 40, 195
Federov, S., 106, 114
feminism, 6
fertility, 56–7
Field, Frank, 53–4, 60, 61
Fitzgerald, F. Scott, 38
flexible working, 149–52, 202
forced labour, 16
France, 9, 157, 162, 193
fraud control, 74
Friedman, A.L., 145

Galbraith, J.K., 101
Gans, Herbert, 45, 60
Gellner, E., 20
Genchev, N., 119
gender *see* women
Genov, N., 22
Germany
industrial democracy in, 157, 162
labour force participation in, 193
unification of, 129–30
trade unions and, 130–40
Giddens, A., 5, 9, 19, 20, 21–2, 23
Gier, H.G. de, 160
Gilder, George, 58
global citizenship, 23, 25
Goodin, R., 88, 93–4
Gorbachev, Mikhail S., 2, 103, 104
Gorz, André, 7–8, 13, 20, 182, 183, 184–5, 230
Grancelli, B., 103
Greece, 193
Grigoriev, L., 106
Grint, K., 7, 8
guild system, 11

Hagenaars, A.J.M., 36, 38

Halsey, A.H., 53
Handler, J., 86
Harrison, M.L., 5
Hayek, F., 120
Heater, D., 2, 4, 13, 17, 23, 25
Heijink, J.Z., 165
Heinze, R.G., 228
Held, D., 1, 5, 6, 12, 18–19, 23, 25, 157, 158, 160, 167, 170, 182
Hemingway, Ernest, 38
Heuval, G. van den, 160
Heycock, Stephen, 147, 148, 149, 150, 151
Himmelfarb, Gertrude, 35, 42, 46
Hindriks, T., 13, 184
Hint, M., 113
Hobsbawm, E.J., 145
Hollingsworth, E., 86
Hooper, J., 55
housework, 7–8
Hövels, B.W.M., 165
Howe, S., 22
Hungary, 114

IG-Metall, 49, 131, 137
illegitimacy, 57–8
immigrants *see* ethnic minorities; migrant workers
imperfect selection, law of, 83
income (wages), 74, 123–4, 151, 203
income guarantees *see* basic income schemes
indebtedness, 40
individualization process, 81
industrial democracy, 19, 126–7, 143–6, 157–9
definition of, 159–60
Netherlands case study of, 160–67
solidarity and, 170–7?
UK case study of, 146–55
workers' autonomy and, 145–6, 147, 149, 151, 152–5, 160, 167–70
industrial relations, 145
German unification and, 130–40

Printed and bound by CPI Group (UK) Ltd, Croydon, CR0 4YY

23/04/2025

14661001-0001